Saber and Scapegoat

Saber and Scapegoat

J. E. B. Stuart and the
Gettysburg Controversy

Mark Nesbitt

STACKPOLE
BOOKS

Published by
STACKPOLE BOOKS
5067 Ritter Road
Mechanicsburg, PA 17055

Maps by John Heiser

Letter from James Longstreet to H. B. McClellan (page 75) from H. B. McClellan Papers, Virginia Historical Society

Printed in the United States of America

First edition

10 9 8 7 6 5 4 3 2 1

Library of Congress Cataloging-in-Publication Data

Nesbitt, Mark.
    Saber and scapegoat : J. E. B. Stuart and the Gettysburg controversy / Mark Nesbitt
      p.   cm.
    Includes bibliographical references and index.
    ISBN 0-8117-0915-9
    1. Stuart, J. E. B. (James Ewell Brown), 1833–1864.   2. Gettysburg Campaign,
    1863.   3. Gettysburg (Pa.), Battle of, 1863.   I. Title.
    E467.1.S9N47   1994
    973.7′349—dc20   94-20509
                                         CIP

To Arthur Vernon Nesbitt and John Pasko
The grandfathers I never got to know

"Stuart is the best cavalryman ever foaled in America."
—Major General John Sedgwick, U.S. Army

"I then concluded my report for General Lee. In doing so I dealt with Stuart in the plainest language, in fact, I had told him before, I thought he ought to be shot."
—Colonel Charles Marshall, aide-de-camp of General Robert E. Lee

Contents

Acknowledgments

Somewhere in the vast pile of paper that accumulated while I was writing this book is a card and perhaps one or two scraps of paper upon which I diligently placed the names and proper spellings of every person who helped me. I will find it, no doubt, a few days after the book is on the shelves. Then again, like many of the dispatches sent among the officers in the Gettysburg campaign, they may never show up.

As well, I know that there were several people in my social circles who, upon hearing the subject of this book, made comments and suggestions and whose names I did not record. If they find their recommendation within these pages but no acknowledgment for it, I sincerely apologize. However, the following people and organizations have surfaced from the mass of paper and my memory. My heartfelt thanks go to them all.

Ted Alexander, historian with the National Park Service at Antietam National Battlefield, read over the section on Stuart's retreat and recommended some changes according to the vast amount of research he has done on that segment of the great campaign.

Gregory Coco, author and historian at Gettysburg National Military Park, pulled a description of Stuart at Emmitsburg, Maryland, from his files. I appreciate his thinking of me while busy with his own projects.

William C. Davis, historian, author, and consultant, is one of my editors at Stackpole Books. He read the manuscript and gave me some sound advice on making it more palatable. Sylvia Frank, also my editor at Stackpole, keeps me to my deadlines—or at least understands when I don't meet them. Dick Frank of Stackpole sells my books. He certainly is appreciated.

Kathy Georg Harrison, along with her endless other duties at Gettysburg National Military Park, still found time to help me find the last few documents in the park's files concerning the cavalry at Gettysburg.

D. Scott Hartwig, also a historian at Gettysburg National Military Park, took time out of his schedule to read the entire manuscript for errors. If there are any mistakes in the book, they exist probably because I didn't follow his suggestions. As well as being an expert on the Gettysburg campaign, he knows military history and pointed out one of the themes of this book: that historians often overlook how binding military orders are; when historians say, "Stuart should have acted in this fashion," it is meaningless unless the actions corresponded with his orders. Scott provided many enlightening conversations on the battle and showed me a new way—the "military" way—of looking at Stuart's role in the campaign. His upcoming book on the Maryland campaign of 1862 should be excellent.

Adele H. Mitchell, Stuart scholar and friend of the Stuart family, through our numerous conversations, virtually inspired this book. She made me look again at Stuart's orders and the absurdity of some of the charges against him. I once was a Stuart accuser myself, but Adele's comments helped me re-analyze his actions instead of just repeating what has been said over the years. And that, of course, is the basis for all knowledge.

Paul Shevchuk, another historian at Gettysburg National Military Park, has written many fine articles on the smaller cavalry actions during the campaign. He gave me a better understanding of those fights and their intensity.

Don Stivers, one of America's premier historical artists, was kind enough to allow Stackpole Books to use his painting "The Homecoming" for my dust jacket. It portrays Stuart at Carlisle, Pennsylvania, at dusk on July 1, showing all the exhaustion from a week-long campaign of marching and fighting and the weight of command. It is just how I always pictured Stuart on the campaign.

Dean Thomas of Thomas Publications in Gettysburg, Pennsylvania—my "other" publisher—secured some of the photos used in this book. As a Civil War author himself, his comments on Stuart's role at Gettysburg were also enlightening.

Robert J. Trout, who wrote *They Followed the Plume* (Stackpole Books, 1993), about Stuart's staff throughout the war, also read the manuscript and helped me stay out of trouble with the details of Stuart's staff officers and his personality. His comments on the charges against Stuart, in addition to those about Stuart in general (gleaned from years of studying what others wrote about him), added immeasurably to my knowledge of the man and his role as innovator of light cavalry tactics. One of my favorite comments from Bob, in response to the old saw that Stuart was "late" for the Battle of Gettysburg, is, "How can you be late for an accident?"

Institutions deserve credit and thanks for maintaining, protecting, and making available the documents upon which all historical study is based. To them and their fine staffs, my appreciation is extended.

The Gettysburg College library is just a block from my office and my friends David Hedrick, Susan Roach, and Peggy Steinour are always more than helpful, even when all I have time for is a phone inquiry.

The Gettysburg National Military Park library and its renowned "vertical files" have, for the last twenty-five years, been my favorite resource for both obscure secondary and still untapped primary sources on the battle. Cindy Stouffer helped locate the rare photo of James Harrison.

The University of Virginia was gracious in allowing me to use the John W. Daniel Papers from its manuscript department.

The Virginia Historical Society has one of the best card catalogue systems in its manuscript division that I have ever seen, detailing on each card the various subjects included in that piece of correspondence. The people there are to be commended and thanked for their assistance.

Finally, I must thank the people at the U.S. Army Military History Institute, Carlisle Barracks, Pennsylvania, for literally years of help. I am particularly indebted to Randy Hackenberg for his help with many of the photos herein.

I would be remiss if I failed to mention Danette Taylor for her reading of the manuscript and, more important, her patience while this book was being produced. The reader knows the price of this book; only a very few know what it cost. Dani is one of them.

Introduction

It was a typical Victorian-era dinner party at the Baltimore home of Johns Hopkins University Professor H. Newell Martin. David Gregg McIntosh, a former officer in the Army of Northern Virginia, was present with his wife, the former Virginia J. Pegram. Also at the dinner were General and Mrs. Bradley T. Johnson; Martin's wife, the former Hettie Cary Pegram (widow of Confederate Major General John Pegram); and Miss Jenny Cary. Perhaps the most distinguished diners were Colonel and Mrs. Charles Marshall; he had been military secretary to General Robert E. Lee.

Though nearly a quarter-century past, the Gettysburg campaign was a topic of conversation. Many interesting comments and speculations probably were made about the controversies of the campaign that had arisen over the years, but demitasses and brandy snifters certainly froze between table and lip when Marshall said that, for his role, he tried to have Major General James Ewell Brown Stuart court-martialed.

"Who?" everyone asked, incredulous. "Not J. E. B. Stuart."

"Yes," Marshall said coolly. "J. E. B. Stuart."

He told his rapt audience that he had written just that in the report of the campaign he had prepared for Lee just after the event and that he had dealt with Stuart in the plainest of language. He said that he thought Stuart ought to have been shot.

Marshall said that he had explicitly charged Stuart with disobedience of orders and "laid the full responsibility at his door." McIntosh, who was so stunned that he wrote Marshall's words down the next morning, said that Marshall then detailed the orders Stuart received to move along the Confederate army's flank and that Stuart confessed that he had pursued a different course.

Marshall sounded disappointed that "General Lee was unwilling, however, to adopt my draft."

In October 1993, as this book was being finalized, the author attended the premiere of "Gettysburg," the first full-length movie on the battle taken from

Michael Shaara's Pulitzer Prize-winning novel *The Killer Angels*. A small part of the four-hour-plus film deals with the meeting between Lee and Stuart after Stuart returned from his ride around the Union army—the act for which Marshall would have had him shot. Lee informs Stuart that some in the army were suggesting his court-martial; Stuart asks for their names, apparently in order to challenge them to a duel. Lee then tells Stuart he was the eyes of the army and that his mission was to screen it from enemy cavalry and report the movements of the Union main body. "That mission," Lee says, "was not fulfilled." Stuart pulls his saber and attempts to hand it to Lee, apparently to resign his commission.

Dramatic and full of tension as the scene is, it is also complete fiction. Though acted well and written by a fine novelist, it still takes bits of history— such as Marshall's statements, or subsequent variations of them and other half-truths—and popularizes and perpetuates yet another tale about the Battle of Gettysburg. The problem is that millions will see the movie and assume that the event actually happened; another Gettysburg myth will be perpetuated.

Even sadder is that Stuart, one of the finest officers ever to draw a saber, has his reputation tarnished for another generation and the fabrications, truth-stretching, and outright lies about the man and the history of the cavalry in the Gettysburg campaign of 1863 will be maintained by the uninformed.

Stuart loved doing reconnaissance himself. He rode in small groups or often alone until the enemy fired upon him. Drawing fire let Stuart know where the enemy was during the war; it may still be so today.

Stuart was an innovator of cavalry strategies and tactics. The U.S. Army had reinstated the cavalry arm, as opposed to Mounted Riflemen and Dragoons, under Secretary of War Jefferson Davis just a few years before, in 1855. Stuart was one of those chosen as an officer in that branch, which then consisted of only two regiments. The cavalry's new role in the American way of war was developing. Stuart learned much about light cavalry tactics on the Plains; he learned more in the first years of the Civil War; he was continually pressing, utilizing, and inno-vating so that his light cavalry could not be mistaken for the heavy horses and men of the old dragoons or the mounted men who simply used their horses to ride to their infantry battles. He wanted to use his men like a light saber instead of a broadsword or simply a shield for the main army. He wanted his cavalry to become the flashing, fluid saber of the Confederate army, parrying the enemy, keeping it at a distance by quick thrusts instead of heavy blows. In using his men this way, his name became—and still is—synonymous with them and the Confeder-ate cavalry. As metaphor, Stuart was—and remains—the saber of the Confederacy. He would not have minded this symbolic metamorphosis.

I must admit that at one time, I too blamed Stuart for a major role in the Confederate defeat at Gettysburg. I was not alone. It is truly amazing what careful study and a few eye-opening observations of fact will do in changing one's opinion. Some of the accusations against Stuart that I and many others have perpetuated include:

- Stuart's absence brought on the Battle of Gettysburg.
- Stuart left Lee with no cavalry to do the main army's reconnaissance.
- Stuart was "late" for the Battle of Gettysburg.
- Stuart was not following orders.
- Stuart was on a joyride around the Union army, wasting time seeking glory and fame.

All those statements are patently false.

Some people may want to call this revisionist history. They are wrong. The revisionists began rewriting history in 1863, with the composition by Charles Marshall of Lee's first report of the Battle of Gettysburg. It went on from there. This is an attempt to unwrite the rewriting of history, done in the nineteenth century by many Southerners in an effort to protect the reputation of one whose reputation needed no protecting—Robert E. Lee.

Historians who are familiar with the topic will notice that a few of my conclusions are similar to others'—most notably those of Colonel John S. Mosby, who wrote defending Stuart for years after the war. That is because many of the conclusions are based on solid logic and analysis that lead you nowhere else. Add to that the fact that I used Mosby himself as a primary source independent of his arguments in favor of Stuart, and Mosby became a documentary source for details as well as a fine advocate for defending Stuart's actions.

I think I also have discovered a few things even the meticulous Mosby overlooked. I have no doubt that there was a missing dispatch from Lee to Stuart, written after or added to the published dispatch dated 5 P.M., June 23, 1863. This is not singular. I realized, as anyone can by reading the *Official Records of the Union and Confederate Armies,* that there are numerous dispatches mentioned or referred to in the published letters that cannot be found. In fact, almost as many are missing as have been published. Nor does this missing dispatch of June 23—mentioned by Stuart's assistant adjutant general, by Stuart himself, and referred to by innuendo by several others—have any bearing on the outcome of the campaign. It contains no history-altering revelation, like the potential "Lee's lost orders" had during the Sharpsburg campaign. Stuart's missing dispatch merely adds information—some previously unanalyzed, even by Mosby—to Stuart's decision-making process and to what Lee knew of what Stuart was doing while he was gone from the army. It must be remembered as well that there were numerous verbal orders sent and received, never to be published. These also had an unknown effect upon Stuart's and others' actions.

This book is a thorough analysis of not just the controversy but also of Stuart and his cavalry's role in the Gettysburg campaign. I examined and included some sources to an extent that no other author has. The papers of Colonel John Bachelder were used almost exclusively for the documentation of the cavalry battle east of Gettysburg on July 3, 1863. This is, I believe, the first time this many of them have been used this extensively for the cavalry battle. Every one of the letters concerning the cavalry fight was examined and most were included to some extent.

The letters of Stuart and Mosby recently published by the Stuart-Mosby Historical Society were used to reconstruct some of the more telling events in Stuart's life according to Stuart himself, as well as some of Mosby's private comments and opinions of the cult that formed in Virginia after the war that attempted to "rescue" Lee's reputation by denigrating others, particularly Stuart. The publication of the letters by these remarkable men is a tribute to their editor, Mrs. Ralph Mitchell.

I also examined the papers in the collection of the Virginia Historical Society written by several members of Lee's staff, including Lee's private letter book, into which all the orders he issued were copied. I searched for a clue as to why Marshall, then others, tried so hard to indict Stuart.

One of the most important things to remember while reading this book is the difference between what are referred to as "orders" and "reports." Orders came first, issued in the field to Stuart and others, directing them as to what to do in the next day or two or even as far ahead as a week. Sometimes these were letters from Lee directing (too often merely suggesting) what the subordinates should do and often leaving a great deal to their discretion. The orders for the Gettysburg campaign are found in the correspondence part of the *Official Records.*[1] Reports were written after the campaigns and battles. This chronology is inescapable. Go to the orders to see what Stuart was supposed to do. The reports tell you what he did, but not always.[2]

Because of the mass of official papers on the war, the records on Gettysburg were not published until 1889. The Union reports came first, Confederate reports second, and the correspondence last. Opinions for articles and books were being formed with the cart before the horse, as the reports were pointed to as the definitive answers to questions about the participants.

Worse, the first of two reports on the battle and campaign of Gettysburg (written by Marshall for Lee's signature) was released by Richmond newspapers shortly after the battle in response to the clamoring for a reason for the costly defeat. Some of the report, like his statements at the dinner party twenty-four years later, bore little resemblance to the orders Marshall himself wrote from Lee to Stuart. Why Marshall would attempt to change, just a month later under Lee's eyes, the orders he had written for Lee is one of the mysteries of

Gettysburg. Marshall continued to change the orders as the years went on, referring to the reports as proof of various indictments of Stuart when the proof is not in the orders.

Nevertheless, the orders told Stuart what to do; the reports, including Stuart's, tell what he did. Though Lee's reports were edited and signed by Lee, they say what Marshall thought Stuart did as well as what Marshall thought Stuart should have done.

My conclusions may stir up a number of people, for the Gettysburg camps are indeed still divided sharply on Stuart's role. But after studying the subject from virtually every angle, I can only hope that my colleagues will give this an open-minded reading and acknowledge some new interpretations.

Under examination, the tales that have grown about Stuart bear little resemblance to what really happened on that arduous, five-week cavalry campaign. A careful analysis of the *Official Records* directing Stuart's action by military orders also diverges from what others thought he was supposed to do in the campaign. The differences between the orders and reports and the criticisms and controversies spawned by them recalls the story of an old Confederate soldier. After telling about his numerous battles with his regiment, another old soldier calls him on it— he had been with the unit and it had engaged in none of those battles. "Damn," said the first Confederate. "Another good story ruined by an eyewitness."

Part One

PRELUDE

CHAPTER ONE

Schooling of the Trooper

*"Contrary to the expectations of all I have been so fortunate
as not to have a single fight since I have been going to school."*
—J. E. B. STUART, 1846

To Archibald Stuart, former officer in the War of 1812, esteemed lawyer, politician, and orator of great wit and personality, and Elizabeth Letcher Pannill Stuart, wife and lover of all things natural and godly, was born on February 6, 1833, a son whom they named after an uncle of the boy. James Ewell Brown Stuart began his life in southernmost Virginia, on a farm called Laurel Hill in Patrick County, the seventh of ten children.

His father was a man of good humor with a gifted voice and love of music that his son James inherited. The elder Stuart often became the center of attention at social gatherings, a trait his son also enjoyed. It is often the sign of a leader that he or she is comfortable in front of crowds. From seeing his father before the masses, young James no doubt felt that it also was his place.

From his mother, James learned of things beyond this world, of faith and nature, and a love of flowers. She kept a beautiful flower garden at Laurel Hill. He picked flowers later in his life and sent them to his wife, or wore them in his lapel, when his decisions then led to men's living or dying.[1]

A little is known of his early life, mostly from John Thomason, who became friends with the family when he was writing his biography on Stuart in the 1920s. Young James loved the outdoors and riding, nature, and the woods, fields, and mountains of his part of Virginia. The early religious teachings from his mother grew deeper as the boy matured. He was honest and honored at least one promise unto death. He swore to his mother that he would never drink liquor, and even as he lay dying from a bullet through the gut, he refused to overindulge in liquor, even to ease the pain, taking only one small sip. There was that promise to his mother and he felt even death—especially death—should not tear him from it.

3

Thomason tells a story of personal fortitude and grace under pressure—what Ernest Hemingway called true courage—related by James's older brother William Alexander, who was fifteen when James was nine. One summer day, they came upon a huge hornets' nest lodged low in a tree. Sticks would not reach it and stones bounced off the limbs surrounding it. There was only one thing to do and that was to climb up and bat it down. The boys inched close when suddenly the hornets swarmed out. William Alexander prudently dropped to the ground and bolted, but when he turned, he saw his little brother, eyes slitted against the stinging creatures, inching closer to the nest with his stick. Young Stuart accepted the stings and dislodged the nest, accomplishing his mission despite the pain. From that day, his older brother thought James might make a decent soldier, for he possessed no little amount of physical courage. Apparently, even at that age, overwhelming odds meant nothing to James.

He was healthy nearly all his life. Thirteen-year-old James wrote to his mother in December 1846 from boarding school in Wytheville that he "deemed it unnecessary to say in this that I was well for you know I am never anything else." But less than a year later, he contracted a fever that caused his hair to fall out until "I am very much laughed at by the gals." It was one of the few times Stuart was ill. At the end of March 1848, he was still without hair.

Shortly after he recovered from the fever, the house at Laurel Hill burned. His mother and sister Victoria went to stay in Floyd County and another sister Columbia (called Lummie by the family) relocated to Pittsylvania County. At the time young James wrote about the tragedy, his father had not decided whether they would rebuild. His brother John, who was studying to be a doctor, returned home to continue to study by mail. John and his father were keeping house in the kitchen, probably a "summer kitchen" common on early American farmsteads, built separately from the main house because of the danger of fire.[2]

Stuart had worked in the Wyeth County clerk's office with his older brother Alexander. Perhaps this is where he began to think about a career in law. As well, at college he began to take Latin as preparation for a possible teaching career.[3] Perhaps at this time another career entered his thoughts. At the age of fifteen, after war had broken out with Mexico, he volunteered, but was turned down because of his youth.[4]

In August 1848, at age fifteen, he entered Emory and Henry College in Emory, Virginia, and joined the Methodist Church, though he was confirmed in the Protestant Episcopal Church in 1859 in St. Louis. His mother was an Episcopalian, but his respect for Christianity was broad and apparently embraced all sects. When he was at the U.S. Military Academy, a classmate called him a "Bible class man." By 1857, when he was in his mid-twenties and stationed at Fort Leavenworth, Kansas Territory, he expressed a desire to build a church on his family's farm, having already put away some money for that purpose. Reading the Bible and fighting battles has a rather Old Testament ring to it, but Stuart was not the first officer of that era to praise God for a victory.

In 1850, Dr. Thomas H. Averett, who had defeated James' father in a senatorial election, appointed Stuart to West Point. He traveled by stage from Wytheville though Salem, Lynchburg, and Charlottesville, where he visited the University of Virginia, Monticello, and Thomas Jefferson's grave. From Charlottesville, he went to Washington, where he called on Averett, perhaps to thank him for his appointment, and attended a Senate session. From his spectator's seat, he saw Vice President Millard Fillmore and the great orator Daniel Webster ("He speaks slowly but forcibly"), but was immensely impressed by Senator Jefferson Davis of Mississippi. Stuart heard Davis and Stephen Douglas of Illinois discuss the "California question" and concluded that "Mr. Davis is hard to beat."[5]

He arrived at West Point and went into summer bivouac with other cadets at Camp Gaines overlooking the Hudson River.[6] Stuart officially became a cadet on July 1, 1850.[7] After being at West Point only a month and a half, he wrote to his cousin George Hairston on August 17 to tell him "how I am pleased with my new situation. So far I know of no profession more desirable than that of the soldier."[8]

The superintendent of the academy at that time was Robert E. Lee. Though Stuart was not a bad student, recollections of classmates indicate that he enjoyed the military aspects of West Point more than the academic. Fitzhugh Lee, who later served under him, recalled after the Civil War that he possessed "an immediate and almost thankful acceptance of a challenge to fight from any cadet who might in any way feel himself aggrieved."[9] Strangely enough, most of his fights were against larger students and, though he was often whipped, he always came back for more. The trait is admirable across the human generations; it is a classic theme of literature and films. Though he fought so often that he received an admonishing letter from his father, Stuart gained great respect from fellow future officers because of this never-give-up attitude. He was also remembered as possessing "a clear, metallic, ringing voice," another asset for a battlefield leader.[10]

Stuart seemed to be a natural scrapper. In the earliest letter from him to be published, dated April 11, 1846, he mentions to his cousin, "Contrary to the expectations of all[,] I have been so fortunate as not to have a single fight since I have been going to school." Apparently, if he had gotten into a fight at that age (thirteen), it would not have been his first. Incidentally, this earliest letter and all the rest were signed "J. E. B. Stuart," his *nom de guerre*.[11] Just before Christmas 1853, he sent a long letter to his father from the hospital at West Point, where he was sent with "another black eye" from fighting with a private in his company whom he had put on report. Stuart was about half the size of his antagonist, but they fought until neither could lift his arms. Stuart's eye was swollen shut and he conceded to the bigger man. His main regret, now that he had eased his conscience by telling his father about the fight, was that he would miss the Christmas party given by Mrs. Robert E. Lee at the superintendent's home.[12]

Among others attending West Point while Stuart was there were George Washington Custis Lee, son of the superintendent and eventual aide to the Confederate president; Alfred Pleasonton, later to command a Federal cavalry corps; William Averell, a future U.S. Army general; John Chambliss and John Pegram, future Confederate generals; and Fitzhugh Lee, who later served under Stuart as a rebel. Because of the political and social turmoil the country was experiencing from slavery and sectionalism, these neophytes found themselves soon driven to a soldier's highest challenges. The country was moving rapidly, inexorably toward armed civil conflict.

At least as well as fighting, Stuart liked the attentions of women. It was a lifelong attraction, expressed in letters from age thirteen.[13] Granted, early on he seemed merely to be scouting out attractive women for his cousin Alexander Stuart Brown to pursue. Other references reflect a youthful frustration with the inscrutability of some young women. Still, the attraction seemed as natural for Stuart as his later ability to see defilade in a battlefield position or discover the flank of an enemy.

At the beginning of his second year at West Point it appears from his letters that Stuart lost his heart to Miss Mary Pegram, a Virginian of a fine family whose brothers served and sacrificed a few years later. At this date, perhaps the affections were traveling only from Stuart.[14] He also wrote poetry to and exchanged gifts with the Berard sisters, daughters of the French teacher at West Point.[15] One of his most enjoyable and lasting correspondents was his cousin Bettie Hairston. It was not uncommon for cousins to marry in the old South, and Stuart's letters to Bettie bordered on the romantic. But taken as a whole, they seem to reflect a fond remembrance of his youth and precious days in Virginia, cavorting with her and other friends while home on summer break. The letters show as deep a love for his home state as they do affection for his relation. He established the correspondence fairly early in his West Point career and it continued at least until his days on the Texas frontier.

He also seemed attracted to Mary Custis Lee, the supremely independent daughter of the revered and often intimidating superintendent.[16] She was a year and a half his junior but closer to his age than any of the other Lee girls. She seemed eventually to take the place of Mary Pegram, the other Virginia belle in his affections: "Mrs. Pegram and Miss Mary have been here for two weeks but left us today. Mrs. Lee and Miss Mary Lee also returned home sometime since.

Of the two Mary's I admire Miss Mary Lee much the more, both as regards beauty and sprightliness."[17] If there ever was an early courtship, we may never know, but the friendship that grew from their acquaintance above the Hudson would last his life. Mary Custis visited him at the camp Stuart called *Qui Vive* near Fairfax Court House in 1861 and Stuart wrote to his wife, Flora, after the visit, expressing the wish that someday she might meet his former superintendent's daughter, since she had always been such a good friend.[18]

In fact, Stuart became very close to the entire Lee family at West Point, being invited to dinners and Christmas parties at the superintendent's home. He watched over Mary Lee as the native Virginian gave her best efforts at learning the Yankee girls' winter pastime of ice skating.[19] He even wrote a testimonial letter to endorse the appointment from Virginia to West Point of William Henry Fitzhugh Lee, the superintendent's son nicknamed "Rooney." Stuart and Mrs. Lee must have established a special friendship. Writing to his cousin Bettie in February of his last year at West Point, he said that every Saturday evening was spent in the "society of the ladies" and that, as he was writing, he had "a bouquet, now on the mantle which was sent to me the other day by Mrs. Lee, who as you are aware is my most particular friend among the ladies. I can never say too much in her praise."[20]

Much like war in nineteenth-century America, love too was a great game with overdrawn hyperboles and intense, high-minded affections. It had the strictest of rules that went just so far and then no further. As his fame spread, Stuart had a number of admirers, many of them women who turned out when he passed through their towns. He also called on them as he rode through, sometimes going out of his way to visit. There is no evidence of impropriety.

According to Fitz Lee, fellow cadets at West Point called Stuart "Beauty," said in a way that implied he was not very good-looking. A photo taken without his beard about the time he graduated belies this.

Stuart was a healthy, robust, restless young man, imbued with the superior energy and aggressiveness of, say, a modern professional athlete. A letter from his father sums it up:

> It is true you have, to start with, good morals fortified by religion, a good temper, and a good constitution, which if preserved will carry you though the trial [of military life] safely. But the temptations of a camp to a young man of sanguine temperament, like yourself, are not to be trifled with or despised. I conjure you to be constantly on your guard, repelling and avoiding the slightest approach towards vice or immorality. . . . Your military training at West Point will

strengthen you greatly in the struggle. By it you have been taught
the necessity of strict subordination to superiors, and of kind and
conciliatory manners towards equals.[21]

According to one biographer, though Stuart infrequently mentioned in his
letters the growing uneasiness between the two sections of the country, he did
deplore Abolitionists and the lack of Yankee understanding for "southern institutions."[22] He wrote in one letter to George Hairston, "One would think that a
place [West Point] situated as this is, in the heart of free-soil-Yankeedom was
strongly tainted with that spirit, but quite the contrary is the fact, for there is a
strong Southern feeling prevalent on the Point. . . . There seems to be a sentiment of mutual forbearance. In a word with us all is harmony."[23]

While at the academy, he frequently expressed his love of riding.[24] Stuart
scored high in cavalry tactics (tenth in his class of forty-six) and even higher in
ethics (ninth). He remained in the top 15 percent of his class through most of
his career, but clearly preferred summer encampments over the classroom: "We
had left our pleasant quarters in Camp Gaines for barracks and were preparing
to enter upon the dull career of the student."[25]

Oddly enough, Stuart's cavalry tactics textbook seems virtually unused. It
shows no underlining, no dog-eared pages, or any of the usual markings of a well-
studied book. Yet the pristine text is dated 1855, in Stuart's hand.[26] Perhaps this
was the textbook he used at West Point and dated later when he was on his first
assignment; perhaps it is a copy he picked up after graduation for reference.
One would like to think that he wore the covers off his original cavalry textbook,
but Stuart was a man of action and nothing in the manual says anything about
how to cross a flooding river in pitch-black night or how to get men to ride for
fifty hours straight on a campaign.

Upon approaching graduation, though he loved the soldier's life, Stuart
was still torn between the practice of law and the military. In July 1854 he
graduated thirteenth of forty-six in his class. He was commissioned a brevet
second lieutenant in the regiment of Mounted Riflemen—basically infantrymen
on horseback—and ordered to Texas.

He wrote that the Mounted Riflemen were "a Corps which my taste, fond-
ness for riding, and desire to serve my country in some acceptable manner led
me to select above all the rest."[27] He was granted leave until October 15. He
visited West Point to equip himself for his duty on the frontier and to see his
cousin Pete Hairston, a plebe.[28] He spent some time in St. Louis when his orders
sending him through New Orleans were postponed due to a yellow fever
epidemic there. He wrote to his cousin Alexander Brown: "The longer I am
detained from the field of action the more anxious I become to reach it. I am

burning with all the enthusiasm of youthful ambition to show my prowess in fight."[29]

By December 1854, he had been promoted to second lieutenant. After a harrowing voyage across the Gulf of Mexico and a visit to Galveston, Stuart arrived at Fort McIntosh in Laredo, Texas, on the Mexican border. His Company G had already left to fight Comanches and Stuart had to catch up with it 450 miles north of Laredo. He traveled with an escort across an almost uninhabited area toward a region called the Limpia. A long series of letters to his cousin Bettie Hairston recounted his journey through places with names like Los Dos Hermanos, Rattlesnake Den, and Eagle Pass. During his early days in Texas, he saw his first mirage; witnessed searing, dusty heat change momentarily into rain, hail, and numbing cold; discovered aboriginal drawings on rocks; and lived through a wind-whipped prairie fire in an arroyo where his unit had camped.[30]

John Thomason, Stuart's biographer and no stranger to the military himself, called Texas "one of the most difficult terrains in the world." The story goes that William Tecumseh Sherman, upon seeing the region and assuming that the entire state was similar, announced, in his own fashion, that if he owned hell and Texas, he would rent out Texas and live in the other place. Other officers stationed in Texas included Major James Longstreet with the 8th Infantry and Captain Richard Ewell of the 2nd Dragoons.[31]

Stuart was in charge of the one cannon his unit possessed. During one march across the savage terrain, Stuart and his men fell behind and finally caught sight of the regiment's encampment at the bottom of a 1500-foot escarpment. He rode down the narrow Indian trail to contact his commander, but, "The Major left no orders." Stuart would have to improvise. Figuring that his horse would never make it back up, he climbed the cliff on foot.[32] To the amazement of his commanding officer comfortably ensconced below, Stuart had the cannon dismantled and lowered piece by piece by ropes down the cliff. In a letter to his brother afterward, a realization of what it means to be a soldier as well as a certain spirit shone through: "I could not and would not forsake [the artillery piece]. . . . Down we went, lowering it by lariat ropes, and lifting it over rocks. We reached the bottom safely, and before night were sipping our coffee at the Major's bivouac. The Major told me that I deserved great credit for my success, and said that he never expected to see me bring the artillery down that mountain."[33]

While stationed in Texas, Stuart heard of Lee leaving the superintendent's post at West Point. He wrote to Mrs. Berard, the wife of his West Point French instructor: "Who will succeed Colonel Lee as Superintendent? I fear his place will never be so well filled. What a loss for the Corps Mrs. Lee's departure will be. It is useless for me to say anything in praise of such a model family, especially as my sentiments on that topic have been often expressed to you orally and concurred in entirely."[34]

In 1855, Secretary of War Jefferson Davis organized two new cavalry regiments. They were to be elite, with hand-picked officers. Because of his overall performance and quite possibly in part from that spectacular feat in Texas, Stuart was selected for the new 1st Cavalry. In August 1855, it was ordered to Fort Leavenworth, Kansas Territory, with Stuart as quartermaster and commissary. This appointment was a surprise to the young officer, since it entailed handling large amounts of money and ensuring supplies for the entire regiment. He bunked with Lieutenant Robert Ransom, Jr., adjutant, and Major John Sedgwick. Both were to become major generals on opposite sides during the Civil War.

By August 1855, Stuart was still pondering choosing between a military or civilian career but was leaning toward the military. During that same time, he assured cousin Alexander Stuart Brown that even on the frontier, refinement could be found, as well as ladies, with whom he had been riding every evening. One especially caught his eye. In September 1855 from Fort Leavenworth, he wrote again to Alexander Brown, asking him to order a silver set with "Stuart" engraved on it. He was to be married to Miss Flora Cooke, daughter of Colonel Philip St. George Cooke, respected commander of the 2nd Dragoons. On November 14 at Fort Riley, Kansas Territory, the wedding took place. The couple left for his duty station at Fort Leavenworth the next day. Sadly, Stuart's father had died just before the wedding; Flora had the duty of writing her betrothed while he was on the Sioux campaign with his regiment. Just a few days before, Stuart had received a letter from him with his blessings for the marriage. "What a shadow is life!" Stuart wrote to Alexander. Yet there was duty, in spite of grief: "I got Flora's letter yesterday while in the midst of an important business transaction and will be heels over head in business for a month yet. I assure you it makes me sick at heart to pursue the details of business in the midst of such melancholy tidings." It would not be the last time duty took precedence over personal suffering.

There was also something greater to lean upon: "These dispensations of an all wise providence must be experienced by all. *His* will *not* mine be done."[35]

By December 20, Stuart had been promoted to first lieutenant. His duties for the next year and a half took him away from Flora a good deal; she remained with her family at Fort Riley. Flora was used to it. She had grown up "in the Army," married into it, and knew exactly what the life was like.

On the North Fork of the Solomon River in Kansas on July 29, 1857, six companies of Stuart's regiment were confronted by 300 Cheyenne warriors, spread out in battle line and marching steadily toward them. The order was given to draw sabers and charge. A few dozen yards before the enemy, the Indians broke and scattered across the plains. Stuart swept in pursuit with two other companies.

As they caught up to the Indians, he saw another officer about to be shot by a dismounted warrior.

Stuart rushed in with his saber to save the life of his fellow officer and slashed the Indian severely on the head. But in so doing, Stuart was shot point blank in the middle of the chest by the Indian.

Miraculously, the heavy lead ball glanced to the left, and lodged beneath Stuart's left nipple, so deep that it could not be felt by the doctor upon examination. With the help of his fellow officers, he dismounted. The colonel rode up and ordered that Stuart be placed in a blanket and carried back to camp. On the night of August 4 the camp was attacked by twenty or thirty Cheyennes. On August 8, the group started for Fort Kearny in Nebraska Territory. On August 14, awakening in the midst of a thick fog, the troopers realized that their Pawnee guides had disappeared in the night. Stuart, though still recovering from his own wound, volunteered to lead a small party to find Fort Kearny. They rode the remaining fifty-five miles and arrived at Fort Kearny on August 17 after some of the most trying marching anyone could have endured. In addition to giving Stuart a soldier's look at death, eye-to-eye, this experience would assure Stuart that, despite hardships, much can be accomplished with dogged perseverance.[36]

The America in which Stuart grew to manhood was on the verge of a second revolution. What was to break out into the bloodiest conflict Americans were ever to see had several flashpoints in the 1850s, all seeming to culminate in the attack on the U.S. arsenal at Harpers Ferry, Virginia (now West Virginia), by the fanatical Abolitionist John Brown in 1859.

From the fall of 1857 to the summer of 1860, Stuart was at Fort Riley with the 1st Cavalry under Sedgwick's command. He spent much of his six-month leave of absence in the summer of 1859 joyfully visiting relatives in Virginia. During his stay in Richmond in October he was called to Washington to negotiate for the sale to the government of a saber attachment he had invented. While there, Stuart visited Arlington House across the Potomac River and called upon his dear friends the Lees and their children, including Mary Custis. Then came word of the attack at Harpers Ferry.

Backed financially by Abolitionists in New England, Brown, bent on the immediate abolishment of slavery by any means, had gathered arms over the summer. His plan was to capture the armory and allow word to spread throughout the South. Then he would arm and lead a slave army to freedom.

Brown was prone to violence, particularly in the Kansas Territory in 1855–56 while it was wavering between admission into the union as a free or slave state. Stuart had been stationed there and, when Brown and his gang took prisoner some pro-slavery men at Black Jack, Kansas, part of the 1st Cavalry, including Stuart, freed them. Thus Stuart got his first look at the man who would become the embodiment of and martyr for the Abolitionists.[37]

Harpers Ferry is built on the steep hill that rises between the confluence of the Shenandoah and Potomac rivers. With two rivers for water power, abundant forests for fuel, and eventually two railroads and a canal converging there, it was a natural place for the manufacture and shipment of goods to the East. Arms had been produced there since 1801. Also located on the arsenal grounds were warehouses and a small firehouse near where the Baltimore and Ohio Railroad bridge crossed the Potomac at "the Point."

By 10:30 P.M. October 16, Brown and his group crossed the B&O bridge, took the watchman prisoner, and left guards on the bridge as they went into the town. They quickly broke into the armory grounds. Brown sent his men out to capture the rest of the town and gather hostages. Hayward Shepherd, a B&O station baggage man, was shot when he refused to halt for the raiders. He later died.

Word of the raiders' occupation of the armory and town spread. Residents armed themselves and started taking potshots at the raiders; several died in the skirmishing. A militia unit from Charles Town drove them from their outposts into the armory with their hostages, and they established a "fort" in the firehouse.

More militia units arrived from Martinsburg, Shepherdstown, and Winchester, Virginia, and Frederick and Baltimore, Maryland. Yet, only one attempt was made to dislodge the raiders and that was driven back. Brown, wondering where were the slaves he expected to rally to him, attempted to bargain for his escape. Offers to free the hostages in return for freedom were rejected.

When word arrived at the War Department early on the afternoon of October 17, Stuart was sitting in the office waiting to present some papers on his saber attachment. He was given orders to deliver at once to Lee at Arlington House: Lee was to take command of a detachment of Marines from the Washington Navy Yard and proceed to Harpers Ferry. He not only delivered the message but volunteered to accompany Lee.[38]

Lee did not even have time to change into a uniform and Stuart had barely enough time to borrow a uniform coat and saber.[39] They met the Marines, commanded by Lieutenant Israel Green, near Harpers Ferry and marched them into the armory yard by 11 P.M. Lee demanded surrender at 2:30 on the morning of October 18 but began to mobilize for an assault while waiting for a reply. Green hand-picked a storming party of a dozen Marines. They were ordered to use only bayonets to avoid injuring the hostages.

With the militia formed outside the armory for crowd control, the Marines gathered at a corner of the engine house. Stuart moved to the door and demanded surrender. Brown came to the door and made a counterproposal. Stuart recognizcd the piercing, blue, killer's eyes above the matted, gray beard. Lee had instructed Stuart to accept no terms other than surrender. Brown tried every tack, all amounting to allowing him and his band to escape. The hostages begged to talk to Lee, but Stuart said that Lee would never agree to any terms but those already laid down.[40] When Stuart realized nothing was to be accomplished in talking with Brown, he leapt to the side and waved his hat, the signal for the Marines to attack.

The Marines broke down the door with a heavy ladder. Bayonets and sabers were used on the resisting raiders. Brown himself was felled by a series of blows from Green. The entire fight lasted about three minutes. No hostage was harmed.

While Brown was unconscious (Stuart thought he was pretending to be dead), Stuart was the first one to expose his identity. That same day about noon, Lee asked Stuart to lead some Marines about five miles into Maryland to confiscate 1,500 pikes Brown had stashed.[41] The next day, Brown was questioned by Governor Henry A. Wise and others. Stuart was there and asked Brown that after all the killings, burnings, and thefts he had committed in Kansas if he did not believe the teachings of the Bible.

Brown did not answer directly, for he was trying to portray himself as a gentle man who only was trying to free an oppressed people. Indicating Stuart, he said, "I believe that the major here would not have been alive but for me. I might have killed him, just as easy as I could kill a mosquito, when he came in, but I supposed he came in only to receive our surrender."[42] Stuart mentioned this remark in a letter to his mother.[43]

What Brown said after that may have chilled the cavalryman even more:

> You had better—all you people at the South—prepare yourselves for a settlement of that question that must come up for settlement sooner than you are prepared for it. The sooner you are prepared the better. You may dispose of me very easily; I am nearly disposed of now; but this question is still to be settled—this negro question I mean—the end of that is not yet.[44]

On October 31, Brown was convicted of treason against the state, conspiring with slaves to rebel, and murder. He was hanged December 2.[45] In a letter to his mother, Stuart praised Lee, saying that he should receive a gold medal from Virginia for his cool, efficient handling of the affair. The young cavalryman was at Lee's side virtually every moment and he confided, "No one but myself will ever *know* the *immense* but quiet service he rendered the State and the Country before and after the particular attack for which all give praise." He also passed on a telling emotion: "The feeling that actuated me was this: I felt duty bound to let no opportunity slip to do my native State service—particularly when menaced with a servile war."[46]

Stuart's reaction to the encouragement by a Northerner of a slave rebellion was probably typical. Writing from Wytheville to Wise less than a month after the Harpers Ferry incident, he touched on the "armament and defense of the State against 'invasion from without, and commotion within.'" He referred specifically to the vulnerability of Virginia to attack from the North, recommending that the state encourage young men to enlist in the military by paying for their uniforms. He also recommended that they be required to drill once a month.[47]

Stuart's assistant adjutant general and biographer, H. B. McClellan, said that Stuart had determined before the war to follow Virginia whichever way it went. Perhaps his experience with Brown had something to do with this; in his letters after the raid, he began to mention his loyalties to Virginia more and more often.

In a letter dated January 11, 1861, after his return to Kansas, Stuart asserted where his deepest allegiances lay: "I for one would . . . throw *my sabre* in the scale consecrated by the principles and blood of our forefathers—our constitutional rights without which the Union is a mere mockery." Finally, he lamented that he was not nearer the scene of the impending conflict and that the country's wounds already were too deep to heal.[48]

On May 3, shortly after Fort Sumter fell, Stuart wrote his resignation from the U.S. Army. Ironically, his promotion to captain arrived simultaneously. His resignation was accepted on May 7 and three days later he was commissioned as a lieutenant colonel of infantry in the Confederate army.[49]

Events happened quickly after that.

CHAPTER TWO

Civil War

"For my part I have had no hesitancy from the first that, right or wrong, alone or otherwise, I go with Virginia." [1]

—J. E. B. STUART, 1861

Stuart wrote to his wife from Richmond and later Harpers Ferry, where he was sent to serve with the odd genius Thomas J. Jackson. He mentioned his mentor, Robert E. Lee, now a general in the Southern army, who was beleaguered with staff duties. Between the lines is a sense of a sorrow for Lee and a regret that Lee's gifts of cool, planned decision-making were being wasted.

He also wrote that many of the young men he studied with at West Point and fought with on the frontier were beginning to gather around the new Confederacy. He was especially eager to see his father-in-law, Philip St. George Cooke, come over. Cooke was considered one of the best cavalry officers in the country.

A change in command brought to ̶ ̶ ̶ ̶ oseph E. Johnston, whom Stuart had seen in comman ̶ ̶ ̶ ̶ thereafter, Stuart got the cavalry command he desir ̶ ̶ ̶ ̶ .t.

In another letter to his wife, n ̶ ̶ ̶ ̶ ̶ ̶ ̶ attention from the ladies he was suddenly receiving: "If you could see the strawberries, bouquets, and other nice things the ladies send me you would think me pretty well off. The young men of the Regiment wonder why it is that I am the recipient of so much favor—they forget that rank will tell." By now the Stuarts had two children. In the same letter he told his wife to kiss "our dear ones a thousand times" and to remind them of their father. He signed in haste, "Your devoted." [2]

Later, some fellow officers and misinformed newspapermen accused Stuart of currying ladies' favors, of wasting military time, and casting aside duty for the attentions of one woman or another. The frank paragraph to his own wife indicates that he was hiding nothing from her. Stuart initially seemed as confused as his younger comrades as to all the attention, but realistically conceded that it was more likely due to his status and accessibility than to himself.

While in camp near Bunker Hill, nine miles north of Winchester, Virginia, a unit arrived under the command of Captain William E. Jones. Even then, he carried the nickname "Grumble." For any number of reasons, Jones took an immediate dislike to Stuart. It was unfortunate, because Jones later served under him. Though the animosity grew into hatred and resulted in Jones' arrest and preference of charges by Stuart, it was too late when "Grumble" finally realized Stuart's worth to the Confederacy.[3]

Stuart operated in the early summer with Johnston's army near Winchester and along the Potomac River. His appearance at this time was a little different than the image he would later assume. According to John Esten Cooke of Stuart's staff, "He wore at this time his blue United States army uniform, and a forage cap covered with a white 'havelock,' resembling a chain helmet, which made his head resemble that of a knight of the days of chivalry."[4] One incident may help to define his character as well as the atmosphere early in the war, when it was more like a grand game than the killing machine it became just a few months hence.

In early July, Stuart was apparently scouting alone in front of the main body of his unit—the commander acting like any common trooper—when he emerged from a thick stand of trees to confront about fifty Pennsylvania infantrymen just on the other side of a fence. Bombast became his best weapon. He rode over and ordered them to throw down a section of fence. He was an officer, no doubt, by his bearing and ease of command, so the soldiers obeyed. He then commanded the men to put down their arms, which they did. A few more commands and the men were in line, filing sharply through the gap in the fence and into the midst of Stuart's cavalry, prisoners by ruse.

George Cary Eggleston, a trooper in the 1st Virginia, wrote:

> [Stuart's] restless activity was one, at least, of the qualities which
> enabled him to win the reputation he achieved so rapidly. He could
> never be still. He was rarely ever in camp at all, and he never showed
> a sign of fatigue. He led almost everything. Even after he became a
> general officer, with well-nigh an army of horsemen under his com-
> mand, I frequently followed him as my leader in a little party of half
> a dozen troopers, who might as well have gone with a sergeant on
> duty assigned them.[5]

In June, Eggleston had been assigned to some paperwork at Stuart's headquarters at Bunker Hill. He was outside with his horse awaiting further orders when Stuart emerged from the house. The lieutenant colonel was immediately drawn to Eggleston's fine horse—poking, patting, and feeling as horse lovers often do. Stuart apparently offered to buy the animal but Eggleston refused. Well then, how about slipping off for a scout? "I'll ride your horse and you can ride mine. I want to try your beast's paces," Stuart said. Off they went.

They rode into the area between the armies. At first they were undetected by enemy pickets. They stopped and looked down upon the Union camps. Soon they were discovered. Federal cavalry pursued as they took to the road back toward Confederate lines. For three minutes, while the blue troopers behind them gained ground and the pair approached Union pickets on the road, Eggleston's concern mounted. Suddenly, they were upon the pickets, riding through them at a gallop from the rear. Shots echoed in the woods and Eggleston distinctly remembered half a dozen bullets whistling past their ears.

Lucky to be unscathed, they approached their own lines and reined their horses in. Stuart was silent for a moment, then turned to Eggleston, who was still unnerved by the close call. "Did you ever time this horse for a half-mile?" Stuart asked nonchalantly.[6]

It was during this time that Stuart gave his recruits some of their best training. Eggleston was said to tell the story of the morning Stuart, after hearing that the enemy was near, led a squadron of unbloodied troopers in column of fours out of camp. Soon they crested a hill and were discovered by some Federal infantry. Stuart spread the column out into battle line. The infantry began firing at Stuart's troopers and they began to look at one another nervously. Then the Yankees unlimbered a cannon. Stuart turned his back almost disdainfully to it as a round was fired. A second later, the boom arrived along with a crashing sound and explosion in the trees above their heads. "There," Stuart told them. "I wanted you to learn what a cannon's like, and hear it." After a few more words of instruction to the wide-eyed troopers, Stuart and his students turned and trotted off.

Facts back up Eggleston's remarks that Stuart seemed often to ride alone or with just a small body of men while scouting, even after attaining high rank. There was an affair at Verdiersville, Virginia, in mid-August 1862 in which Stuart, a newly appointed major general, was nearly captured while riding in a small group. There were numerous other instances where he rode alone and was nearly captured or killed. He enjoyed independent command and realized that light cavalry needed independence to strike swiftly and escape. Stuart always seemed confident that *he* could escape using his wits and a fast horse. He expected it of his men, too.

One of the reasons he liked to scout alone or with just a small group was to gather information about an area in which he was to operate. Knowledge of the terrain, of roads and trails and where they led was essential, not only to protect his own command but to pass vital information on to infantry units. Considering the lack of reliability of others, he used the only scout he knew he could trust implicitly: himself.

He also liked to see the war from the trooper's point of view, to see firsthand the defilade and ground he was asking his men to die for. Everything was different under fire, and Stuart knew it. More than once, Yankee lead had bored holes in his clothes and torn the warm fur collar his wife made from his throat. On one occasion a group of his men was not standing under fire and Stuart rode up. Union officers could be heard commanding their men to shoot the rebel officer on the horse. His staff begged him to get under cover, but his men must stand and he knew they would if he did. The fire got even hotter, but the men were steadied. They saw Stuart put a curious hand to his face. He turned his horse to ride back and when he dropped his hand to rein, they saw that a Yankee minie ball had shaved half his moustache, as clean as a well-stropped razor.

In July 1861, the Northern military plan was simple enough: Keep the Confederates under General Joseph E. Johnston in the Shenandoah Valley busy with troops under Major General Robert Patterson. Federal forces would then strike out from near Washington and destroy General P. G. T. Beauregard's forces near an important Virginia rail center, Manassas Junction, twenty-five miles west of the capital. Then they could march south on Richmond and the war would be over in a week.

Stuart's 1st Virginia scouted with Johnston in the valley and guarded Jackson's flank. As an attack on Beauregard seemed imminent, Johnston's men went by train to Manassas. Stuart kept Patterson's force occupied for a while, then followed Johnston. After thirty-six hours in the saddle, his regiment arrived at Manassas to engage the enemy in a spectacular way.

The fighting at Manassas had gone on most of the day of July 21. It seemed as if no commander remembered that he had cavalry. Stuart, eager to participate but still without orders, scouted across the stream at Hull Run, then returned. It must have been agony for the restless Stuart, surrounded by the sights and sounds of the biggest battle he had seen to date but without orders to do anything. His apprehension increased as some South Carolina troops, panic-stricken and fleeing the enemy, ran out of some woods and disappeared into the distance.

In the afternoon, just a couple of hours after Jackson became immortalized with his nickname "Stonewall," Stuart's regiment was on the left flank of the army. A courier rode up with orders for Stuart to attack where the firing was hottest. It was exactly what he wanted to hear.

To the bugle call of "Boots and Saddles," the men tightened girths and adjusted reins, their movements quickened by nervous anticipation. As they trotted off in column of fours, they could not have been encouraged as to the prospects of glorious war as they passed through a field hospital. Surgeons slick with gore sawed at the limbs of screaming men and heaved the still-warm limbs into growing pyramids of human flesh and bone. Those with whom the surgeons had finished calmly shooed the flies from their fresh stumps, or moved not at all as the flies gathered in their eyes and noses—too far gone for the doctor, but not for the undertaker. The gory scene was too much for some stomachs already twisted with pre-battle nerves.

From Stuart's position at the head of his troopers, the field was a cloud of white and blue smoke covering the artillery and lines of infantry. Flashes could be seen from the cannon through the vaporous, ghostly field, then the wind would pick up and the view of thousands of men in mortal combat would emerge, only to be covered up again in a moment.

As Stuart led his column, a bright line of Zouaves—dressed in red caps and trousers, and short blue jackets—suddenly appeared marching down a sunken part of the Sudley Road. Stuart ordered a charge, but pulled up; whose troops were they? Both sides fielded men in the uniform of the vaunted French troops.

The regiment was on the double quick, but seemed to Stuart to be greatly disorganized. He was near enough by then to shout to them, "Don't run, boys, we are here!" The Zouaves ignored him and ran on in column of twos. As he was passing through a gap into the same field they were entering, suddenly, from behind the hill emerged the U.S. flag. The Zouaves were New Yorkers, so intent upon the battle ahead of them (or perhaps upon escaping) that they did not notice the enemy cavalry on their flank.[7]

Stuart spread his men out in battle line, charged, and covered half the distance between the two lines before the Yankees realized what was happening. The Zouaves turned and fired a volley. The smoke obscured Stuart's charging horsemen and the Zouaves, instead of preparing to repulse the attack, assumed they had blown away the enemy with the one volley. The Yankees were reloading when Stuart's men hit them at full speed. The Zouaves scattered.

Stuart turned his men around and charged back through what was left of the Zouave line. He had only two companies, but they seemed huge and unstoppable as they plunged through the smoke into the natty New Yorkers.

Stuart's men were scattered now and adjutant William Blackford tried to re-form them. Some of the men returned, but others, perhaps shaken by the experience, headed off down the road behind the rallying point, seemingly heading for home. Blackford brought them back and Stuart laughed off the incident. Blackford thought that Stuart had been a bit scandalized at the troopers' reluctance to re-form after their first taste of real action, but "he [Stuart] was so brave a man himself that he never seemed to attribute unworthy motives to his men, and this was one of the secrets of his great influence over them in action. They were ashamed to be anything but brave where he was."[8]

Stuart soon acquired some artillery commanded by Lieutenant R. F. Beckham. After the men had re-formed, Stuart moved two guns across the Sudley Road. Screening the artillery behind some foliage about 500 yards from the right rear of the enemy, he opened fire. The pines dispersed the smoke from the pieces so the Yankees could not locate them to return fire. He placed his cavalry behind the guns, ready for action, and sent observers far out on the high ground to spot for the artillerists as well as for the infantry.[9] Beckham cut the fuses long and lowered the guns so that the shells bounded along the ground, mowing through the enemy's packed ranks, before exploding. Blackford proposed, "But for our charge and the fire of these guns, there can be no question that the flank of Jackson's 'stone wall' would have been turned before [Jubal A.] Early arrived with his brigade, in which case the day would have been lost."[10] Just two years after the war, Early himself wrote, "Stuart did as much towards saving the battle of First Manassas as any subordinate who participated in it; and yet he has never received any credit for it, in the official reports or otherwise. His own report is very brief and indefinite."[11]

Blackford watched as the whole field was suddenly transformed into a confused, running mass of Yankees headed for a small bridge over Cub Run that soon was blocked by an overturned wagon. Stuart decided to pursue. In his after-action report, Stuart wrote that he was so encumbered with prisoners and had to detail so many of his troopers to guard them that his combat command was reduced to a squad. Stuart and his men followed the Union retreat nearly a dozen miles before they turned back, their role in the battle completed.

Johnston had seen Stuart in action in the Valley and at Manassas. On August 10, the general wrote to President Jefferson Davis:

> He is a rare man, wonderfully endowed by nature with the quali-
> ties necessary for an officer of light cavalry. Calm, firm, acute, active,
> and enterprising. I know no one more competent than he to estimate
> the occurrences before him at their true value. If you add a real brigade
> of cavalry to this army, you can find no better brigadier-general to
> command it.[12]

Small fights and scouting missions toward Washington filled the rest of the summer and fall. Typical was a battle fought on September 11 at Lewinsville, Virginia, where Stuart attacked with 300 men an already retreating Federal force of 1,800. He reported "not a scratch to man or horse."[13]

Promotion always comes rapidly in wartime, but the Confederacy needed experienced officers desperately. On September 24, just four-and-one-half months after he resigned his commission as a first lieutenant in the U.S. Army, Stuart was commissioned brigadier general.

In the third week of November, he wrote to his wife from Camp *Qui Vive* to ask her to keep her own name out of the newspapers. There may have been some scandal after the Washington Star published her father's promotion as a Union brigadier general. He recommended that they just "let it go and be forgotten. By calling attention to the matter no one will regard what you say and it will only revive the recollection of your Pa's course. . . . Let us determine to act well *our* parts and bear with the mistakes and errors of others, however grievous, with the charity of silence."[14] It sounds like something Robert E. Lee might have counseled.

On December 1, he wrote her to ignore the teasing of her cousin, John Esten Cooke, about some "hand-kissing affair." "My darling if you could know—(and I think you ought) how true I am to you and how centered in you is my every hope—and dream of earthly bliss, you would never listen to the idle twaddle of those who knowing how we love each other amuse themselves telling such outlandish yarns."[15] In other letters in December, he talked about the possibility of death in battle—that he would not sacrifice himself rashly but would leave a fine legacy for his children. He said that he had heard that Flora's mother was staying in a hotel in Washington and that she would like to hear from her daughter. Stuart told his wife that if she would write a note, he would have it placed under her breakfast plate within the week.[16]

At this time, Stuart began organizing an important branch of his cavalry, the artillery, under the energetic drills of John Pelham of Alabama. Pelham named the units the "Stuart Horse Artillery." By December 20, Stuart commanded four regiments of infantry (about 1,600 men), about 150 cavalry troopers and a battery of artillery. Near Dranesville, Virginia, he fought against a force of 3,950 and was forced to withdraw to Centreville.

Through the winter, Stuart and his men stayed on outpost duty. He made the telling statement in a letter that as long as the war lasts, "I will not *leave* the *van* of our Army unless *compelled* to." He did not care what the other generals did; for him, duty came first.[17] Flora understood how devoted he was to duty; she visited him at Camp *Qui Vive* at the end of December.[18] Around this time, he seemed in his own mind to have put to rest the family problems caused by his father-in-law's decision to fight for the Union. Stuart wrote to Flora's brother, John R. Cooke, who fought for the Confederacy, about their father's decision: "He will regret it but once and that will be continually."[19]

Spring brought increased action from the Yankees. Major General George B.

McClellan, the new commander of the Army of the Potomac, began a strategy that drew Confederate forces away from Washington. First planning a massive march from Urbanna, Virginia, to Richmond, McClellan was stymied by the menacing appearance in Hampton Roads of the ironclad *Virginia,* built out of the former U.S. vessel *Merrimack.* McClellan remained near Washington for fear that the seemingly unstoppable craft would sail up the Potomac and shell the capital. After the *Virginia* fought its inconclusive battle with the ironclad *Monitor* on March 9, McClellan could move. By then, he had abandoned his Urbanna plan and instead launched the largest amphibious operation to date: transporting his entire army down the Chesapeake Bay and landing at the tip of the Peninsula, which runs between the James and York rivers and leads directly to Richmond.

In response, Confederates withdrew from lines around Manassas and entrenched in Yorktown, Virginia, rebuilding some of the earthworks constructed by the British during the siege there eighty years before. McClellan brought in huge artillery pieces and dug lines in preparation for a siege. After a month of backbreaking work, McClellan's men were amazed to discover that the Confederates were no longer in their lines. They had begun a retreat up the Peninsula toward Richmond.

Stuart guarded the army's rear and other vital points along the Peninsula, fighting around Fort Magruder near Williamsburg. He was pleased with the cool actions of the Horse Artillery under young Pelham as well as the charges made by his cavalry against the enemy. Someone told Stuart that he had come close to capturing his own father-in-law, Philip St. George Cooke.

On June 1, 1862, Confederate commander Joseph Johnston was wounded at the Battle of Seven Pines east of Richmond. Robert E. Lee became commander of the main Confederate army in the East, which he soon named the Army of Northern Virginia.

Even though he had known Lee for years, socialized with him, and even served under him at Harpers Ferry, Stuart was still testing their new respective roles in June 1862. Through little fault of his own, Lee had been conspicuously unsuccessful in his first campaign in western Virginia. Boldly in a letter, Stuart suggested to Lee some campaign strategy, after apologizing for being presumptuous. He went on to say that he had studied the enemy's movements, system of war, and conduct in combat over the previous several months and concluded that the Confederate army was better suited for attack than defense: "Let us fight at advantage before we are forced to fight at disadvantage."[20] No matter what Lee's course, Stuart assured him that he would support him.

Stuart's strategy was not what Lee had in mind. Stuart wanted to attack south of the Chickahominy River; Lee sent him north of it. But the correspondence surely reminded Lee of the kind of soldier Stuart had always been. Lee was aware of Stuart's reputation at West Point for aggressiveness; he also may have realized the potential in this type of personality.

Early in June, Stuart sent John Singleton Mosby scouting along the Union army's supply line from White House Landing on the Pamunkey River. After Stuart conveyed Mosby's report, on June 11 Lee told Stuart to scout the Union rear. His orders seemed to address Stuart's strengths and faults.

> You are desired to make a scout movement to the rear of the enemy now posted on the Chickahominy, with a view to gaining intelligence of his operations, communications, etc. . . . Another is to destroy his wagon trains. . . . You will return as soon as the object of your expedition is accomplished; and you must bear constantly in mind, while endeavoring to execute the general purpose of your mission, not to hazard unnecessarily your command, or to attempt what your judgement may not approve; but be content to accomplish all the good you can, without feeling it necessary to obtain all that might be desired. . . . You must leave sufficient cavalry here for the service of this army, and remember that one of the chief objects of your expedition is to gain intelligence for the guidance of future movements.[21]

He updated Stuart on information he had received the night before on the strength and position of Federal forces. He also warned him that if the enemy were too strong or reinforced in the area where Stuart was to go, he must return immediately to his former position.

Twenty-eight-year-old Stuart must have been thrilled at the opportunity. This was much better than trying to locate the ubiquitous and inscrutable Indian in the vastness of the Southwest. Until this point, Stuart had only read about such an operation.

Gathering a force of about 1,200 troopers and some artillery on the morning of June 12, Stuart set out on his greatest mission so far during the war. Heading first northwestward from Richmond to deceive the enemy as to his planned route, he suddenly turned to the southeast, crossed the Richmond, Fredericksburg and Potomac Railroad, and encamped that night at Winston's Farm. Any enemy scouts seeing the column during the day would have informed their commanders that night that a large Confederate cavalry force looked to be heading across the South Anna River, perhaps on a raid north or to reinforce Stonewall Jackson, who was running wild in the Shenandoah Valley.

After putting his men to bed without fires, Stuart rode five miles with

Rooney Lee to Hickory Hill, where Lee's wife lived at the family home. Stuart caught a couple of hours sleep in a chair and by daylight had ridden back to lead his troopers. It was because of this restless energy that Stuart was called indefatigable.

At 9 A.M. Stuart ran into a small body of Federals at Hanover Court House. He sent Fitzhugh Lee around to the right in an attempt to get into their rear, but the enemy retreated south so quickly that Lee did not even have time to get into position. At Hawe's Shop, the Confederates struck pickets of the 5th U.S. Cavalry, sent out from Old Church to the southeast. Stuart attacked, drove the Union troopers back, and burned their camp. The Confederates then headed southward toward Tunstall's Station.

Late at night on June 13, Stuart made a decision with Lee's orders in mind. He had accomplished everything he was supposed to: he had scouted the enemy's right flank and fortifications and had destroyed wagons and supplies. The question was how to return safely. The enemy would expect him to retrace his steps rather than ride completely around its rear. Stuart decided to use light cavalry the way it was always meant to be used. He ordered his column into a trot and headed toward McClellan's lines of communication. It was bold but not necessarily impetuous. He made the decision in the field, according to circumstances, following orders, and relying on his wits and well-trained troopers to get him through.

On the road from Old Church to Tunstall's Station, Stuart captured a wagon train[22] and at Putney's Ferry burned two large transports on the Pamunkey River as well as a number of wagons. At Tunstall's Station, McClellan reported that more wagons were burned, along with railroad cars full of corn and forage. Telegraph poles were destroyed and the railroad bridge over Black Creek burned. Stuart was mightily tempted to race to White House, the supply center for the huge Union force on the Peninsula, but, perhaps remembering Lee's instructions, he resisted temptation and rode on.

By now, a pursuit was being organized by Stuart's father-in-law. For some reason, it was laggard and lethargic. While Cooke poked around, Stuart's troopers burned stores everywhere, cut telegraph wires, and obstructed the railroad. Rations and forage were collected when they could be; the rest was destroyed.

Stuart put the 165 prisoners he had gathered on captured animals so as not to slow him down[23] and the column headed toward Talleysville. Many of Stuart's men had grown up in the area and knew every pig path. After a brief rest at Talleysville, Stuart pushed on toward the Chickahominy River, with infantry and cavalry in pursuit.

After unsuccessfully trying to ford, his men dismantled a warehouse and built a bridge at Forge Bridge. Once on the other side, Stuart himself hurried to Richmond to report to Lee while his men strengthened and widened the bridge for the passage of artillery and wagons.

The physical results of the raid were impressive, but more important was the information obtained on the Union army's right wing. Stuart also gained valuable information on the area through which Lee would be fighting in just a couple of weeks. In addition, the ride boosted morale in the cavalry, the army in general, and among civilians who now knew Stuart's name intimately from the newspapers as the man who humiliated the vast Yankee foe at the doorstep of their capital.

While Stuart was in Richmond, Virginia Governor John Letcher presented him with a sword. A crowd stopped him in front of the Governor's Mansion and demanded a speech, which he gave.

During the week that the accolades flowed into cavalry camp, Lee was planning how to drive the Union army from its position just outside of Richmond. Fortunately, McClellan was cooperating. He placed his base of supply at White House on the Pamunkey River and stretched his army across the Peninsula, straddling the Chickahominy River. This normally sluggish creek, draining the swamplands north and east of Richmond, flooded when it rained heavily, as it had in June. It now impeded support of either wing of McClellan's army by the other. Lee planned to attack the Union force near Mechanicsville and drive him back down the Peninsula. Jackson, who was marching from the Shenandoah Valley, was to turn the Union right flank at Beaverdam Creek. Stuart's cavalry was to guard Jackson's left flank as he marched.

Though Jackson was delayed, Lee began his attack on the afternoon of June 26 at Beaverdam Creek. Losses were heavy, but the Confederates kept the pressure on. Jackson finally made it to the field and gained a position that forced the Union army to withdraw to Gaines Mill. Stuart guarded Jackson's left to Old Church and found artillery positions for him, with Pelham taking two guns and effectively countering two entire batteries of Federal artillery.

Stuart continued to work his way around the Union right flank on ground he knew intimately from his ride just a few days before. This time, however, he advanced to White House. Sadly, when they arrived, the house for which the landing was named was burning. Riding with Stuart was its owner, Rooney Lee.

On June 29, Stuart skirmished with a gunboat, the *Marblehead*. Using sharpshooters and one of Pelham's artillery pieces, he drove it back down the Pamunkey toward the York River. Stuart took White House Landing and told Lee that the Federal army had abandoned its supply base on the north side of the Peninsula. Swinging southward again with orders to hook up with Jackson, Stuart reached the Chickahominy on July 1 but found that the army had moved farther south. Unable to connect with Jackson from where he was located, he improvised, retraced his steps, and forded the river lower down. In the meantime, Lee battled the Federals as they continued to retreat across the Peninsula. Lee's advance was finally stopped on July 1 by massed Union artillery on Malvern Hill. By then, the Federal army had changed its base to Harrison's Landing on the James River.

As the Army of the Potomac lay under the protection of gunboats on the James, Stuart and Pelham shelled their camps on July 3. Walter Taylor, Lee's adjutant general, later wrote, "Stuart, glorious Stuart! always at the front and full of fight, gained these hills." [24] Taylor's statement could be taken two ways. Actually, it was a sarcastic attack, saying Stuart should have waited for the rest of the army to come up instead of provoking the enemy to occupy the heights. Taylor's prejudice against Stuart would emerge later when writing of Stuart's role in the Gettysburg campaign.

Looking at it from Stuart's point of view on Evelynton Heights brings it into sharper focus. First, Stuart believed the rest of the army was where it was supposed to be, nearby instead of lost and wandering. Using locals in his ranks as guides, Stuart found the enemy and engaged him.

Regardless of what Taylor thought at the time or years afterward, Stuart soon after his action on the Peninsula got his commission as major general, on July 25.[25] Other promotions among his officers followed and the cavalry brigade was filled out into a division.

At Verdiersville, Virginia, on August 17, while riding with only five of his staff to contact Fitzhugh Lee at Raccoon Ford, Stuart stopped at a house for the night. Horses were left saddled in the back yard and the officers rolled themselves up in their blankets on the front porch. About dawn, Stuart heard cavalry moving toward the little clump of houses. John Singleton Mosby and another man were sent down the road to contact what Stuart thought were Lee's men. Without hat, cloak, or haversack, Stuart walked to the gate to welcome Fitz.

Suddenly, pistol shots echoed down the road through the early morning haze. Mosby and his comrade, faces pressed against their horses' manes and whipping hard, came around the bend shouting that Yankee cavalry was behind them. Stuart and the rest bolted for their horses and tore off in different directions, with most of the Yankees chasing huge Major Heros von Borcke, a Prussian who was Stuart's assistant adjutant. Stuart hid in the woods nearby and watched as the blue troopers rifled his equipment, taking his famous plumed hat. He rode the next day wearing a bandanna around his head and suffered the ignominy of the infantry he passed: "Hey cav'ry! Where's yer hat?" He wrote to his wife of the incident and added savagely, "I intend to make the Yankees pay for that hat."[26]

On August 22, Stuart proposed to Robert E. Lee a ride to the rear of Major General John Pope's army, a force of about 50,000 operating in north-central Virginia. Lee agreed. Stuart reached the rear of Pope's army at Catlett's Station, but a downpour made any action virtually impossible. Stuart did, however, capture some of Pope's staff, some money, and Pope's dispatch book and baggage. Because of the rain, they could not burn the railroad bridge over Cedar Run and could not cut it down with the few axes they could find. Stuart withdrew to Warrenton Springs with 300 prisoners and Pope's uniform, which was displayed in Richmond, just recompense for the loss of Stuart's plumed hat less than a week before.

There also were those in his own ranks who, for whatever reason—jealousy, egocentricity, mule-headedness—began to make an enemy out of Stuart. Old Brigadier General Isaac R. Trimble got upset with Stuart during the capture of Manassas Junction, just before the second battle there.[27] William E. Jones still cared little for Stuart. It could have been because of Stuart's youth and his being in command of his elders. Occasionally, seniority takes it hard when someone with vivacity, strength, and sheer energy of will comes along.

During the maneuvering around Manassas Junction in the last few days of August, Stuart again worked with Jackson. During a crucial time in the campaign, Longstreet had to fight his way through Thoroughfare Gap in the Bull Run Mountains to connect with Jackson before Jackson's troops were overwhelmed. On the evening of August 28, Jackson had attacked a much larger Union force marching temptingly in front of him. Jackson knew Longstreet was on his way and that if he got in trouble, he always had darkness to rely on to end the battle. After Longstreet fought his way through the gap, Stuart opened communications between the two commands as Longstreet moved to support Jackson.[28]

Longstreet and Lee rode ahead of Longstreet's columns. Stuart gave his commander his first appraisal of the battlefield and the action so far.[29]

A portion of Stuart's cavalry—actually his Horse Artillery, under Pelham, on loan to Jackson—helped save Jackson's wagon trains on August 29 near Groveton,[30] Virginia, and a ruse by Stuart helped delay a Federal attack until the next day, resulting in the court-martial and dismissal from the service of Union Major General Fitz John Porter. Porter was supposed to attack Jackson's right flank, but if Longstreet's troops arrived on the battlefield, it would make his move impossible. Porter's preparations for attacking were discovered by William W. Blackford of Stuart's staff. After he told Stuart, Stuart sent word to Lee, who promised reinforcements. While waiting, Stuart had his men tie pine branches to their horses' halters and drag them along a road behind the lines. Clouds of dust rose behind the Confederates, convincing Porter that Longstreet's infantry was massing where he was to attack. He postponed his attack and brought down the wrath of his enemies in his own army.[31]

On August 30, Stuart helped defend Jackson's line as Longstreet's men attacked the Yankees on the right. Stuart put T. L. Rosser in command of four batteries to help enfilade the Union line.[32] After Second Manassas, Stuart's cavalry occupied Fairfax Court House, within striking distance of Washington.

Barely taking a breath from his victory at Second Manassas, Lee wrote to Davis on September 2 of an invasion of the North. Most of the Federals were beaten out of Virginia at this time, he reasoned; provisions and potential man-power were just across the Potomac in Maryland; a raid into Pennsylvania could bring recognition of the Confederacy by European powers. Davis agreed.

Stuart's cavalry waded across the Potomac into Maryland near Leesburg, Virginia, on September 5. He established headquarters at Urbana with his cav-alry stretched from New Market to Sugar Loaf Mountain and Poolesville until September 11 while Lee's army concentrated near Frederick.

In war, there is little enough time for fun, and when Stuart found the time, he made the most of it. At lunch one afternoon, there was talk of the local sights and of an abandoned girls' school just down the road from Urbana. Upon examination, Stuart declared it the ideal place for a ball and ordered von Borcke to arrange it. A regimental band was procured and the hall was decorated with regimental battle flags and sabers. Cavalry boots and crinolines swirled to the happy music, and for hours there was no war. Ominously, the horses remained saddled just outside the door.

A good thing, too. Almost on cue around 11 P.M., artillery fire was heard down the road toward Hyattstown. Musketry crackled, too. The sabers came down and the girls stood rooted to the floor as the young men tried to assuage their fears—"We'll be back. Just a little tussle." By 1 A.M., the skirmish was over. The men returned and the dancing continued. But a few of the faces seen earlier were missing. Soon, the rest returned, some on stretchers, some walking and bleeding. The proper thing for Southern women to do at such a moment was to swoon, but instead they tore linen into bandages, hauled water, and held trembling hands while surgeons worked. Dressed in their white dancing dresses, bending over the sufferers, Blackford thought they looked just like angels.[33]

Stuart wrote to Flora that his health was fine and that he was sending some spoils of the invasion—shoes for the children, gloves, needles, and flannel. He told her frankly that the ladies of Maryland were making a great fuss over him, "loading me with bouquets, begging for autographs, etc. What shall I do?"[34]

On September 15, Jackson forced the surrender of the Union garrison at Harpers Ferry, capturing 11,000 men, seventy-three cannon, 13,000 small arms, and large stores of supplies and ammunition. Meanwhile, as Lee's army marched through the gaps and behind the temporary protection of the South Mountain range in Maryland, Stuart and Brigadier General Wade Hampton held Turner's Gap in the Catoctin Mountains west of Middletown until relieved by the infantry of Major General D. H. Hill.[35]

There was fighting near Turner's and Boonsboro Gaps on September 13, but even more ominous was the fact that McClellan had a set of Lee's orders— lost by a Confederate officer at a campsite near Frederick—for the movements of his divisions for the next few days. McClellan made little use of the information, continuing the slow pace that had plagued him on the Peninsula.

Still, with the knowledge in hand, he pushed toward the rebel army. The Federals hammered their way through Turner's Gap on September 14, but Lee had gained time.

Stuart left Boonsboro early on the 14th for Crampton's Gap, where Colonel Thomas Munford held off Union infantry nearly all day; he then retired toward Boonsboro. At daylight on the 15th, Fitz Lee and his men had a spirited fight east of Boonsboro, holding up a Union advance from Turner's Gap. The fighting descended like a rolling wave from the mountain pass into Boonsboro when suddenly the Federal infantry column split to let out a force of charging cavalry. Fitz Lee's 3rd Virginia Cavalry met the charge and drove it back, but eventually Rooney Lee and his 9th Virginia had to be called in to help extricate the Confederates from the narrow streets of Boonsboro. Union sentiment ran high in Boonsboro and the rebels were sniped at from houses. Rooney Lee was nearly captured when his horse fell on a bridge and he was knocked senseless. He crawled to some woods and Confederate troopers helped get him back to the army.

Stuart knew this area of Maryland well from his experiences with Robert E. Lee during John Brown's raid on Harpers Ferry. Now, his subordinates were learning the lay of the ground, the difficult gaps and mountainside towns, and the intricacies of fighting through them. They were fighting through this same area less than a year later, after Gettysburg.

McClellan's forces finally caught up with Lee outside of Sharpsburg, Maryland, near a small creek called the Antietam. Although the cavalry fighting had been fierce in the mountain gaps, at the Battle of Antietam on September 17, the infantry and artillery slugged it out with little finesse, and there was hardly an opportunity to use cavalry. Still, Stuart was constantly active. His artillery fought against the Union right from near the Dunker Church. Both Jackson and Jubal Early praised Stuart for his bold use of artillery during the battle.[36]

Fitz Lee covered the withdrawal of the army from Sharpsburg with Munford on the right, fighting along the Chesapeake and Ohio Canal. In his rear-guard action, Munford almost got caught, but eventually crossed the Potomac at Boteler's Ford. Stuart, with Hampton's troopers and two sections of artillery, rode up the Potomac on the evening of September 18 to Williamsport, Maryland, to divert the enemy, while Lee and his infantry and artillery re-crossed the Potomac near Shepherdstown, Virginia (now West Virginia). On the night of September 20, Stuart and his troopers re-crossed at Williamsport.

From camp near Winchester, Virginia, on October 8, Lee ordered Stuart to take a force of up to 1,500 men, re-cross the Potomac at Williamsport, and ride to Chambersburg, Pennsylvania, in order to destroy the railroad bridge over the Conococheague Creek. "Any other damage that you can inflict upon the enemy or his means of transportation you will also execute. You are desired to gain all information of the position, force, and probable intention of the enemy which you can," Lee added. He also told Stuart that he could take local officials hostage so that they could be exchanged "for our own citizens that have been carried off by the enemy. . . . Having accomplished your errand, you will rejoin this army as soon as practicable. Reliance is placed upon your skill and judgement in the successful execution of this plan, and it is not intended or desired that you should jeopardize the safety of your command, or go farther than your good judgement and prudence may dictate."[37]

Stuart selected 600 of the best men from each of Hampton's, Fitz Lee's, and Robertson's brigades, which were commanded respectively by Wade Hampton, Colonel W. H. F. Lee, and Colonel William "Grumble" Jones. Pelham's four guns were taken along for artillery support.

One-third of each brigade was to be detailed to seize horses and other property, giving receipts when requested so that private individuals could seek reparations from the U.S. government. Individual plundering would not be tolerated. Maryland was exempt from property seizure; the Confederate government was still courting this border state.

Through the morning autumn mist of October 10 at McCoy's Ferry came a few dismounted Confederate troopers, leading their horses across the Potomac, barely disturbing the water. Pistol shots drove away Federal pickets and the main column charged across, artillery wheels making rooster tails in the water.

Farther north on the C&O Canal, the commander at old Fort Frederick got a warning, but there was virtually nothing he could do against a force he estimated at 2,500 troopers with artillery. Through the fog and early-morning eyes, the force must have looked that size to the surprised pickets.

Word spread quickly and Stuart knew he had to move swiftly, keeping one step ahead of the pursuit that was being organized. Once in Pennsylvania, the Southerners took much-needed boots and shoes and gathered in horses.

William Blackford of Stuart's staff said the cavalry was organized so that 600 men formed the advance, another 600 formed the rear guard, and the middle 600 collected horses. He said that because of the drizzly weather, most farmers were inside their barns threshing and their horses were easily collected. The foul weather also prevented word from traveling quickly from farm to farm, so they gathered many more horses than would otherwise have been the case.[38]

They reached Chambersburg at 8 P.M. October 10 in a drizzling rain. Stuart demanded money from the bank, but it had been sent away that morning. Apparently, word of Stuart's column had been telegraphed from Fort Frederick to major towns. Colonel A. K. McClure of Chambersburg described Stuart as sitting on his horse in the center of town with his staff while his riders brought in horses. He also wrote, "In several instances his men commenced to take private property from stores, but they were arrested by General Stuart's provost-guard."[39]

Stuart burned the government depot, machine shops, firearms, and a warehouse of ammunition, which continued to explode all morning.[40] He did not burn the Cumberland Valley Railroad bridge across the Conococheague, a main line of communication from southern Pennsylvania to the state capital, Harrisburg. It was one of Lee's specific objectives, but it turned out that the bridge was constructed of iron.

Stuart's assistant adjutant general, H. B. McClellan, offered an enlightening view on how Stuart conducted the raid:

> Certainly this was a remarkable scene. It did, however, but illustrate the control which Stuart had over his men. They were accustomed to feel his hand upon them in the camp as well as on the field of battle; and they knew that when occasion required that hand was a heavy one. Orders were issued to be obeyed, and not as an empty sound. And then, the ranks of Stuart's regiments were largely filled with men from the highest class of Southern society— men who intelligently appreciated the importance of obedience, and who yielded it as readily as they did their lives at their country's call.[41]

If great latitude were given to Stuart by Lee in his orders, it was because Lee knew the orders would be obeyed. Military exigencies may alter plans, but orders were to be followed. Stuart was certainly as appreciative of this as any of his men.

In the early morning of October 11, Stuart's men were ready to ride. Colonel Williams C. Wickham had his regiment facing westward, expecting to re-trace the ride back to McCoy's Ferry. Suddenly, he was ordered to about-face and his men rode off to the east. Months later, Wickham asked Stuart why orders were changed so abruptly. "Was it intuition?" Wickham asked, trying to peruse Stuart's military character. "No," Stuart said, "rather say judgement."[42]

On the 11th, after bivouacking at the tollgate on the Gettysburg Road, Stuart's force indeed headed toward the east, rather than back to McCoy's Ferry, apparently to the confusion of not just Wickham but everyone. Blackford said, "No one knew when day broke what our movements were to be, as General Stuart had preserved absolute reticence upon that subject." Stuart took out a map and told Blackford, "You see, the enemy will be sure to think that I will try to recross above, because it is nearer to me and further from them. They will have all the fords strongly guarded in that direction, and scouting parties will be on the lookout for our approach, so that they can concentrate to meet us at any point. They will never expect me to move three times the distance and cross at a ford below them and so close to their main body, and therefore they will not be prepared to meet us down there." Blackford agreed with his reasons.[43]

It is a classic tactic of doing the opposite of what your enemy expects you to do. It is perhaps the most fundamental principle in commanding light cavalry. It is bold, but not necessarily reckless; its safety lies in its audacity. But it takes more than your average commander to make such decisions and it takes superior confidence from his men to carry them out.

Swinging around in a huge arc to the east and south, Stuart and his brigade approached Gettysburg—they would visit it again in July 1863—and, moving into Maryland, neared the Potomac River on a small farm road. He was looking to cross at White's Ford with his spoils of war. By now the tired horses were staggering against one another and the men swaying in their saddles from the exhaustion of riding through the night.

Stuart determined to re-cross the Potomac near White's, where the Monocacy River empties into the Potomac. By the morning of October 12, his troopers were sleepy but buoyant after one of the more daring cavalry raids yet in the war. Along with food and horses, they had gathered clothing, much of it Union blue, which they exchanged for their worn gray and butternut uniforms.

Less than a mile from the river, the Confederates ran into a column of Federal cavalry. Stuart charged immediately and drove the troopers from his front. The Confederates rode up the ridge overlooking the Little Monocacy River and saw the Federals digging in.

Stuart sent Rooney Lee with the main column toward White's Ford; Stuart, Pelham, and the Horse Artillery handled the rear guard, the most dangerous part of any ride.

There was a quarry near the ford. Its rim was lined with Union troopers. Rooney Lee's plan was to attack and occupy the enemy at the quarry while some horsemen and artillery forced a crossing at the ford. They were then to set up positions on the other side and cover the rest of the column's crossing. Time counted, too, because the rains were pushing up the Potomac each minute. Lee sent a note under a flag of truce to the Union commander stating that Stuart himself was there with a large force and that he must surrender within a quarter-hour or the Confederates would attack.

The fifteen minutes passed. The Confederates opened fire with two cannon. To their surprise, their bluff worked and the Union troops began withdrawing. Stuart had a little trouble bringing off his rear guard but by 10 A.M. his columns were safely in Virginia.

They brought back 1,200 to 1,500 horses, destroyed about a quarter of a million dollars worth of supplies in Chambersburg, and once again established their ability to go anywhere they wanted, fearless of the Union army.[44]

Stuart was supremely confident in his hand-picked troopers, who could by now fight well mounted and dismounted.

The raid had political ramifications as well. President Abraham Lincoln was getting tired of hearing that the Confederates were doing what they wanted with apparent impunity. What was McClellan doing? To his Cabinet, in reference to a children's game called Three Times Around and Out, he said that if Stuart got around McClellan a third time, the commander of the Army of the Potomac would be the one out . . . of a job.

John Thomason wrote in his biography of Stuart that during the raid, Robert E. Lee was anxious about Stuart and learned from a Baltimore paper on October 12 that he had reached Chambersburg. Thomason, a soldier, also said that leading 1,800 mounted men eighty miles in one day and keeping them together enough to force their way across White's Ford was unheard of: "I know of no equal exploit in the cavalry annals."[45]

Stuart, who was there and rode the distance, calculated time and distances a little differently. It was a march without parallel—90 miles in 36 hours in one stretch in addition to the previous days' rides.[46]

Promotions were recommended by Stuart, but he opposed one for Grumble Jones. Stuart saw Jones as insubordinate and subversive of authority.[47]

Fighting went on during November. Stuart's only wound was to his heart; his little daughter Flora had died in Lynchburg, Virginia, on November 3, and he could not remove himself from duty to see her as she was dying. The letter to his wife expressed a loss so deep that he closed, "God has shielded me thus far from bodily harm, but I feel perfect resignation to go at his bidding, and join my little Flora. I cannot write more."[48]

In the late autumn, the Army of Northern Virginia moved to Fredericksburg to contest Major General Ambrose E. Burnside's winter campaign toward Richmond. Stuart established his headquarters on Telegraph Road outside of the colonial-era city. Blackford said the cavalry maintained pickets along the Rappahannock River for thirty miles above and twenty miles below Fredericksburg. He noted that Stuart and the Horse Artillery went down to Port Royal a couple of times to shell Union gunboats attempting to come upriver.

In early December Stuart attempted a grand gesture. Mary Custis Lee, his friend from West Point days, was caught behind Yankee lines by the shifting tide of war. He sent two of his most trusted aides across the Rappahannock River to rescue her. But the eldest daughter of Robert E. Lee was also the most independent, and feeling no threat from an entire Federal army just a few miles away, she refused Stuart's offer and remained where she was.[49]

Stuart's cavalry covered the right flank of the army, but as at Antietam, the ground was little suited to its use. During the Battle of Fredericksburg on December 13, Pelham and two of his guns held up the advance of an entire Union division against the Confederate right wing. He drew the attention not only of the enemy but of Lee and Jackson. Stonewall asked Stuart, "Have you another Pelham, general? If so, I wish you would give him to me!"[50] Lee remarked, "It is glorious to see such courage in one so young!"[51] He would afterward refer to the twenty-four-year-old as "the Gallant Pelham."

Christmas 1862 was a relatively happy time for Stuart's command. Lee had just whipped another Yankee commander, redeeming the stalemate and losses suffered at Antietam. Cavalry horses were short of food and the men needed blankets and shoes, but their spirits were high. Stuart prepared for a Christmas celebration on December 24, inviting family and neighbors, but also made ready to cut it short the next morning. Lee again had ordered him to gather information on Burnside's army and harass his communications.

On the day after Christmas, 1,800 cavalrymen under Wade Hampton, Rooney Lee, and Fitz Lee crossed the Rappahannock at Kelly's Ford. Stuart had planned a rare and potentially complicated division of forces, sending Fitz Lee south of Quantico, Rooney Lee to Dumfries, and Hampton to Occoquan, cutting fifteen miles of the road between Fredericksburg and Washington. Hampton had reconnoitered this area twice that month and was familiar with it.

The raid accomplished nearly every goal, capturing prisoners, cutting Burnside's communications, and gathering information. It also provided some interesting insights into Stuart and his men. Splitting one's forces to come together again in the face of the enemy is a feat that can only be accomplished by excellent soldiers, commanded by efficient officers. The raid also included a maneuver that had practically become Stuart's trademark. When all the enemy was looking for him to return to the main army, Stuart rode away from it, completing a wide circuit of the Yankees. Finally, after capturing Burke's Station on the Orange and Alexandria Railroad, just fifteen miles from Washington, he listened in on the telegraph line from the Yankee capital for a while. Then he sent a telegram to Major General Montgomery C. Meigs, quartermaster general of the U.S. Army. He complained about the poor quality of Federal mule-flesh furnished lately, which slowed the removal of the wagons he had captured. He signed the telegram, "J. E. B. Stuart."[52]

The spring of 1863 was spent moving cavalry headquarters to Culpeper Court House, about thirty miles northwest of Fredericksburg, and in reconnaissance across the upper Rappahannock. One battle stood out, not necessarily for its own sanguinary nature but for the blood shed by one individual.

On March 16, Major John Pelham, the shy, handsome Alabamian, had met Stuart at Culpeper as the general testified in a court-martial hearing. Afterward, Pelham visited Miss Bessie Shackleford, who lived in Culpeper. At dawn the next day, Union Brigadier General William W. Averell's cavalry crossed the Rappahannock at Kelly's Ford and advanced toward the Orange and Alexandria Railroad. Borrowing horses, Stuart and Pelham rode toward the sound of the guns.

Once on the battlefield, Pelham rode off to help find some good artillery positions. Soon he was before a stone fence where the Yankee cavalry had placed skirmishers. Pelham watched as a column of the 3rd Virginia Cavalry charged the Union skirmishers behind the fence, which was too high for their horses to jump. They turned and rode along the fence, yelling and firing at the Yankees behind it, looking for a gap or gate.

Pelham drew his saber and cut toward the head of the column. The troopers had found a gate and the youngster rode up to it, standing in his stirrups, smiling, and shouting "Forward!"

A shell burst above. In the melee, hardly anyone saw the young man tumble from his horse. Two officers who did notice lifted him over the saddle of one of their horses. They probably never saw the tiny wound in the back of his skull at the hairline, where a shell fragment had entered. An ambulance took him to the Shackleford home in Culpeper, where he died.

The vivacious Pelham's death had a profound effect on Stuart. The cavalry mourned his passing and it seemed that death, now, was stalking its ranks. Stuart's thanatopsies were revealed in a letter to his wife just two days after Pelham's passing: If his Flora survived him, which seemed probable, "I wish an assurance on your part . . . that *you will make the land for which I gave my life your home, and keep my offspring on southern soil."*[53]

Stuart ordered members of the cavalry division to wear black mourning cloth on the left arm, closest to the heart, for thirty days.[54] By the end of April, cavalry headquarters was named Camp Pelham.[55] His next child, a girl, was named Virginia Pelham Stuart.

Major General Joseph Hooker took command of the Army of the Potomac in April 1863. With Lee still on one side of the Rappahannock and his army on the other, Hooker devised a plan to keep Lee's army busy with attacks at Fredericksburg, then move swiftly westward to swing around the Confederate rear.

Lee recognized the plan and maneuvered so to not only counter Hooker's move but to pull off a flank march of his own. The resulting battle around Chancellorsville in May allowed Stuart to command a large force of attacking infantry for the first time, but his opportunity came at a horrible cost.

As Stonewall Jackson marched along the dusty road through an area west of Fredericksburg known as the Wilderness, his column was led by the 1st Virginia Cavalry under Fitzhugh Lee.[56] The 2nd, 5th, and part of the 3rd Virginia Cavalry regiments screened the flank movement from Union eyes.

Stuart rode with Fitz Lee on the right of Jackson's column between him and the enemy. When Jackson thought he was in position on the Orange Plank Road, Fitz Lee encouraged him to ride farther north to the Orange Turnpike. There Jackson saw the end of the Union line and altered his orders to move his attack a little farther to the north to take advantage of being able to strike more into the rear of the Union XI Corps.[57]

By 6 P.M., Stuart's work in leading the column was done and he headed off to Ely's Ford to do some damage to Union wagon trains there. With Jackson, however, he left the Horse Artillery commanded by Major R. F. Beckham, who took Pelham's place. Placing two guns in the road and the others in reserve, Stuart told Beckham to advance along with Jackson's line but to stay just in the rear of the skirmish line. Using artillerymen as skirmishers was unheard of, except for Stuart. This was horse artillery, and it was attached to light cavalry. To Stuart, there was no other way to use it.

That night at Ely's Ford, however, he received the shocking message of the wounding of Jackson and Major General A. P. Hill. He was ordered back to the battlefield to command Jackson's entire Second Corps.

Though ill and not present during the battle of Chancellorsville, Blackford recounted the difficulties Stuart had to overcome. First, he had to return several miles to take command, knowing virtually nothing about the disposition of the lines or plan of attack; it was night and Jackson's corps was in a wooded area (the Wilderness, no less) and Stuart did not know the troops or officers' special talents or weaknesses. He also came from a different branch of the service. As a cadet at West Point, he had studied infantry tactics, but he had never commanded such a large group of infantry in combat. Jackson left no orders, since he always kept his plans to himself. Also, after being wounded and partially anesthetized, he was in no condition to give any orders. When asked what Stuart should do, Jackson, still woozy, replied with great difficulty, "I don't know: I can't tell: say to General Stuart that he must do what he thinks best."[58] Stuart took command of the corps between 11 P.M. and midnight May 2 and fought the main battle through May 3.

Jackson's men had had nothing to eat for twenty-four hours, except what they took from the haversacks of the casualties of the Union XI Corps. Some of the officers wanted to wait until food was brought up, but Stuart had orders from Lee to press the attack as early as possible. Twice he led the 28th North Carolina in a charge. His horse, Chancellor, was mortally wounded beneath him. He remounted and rode into a Southern regiment that had broken before the Yankees, grabbed its colors, and rallied the men.[59]

Everyone in Jackson's corps had heard of Stuart and many may have even seen him before when he visited Jackson in camp. But this was the first time most had seen him lead men in battle, and it was intoxicating. General James H. Lane wrote:

> That afternoon, when the 28th [North Carolina] rejoined me on the left, where I had been ordered to support Colquitt, its colonel, Thomas L. Lowe, was perfectly carried away with Stuart. He not only spoke of his dash, but he told me he heard him singing, "Old Joe Hooker, won't you get out of the wilderness!" and he wound up by saying, "Who would have thought it? Jeb Stuart in command of the 2nd army corps!"[60]

Lee wrote Stuart shortly after the battle, "In the management of the difficult operations at Chancellorsville, which you so promptly understood and creditably performed, I saw no errors to correct, nor has there been a fit opportunity to commend your conduct."[61]

Years later, H. B. McClellan quoted in his book from a letter he received from E. P. Alexander, esteemed artillerist of the Army of Northern Virginia. Writing of Chancellorsville, Alexander said:

> Altogether, I do not think there was a more brilliant thing done in the war than Stuart's extricating that command from the extremely critical position in which he found it as promptly and boldly as he did. . . . Stuart never seemed to hesitate or to doubt for one moment that he could just crash his way wherever he chose to strike. . . .
>
> I always thought it an injustice to Stuart and a loss to the army that he was not from that moment *continued in command of Jackson's corps*. He had *won* the right to it. I believe he had all of Jackson's genius and dash and originality, without that eccentricity of character which sometimes led to disappointment. . . . Stuart, however, possessed

the rare quality of being always *equal to himself at his very best*.
[Emphasis Alexander's.][62]

To be always equal to oneself at one's very best is both compliment and
curse, for it is something of never-ending, constant aspiration.

After Chancellorsville, cavalry headquarters were moved to Orange Court
House, where Stuart heard of Jackson's death on May 10. Partially because of
this loss, Lee re-organized the Army of Northern Virginia into three corps of
infantry and a cavalry corps composed of three divisions (actually brigades)
commanded by Wade Hampton, Fitzhugh Lee, and Rooney Lee.

On May 20, cavalry headquarters moved again, to Culpeper Court House.[63]
Two days later, Stuart reviewed the three brigades, about 4,000 men in all, near
Brandy Station, a small depot on the Orange and Alexandria Railroad between
Culpeper and the Rappahannock River, a few miles outside of town. Within a
few days, the brigades of Beverly Robertson and Grumble Jones were encamped
near Brandy and Stuart's cavalry grew by another 4,000.[64] By the end of May,
thirty-year-old Stuart had between 9,000 and 10,000 men in his corps, the largest
force he ever commanded.[65]

On June 5, he had his unit prepared for another review, this time by Robert
E. Lee. Lee had to cancel at the last minute, but Stuart held the review anyway,
having invited many local people, who were enthralled by the spectacle. Lee
was able to come on June 8 but recommended that the horses not be galloped
and the cannons remain silent to save both for the near future.[66]

Camp was awakened by firing at daylight June 9. Part of Union Brigadier
General John Buford's 1st Cavalry of the Army of the Potomac was forcing
Jones' 6th Virginia from its picket post at Beverly Ford on the Rappahannock.
Jones personally led an attack that slowed Buford's advance, but he was driven
back into his own guns by the Yankees. The rest of Jones' brigade arrived along
with Rooney Lee's men to attempt to stem the tide. The rest of Buford's division was thrown into the fight, including the reserve cavalry brigade, and an
infantry division under Adelbert Ames was brought up.

Stuart came up as the units were maneuvering. H. B. McClellan stayed on
Fleetwood Hill maintaining Stuart's headquarters, which had been placed on the
highest ridge in the vicinity to be close to his pickets.

While Stuart was directing Rooney Lee and Jones at the Beverly Ford
sector, Union Brigadier General David M. Gregg had crossed the Rappahannock at Kelly's Ford, moved around Robertson's right flank, and was heading
directly for Fleetwood. McClellan discovered them and sent an urgent message
to Stuart that they were about to be overrun. Stuart at first did not believe that
Robertson would not have sent a message, but upon hearing the cannon fire, he

sent Jones' 12th Virginia Regiment and 35th Virginia Battalion, dispatched orders to Lee, Jones, and Hampton, and then followed them to Fleetwood between 10 and 11 A.M.

The battle swirled up and around Fleetwood Hill. The openness of the countryside, after war had denuded it of fencing, and the solidness of the turf dictated tactics as ancient as Alexander. Pistols and artillery were rarely heard; men plying the saber was the order of the day. Blackford recalled the fighting on Fleetwood:

> The enemy had gotten a battery almost to the top of the hill when they [reinforcements ordered by Stuart] arrived. This was taken and retaken three times, we retaining it finally. The lines met on the hill. It was like what we read of in the days of chivalry, acres and acres of horsemen sparkling with sabres, and dotted with brilliant bits of color where their flags danced above them, hurled against each other at full speed and meeting with a shock that made the earth tremble.[67]

Blackford soon discovered Union infantry reserves coming up. Robert E. Lee sent some of Longstreet's corps, but in the end, neither side used infantry. The battle would be called Brandy Station or Fleetwood Hill and was strictly among cavalry, the largest such battle ever in North America.

Stuart claimed victory because the enemy retired back to the Rappahannock and Confederate forces retained the field. However, he appeared to have been failed by Robertson, who had allowed the enemy around his flank. Robertson was not relieved of command, at least one historian said, probably because he was a North Carolinian and politics came into play. North Carolina Governor Zebulon Vance was taking advantage of the loose organization of the Confederacy by keeping thousands of shoes in storage for North Carolinians while thousands of soldiers from other states went barefoot, and he was playing his games with Jefferson Davis about this time.[68] Robertson first submitted his official report, then followed it up with an explanation of his role and his reason for not becoming engaged in the fight. He then issued a challenge for an official investigation. Stuart finally agreed that Robertson's courier indeed reached him too late in the battle to accomplish anything. But the correspondence continued. Robertson wrote three other explanations and Stuart responded to them twice. Then, almost in exasperation, Stuart wrote tersely that "General Robertson's report appears satisfactory." If Stuart did not have reason after Brandy Station to question Robertson's wholehearted devotion to him, he soon would.

Casualties in the officers' ranks ran high. Rooney Lee was seriously wounded and would not return to the cavalry for a long while. Lieutenant Colonel Frank Hampton, brother of Wade Hampton, was mortally wounded, as were other subordinate officers and valuable aides. The attrition was mounting among Confederate cavalry officers and there was nothing anyone could do about it.

Federal losses were high, too—nearly 1,000 casualties, almost 10 percent of those engaged. But something was suddenly different with the Union troopers. They were more aggressive, more capable, finally responding to training, and better organized. No one could put a finger on it exactly, but even Stuart must have somehow felt it, although he never wrote about it anywhere. He knew too much about fighting men not to realize it.

In a letter to his wife just after the battle, Stuart said that the "papers are in great error, as usual, about the whole transaction." He had seen the *Richmond Examiner* of the day that he wrote, June 12, and said that it had lied from beginning to end.

Indeed, the paper called Stuart's cavalry "puffed up." Overlooking Stuart's actions at Chancellorsville, the writer charged him with "negligence and bad management," called him and his officers "vain and weakheaded," and wrote that his cavalry was "carelessly strewn across the country."[69]

"I understand the spirit and object of the detraction and can, I believe, trace the source," Stuart continued to his wife. "I will, of course, take no notice of such base falsehood."[70]

Part Two

GETTYSBURG

CHAPTER THREE

Raiding on a Grand Scale

"I realize that if we oppose force to force we cannot win, for their resources are greater than ours. We must make up in quality what we lack in numbers. We must substitute esprit *for numbers. Therefore, I strive to inculcate in my men the spirit of the chase."*
—J. E. B. STUART TO HIS BROTHER

Before the Battle of Brandy Station Robert E. Lee had made several trips to Richmond to confer with President Jefferson Davis, Secretary of War James A. Seddon, and eventually all of Davis' Cabinet.

In the Western theater the war was going badly for the South, with Major General U. S. Grant besieging Vicksburg, Mississippi. Davis and his Cabinet debated what to do, but Lee's mind was clear on the matter: go on the offensive and invade the North to relieve some of the pressure on Vicksburg.

Morale in his Army of Northern Virginia had never been higher. It was rolling off great victories at Fredericksburg and Chancellorsville. As well, the Peace Democrats in the North were agitating for a negotiated peace with the Confederacy; success north of the Mason-Dixon line would surely add credence to the cause and a negotiated peace would mean Southern independence. Britain, though wavering more than ever over whether to recognize the Confederacy, might still be interested should Lee happen to fight and win a major battle in Maryland or Pennsylvania. The time for an invasion of the North seemed right.

Lee enumerated his objectives in his post-campaign report: to draw Hooker out of Virginia and pull Union troops from other parts of the country to his support. This would disrupt any plans Union leaders may have had for a summer campaign of their own in Virginia.

As well the farmers in Northern Virginia and the Shenandoah Valley had been supporting two huge armies nearly non-stop for two years and could use a full year's growing season without the pressure of feeding soldiers, voluntarily or involuntarily. Lee could gather supplies from Northern farmers over the

43

summer and bring what he could back south of the Potomac. This, according to his dispatches, would soon become one of the primary reasons for the campaign.

And there was always the possibility, with the Yankees strung out on the march, that Lee could turn and destroy the Army of the Potomac piece by piece. So, by the second week of June, Lee's army began moving northward.

After the death of Stonewall Jackson, Lee reorganized the Army of Northern Virginia in hopes of making it more efficient. He broke two large army corps of about 30,000 men apiece into three corps. The First was still commanded by Lieutenant General James Longstreet, Jackson's Second Corps was given to Lieutenant General Richard S. Ewell, and the Third Corps was created from divisions from the other two plus a new one and placed under Lieutenant General A. P. Hill.

The artillery was reorganized as well. From an old military custom that attached batteries of four (or sometimes six) guns to certain brigades, Lee placed four batteries into battalions, with each battalion attached to the infantry divisions within each corps. Two battalions were held in reserve. This method took the pressure off of brigade commanders who, under the old system, had to handle artillery along with their infantry in battle. The new organization placed command of the artillery in the hands of a chief of artillery in each corps.

The reorganization of the infantry was necessary after the death of Jackson. The only problem was that two of the three corps commanders were untested in handling such large bodies of troops in battle.

By June 15, the Confederate army was moving northeastward along the Shenandoah Valley, using the formidable Blue Ridge to the east as a screen from Federal cavalry. There were passes through the forested, rocky hills, but even by the nineteenth century—when the roads were somewhat improved from Indian days—there were still steep, twisting climbs to the gaps for man and animal.

By mid-June, the Confederate cavalry's mission was to clog the gaps as the army trudged behind them on its way north. The infantry would send reinforcements if it looked like the cavalry was about to be pushed from the passes. For the most part, the cavalry's tactics tied it to the gaps as a shield for Lee's invasion.

On June 15, Longstreet's First Corps advanced from Culpeper, Virginia, to bottle up Snicker's and Ashby's gaps, two passes in the Blue Ridge leading from Clarke County eastward over the mountains into Loudoun County.

Thomas Munford was temporarily commanding Fitzhugh Lee's troopers; J. R. Chambliss was commanding the wounded Rooney Lee's men. They and Robertson took their brigades, on order from Stuart on the 16th, in the advance and to the right of Longstreet's moving columns. Hampton and the 15th Virginia of Rooney Lee's brigade were left on the Rappahannock to assist A. P. Hill's Third Corps in leaving its lines without harassment. Grumble Jones' brigade followed.[1] On the night of the 16th, Stuart's men went into bivouac near Salem. Scouts

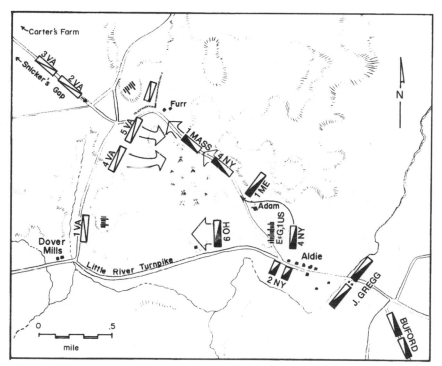

The Battle of Aldie

reported that night that the enemy had withdrawn from Warrenton to Centreville the day before.[2]

The road from Ashby's Gap descends the mountain toward the east, first
passing through Paris, then through Upperville in Fauquier County. Seven more
miles down the mountain the road crosses northeastward into Loudoun County
and runs through the town of Middleburg. Just five more miles down the road is
Aldie, situated in a little gap in a long line of hills that appears on Civil War
maps as Hog Back Mountain. The road then descends into a plain and crosses
the main north-south road leading north to Leesburg near the Potomac River.
Aldie's importance lay in the fact that another road entered the road to Ashby's
Gap there. This road led directly to Snicker's Gap, the next pass in the Blue
Ridge to the north of Ashby's. By holding Aldie, the Confederates controlled
two gaps. The next-nearest crossing point over the mountains was Harpers Ferry,
nearly twenty miles to the north.

On June 17, the 2nd Virginia of Fitzhugh Lee's brigade, under Munford,
marched from Upperville through Middleburg toward Aldie. Munford sent a company out to the junction of the Leesburg Turnpike to warn him of any approaching
enemy. The rest of the regiment went north to Carter's farm near Mountville to
gather forage.[3] The rest of the brigade—the 1st, 4th, and 5th Virginia—had ridden
from Piedmont through Middleburg and halted just short of Aldie at Dover
Mills.[4] Rooney Lee's brigade remained south about fifteen miles from Aldie to
watch Thoroughfare Gap while Robertson was ordered to Rectortown so he
could support either brigade.

The Confederates mainly wanted to gather the forage. However, the little
gap at Aldie was tactically vital and to hold Aldie meant denying Yankee cavalry
access to the northern Shenandoah Valley, where the Confederate army was
marching.

Around 4 P.M. Munford heard reports of firing from his pickets and rode
toward the site. Soon the 2nd Virginia's pickets were being driven back upon
Rosser's 5th Virginia by a large force of Union cavalry from Judson Kilpatrick's
brigade. Two other brigades backed up Kilpatrick, so after buying time to warn the
rest of his brigade, Rosser withdrew up the Snicker's Gap Pike northwest of Aldie.[5]

On both sides of the pike, sharpshooters were placed behind haystacks and
a stone wall.[6] Along with a small reserve, they were to hold until the rest of the
2nd and 3rd Virginia arrived. It was a small force to attempt to hold against what
appeared to be several Yankee regiments.

Farther to the south, Wickham placed the 1st and 4th Virginia, supported
by Breathed's two-gun section of Horse Artillery, on the high ground just west
of Aldie to hold the Ashby's Gap road. The 4th covered his left on one of the
crossroads that led from the Snicker's Gap Pike. The 1st Virginia and two of

Breathed's guns were to support Rosser and the 5th, who were by then being pushed back. Breathed's guns stopped the Yankees advancing in that area[7] but some of the ammunition was faulty and exploded short, causing some casualties in the 5th Virginia's sharpshooters, the last to retire before the Federals were stopped.

Kilpatrick had already gotten his teeth into the Confederate units north on the Snicker's Gap Pike and charged the sharpshooters behind the haystacks. This was repulsed, as was another charge by Kilpatrick, but the action on the Snicker's Gap Pike made Munford realize how weak the position was. Still, Munford sought to bring the 4th Virginia Cavalry and one gun from Breathed's battery from where they were positioned above Aldie to back up his men behind the stone wall.

Before the reinforcements arrived, they had repulsed two mounted charges. The Yankees sent a dismounted group around their flank, and they were forced to withdraw fifty yards behind a farmhouse and orchard, from where they could pour fire into the only opening through which the Yankees could come.

Munford knew that the troopers on the Snicker's Gap Pike could not hold out forever against the much stronger Union force. The terrain would help, but they needed to see the 2nd and 3rd Virginia regiments behind them, and soon. The Union troopers were trying to drive a wedge into the Confederate position between the Little River Turnpike to Ashby's Gap and the road to Snicker's. They kept up a steady pressure. In all, three separate charges from the Union troopers were met by countercharges and turned back.[8]

The 2nd and 3rd Virginia finally arrived. Munford dismounted two squadrons and sent them to help bolster up his left.

Munford now let the particularities of the terrain work for him. His flanks were protected by the Little River and the deep gullies its tributaries had cut. The only access to his line was up the road that would funnel any attack into columns of fours—horsemen four abreast instead of being able to spread out across the fields—a perfect target for concentrated carbine fire from dismounted cavalry. Sure enough, with no other tactic available to them, up the road in columns of fours came the Union troopers, attempting to crack Munford's line.

The 2nd Virginia moved down the road to meet the Yankees. The vanguard of the 2nd Virginia crashed headlong into the front fours of the Union column. With nowhere to go, the two columns drew sabers and slashed away in numerous hand-to-hand encounters. While the two main columns were occupied slashing, stabbing, and firing pistols point-blank, the Confederates' rear squadron enfiladed the enemy left flank. Another squadron did the same on their right. By then the Union troopers were being fired upon by the sharpshooters of the 2nd and 3rd Virginia in their rear. Assailed from four sides, they broke and began to retreat.

A supporting Union column was charged by the 2nd Virginia.[9] The regiment captured the colors of the 4th New York Cavalry and its colonel. Completely disorganized by the two charges, the 2nd was moved to the right to regroup.[10]

So far, the regiments from Kilpatrick's five brigades had failed to do any more than push the Confederates into a fine defensive position. Dusk was falling rapidly while Kilpatrick quickly organized for another assault upon Munford's position across the Snicker's Gap Pike. The 3rd Virginia took the road and charged the disorganized Yankees. The 2nd Virginia had reorganized on their right and the 5th Virginia joined on the left. In what Munford called the most spirited charge of the day, his men plied their sabers hand to hand and drove the Yankees back almost to the village of Aldie. Several more charges were made by both sides. Afterward, Munford recalled,

> I have never seen as many Yankees killed in the same space of ground in any fight I have ever seen, or on any battle-field in Virginia that I have been over. We held our ground until ordered by the major-general commanding [J. E. B. Stuart] to retire, and the Yankees had been so severely punished that they did not follow.[11]

Casualties for the Confederates in the battle were 119; for the Union troopers, 305.[12]

During the fighting at Aldie through the evening of June 17, additional Union troopers under Colonel Alfred N. Duffié were swinging in an arc southward, then to the north, attempting to work their way through the flank of the Confederates at Aldie to reach Middleburg, five miles to the west. Duffié pushed back Chambliss' pickets at Thoroughfare Gap in the Bull Run Mountains to the south. By 11 A.M., he was pounding northwestward toward Middleburg, where Stuart had established his headquarters to keep an eye on the fighting at Aldie. Duffié was to encamp at Middleburg for the night, then march toward Snicker's Gap the next day on an extended reconnaissance. However, at 7 P.M., he was attacked on three sides by Robertson's brigade. His men fought from behind walls and breastworks and repelled at least three charges, but were finally driven back down the road that led to Thoroughfare Gap. Unfortunately for Duffié, Chambliss' men had silently moved in behind them, forming a trap in the night. Scouts sent out into the dark came back with bad news: Every road was covered by rebel cavalry. At 3:30 A.M. on June 18, Duffié's men fought their way along the darkened roads until they reached the road to Hopewell Gap.[13]

Duffié, four of his officers, and only twenty-seven men made it all the way back to Centreville early in the afternoon of June 18. A few more wandered back into their lines over the next two days, but his losses stood at about 200.

On June 17, after the fighting died down along the Snicker's Gap and Ashby's Gap turnpikes, Munford withdrew from Aldie to Middleburg, but not in time to engage in Duffié's defeat. Robertson also encamped at Middleburg, followed by Rooney Lee's brigade, under Chambliss, the next morning.

Earlier on June 17, before any fighting broke out, John Singleton Mosby and thirty to forty of his band of rangers had met with Stuart. Though Stuart knew Mosby well, it was the first time he had seen any of Mosby's men. He made some humorous comment about them, probably noticing their unmilitary look. Nevertheless, he appreciated their remarkable ability to gather accurate information. That morning, Stuart approved an expedition across the Potomac by Mosby and his band to create a diversion for Lee's army. Though the guerrilla leader never made it across the river, the expedition reaped something more substantial than just a diversion.

That evening, Mosby relieved two Federal officers of valuable dispatches from Union General Hooker's headquarters. One of the men was Hooker's chief signal officer on his way to Snicker's Gap to establish a signal station. In typical Mosby fashion, the feisty Confederate rode right up to the house they were in, grabbed their guard by the collar and whispered in his ear that he was now the prisoner of Mosby. Confused because of the darkness and thinking that this stranger was insulting him by calling him the name of the rebel Mosby, the guard retorted: "You are a damned liar. I am as good a Union man as you are." Mosby produced a pistol and the orderly suddenly understood the situation with crystal clarity.

The officers emerged from the house into the night and assumed, from the familiarity of the strangers with their orderly, that they were Federals and began giving Mosby information on their important mission. A flourish of pistols from Mosby's men, and they knew that they had said too much. Mosby took the documents and sent them to Stuart. Receiving them about daybreak on June 18, Stuart sent Hampton's brigade to Warrenton; he whipped the Union force there. Stuart also realized from the information that he did not have enough men to continue his fight in the open terrain around Aldie and would have to wage defensive battles closer to the mountains during the next few days to keep clogging the gaps leading to Lee's army.[14]

On the 18th the Yankees began moving around Stuart's flank, forcing him to pull back from the town of Middleburg. His pickets east of the town were driven through it but regained their position later when the Union cavalry withdrew.

Again, early on the morning of June 19, Stuart's pickets were driven through

Middleburg by a charge of the 4th Pennsylvania Cavalry.[15] The main body of cavalry, consisting of Robertson's and Rooney Lee's brigade commanded by Chambliss, was posted far enough west of the town on the Ashby's Gap road so as not to bring the town under "friendly fire."

Chambliss' men were stretched out in line of battle to the left and Robertson's men extended the line to the right. Far to the left, Fitzhugh Lee's brigade held the Snicker's Gap road. Backing up the cavalry was Hart's battery of Horse Artillery.

Union cavalry advanced and attacked dismounted, fighting like infantry, and were held back for a while. They eventually gained the protection of some woods in front of Stuart's line. On Stuart's right flank, the enemy charged with dismounted cavalry and two mounted regiments. Stuart began an orderly withdrawal under fire to about half a mile to the rear. Shot at Stuart's side was Heros von Borcke, the huge Prussian who crossed the Atlantic just to fight for the independence of the Confederate States.

In their new position behind Middleburg, Stuart's men readied themselves for an attack that never came. That evening, Grumble Jones' brigade arrived and was sent to the left near the village of Union with Fitz Lee's brigade extending that line all the way to the left toward Snicker's Gap. Stuart was attempting to cover nearly fifteen miles of battle line.

On June 20, Hampton's brigade reached the field, but darkness and a heavy rain discouraged any attack upon the Union position in Middleburg. Tom Rosser and the 5th Virginia, however, attacked north of the town and drove the Yankees beyond Goose Creek. Jones' brigade was in support.

With all his brigades finally within supporting distance, Stuart began contemplating offensive operations again. June 21 was a Sunday and he decided to postpone his attack because of the Sabbath. The Yankees were not in a mood to pray and began advancing at 8 A.M.[16]

Three brigades from John Buford's cavalry division moved up the road from Middleburg toward Union, in an attempt to loosen Stuart's hold on the road leading to Snicker's Gap.

Buford's column encountered Goose Creek after riding northwest out of Middleburg. At the creek he turned and took his command along the right bank until he could see that the left flank of Jones and Chambliss was in such a fine defensive position that an attack from that area was impractical. Retracing his hoofprints, he crossed at a ford and started up Goose Creek again, intending to re-cross at Millville. Chambliss and Jones responded by sending three regiments to impede his progress. Buford slowly pushed back the Confederates until he began to feel uneasy about his left flank. He ordered his reserve to close the gap between his division and that of Brigadier General David Gregg farther south.[17]

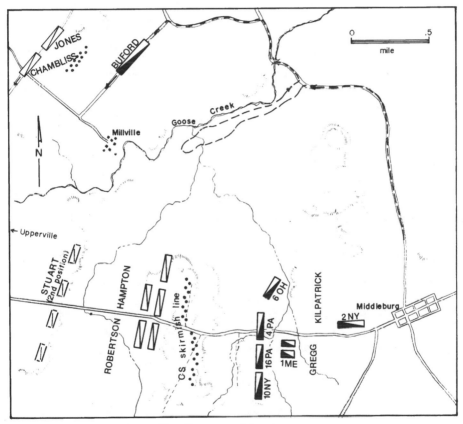

The Battle of Middleburg

It soon became apparent to Buford that he had not found the Confederate left flank. He sent word to Gregg and began to push west toward Upperville. Stuart, desiring to join his divided wings there, had ordered Jones and Chambliss to withdraw in that direction.[18]

Meantime, on the Ashby's Gap road, Kilpatrick had renewed the fight. In an hour-long artillery duel, Stuart's Horse Artillery lost its first gun to the enemy. A Federal shell destroyed a limber chest, killing or disabling three of the six horses. Thus, a Blakely gun had to be left behind while Stuart was retiring Hampton's and Robertson's brigades and Gregg was pushing forward. Kilpatrick's men also advanced.[19]

Stuart continued his withdrawal to a second position on the west bank of Goose Creek, where he was attacked by infantry skirmishers from the 1st Division of the V Corps. A charge of the 2nd and 4th New York Cavalry regiments across the bridge added to the pressure on Stuart's position.

In his report, Stuart wrote that as he continued to withdraw under fire, "Nothing could exceed the coolness and self-possession of officers and men in these movements, performing evolutions with a precision under fire that must have wrung the tribute of admiration from the enemy, even, who dared not trust his cavalry unsupported to the sabres of such men."[20] Gregg, apparently not as impressed, wrote merely that Stuart's retreat was "rapid."[21]

The fight around Middleburg fizzled out into skirmishing while Chambliss and Jones withdrew toward Upperville. Closing to within a mile of town, Buford could see Gregg's men fighting. To Buford, they appeared to be outnumbered, so he hurried. The terrain was covered with ditches and stone walls that broke up any organization and slowed the column. Perhaps feeling he could not get to Gregg in time, Buford, noticing a large Confederate wagon train to his right, for some reason decided to attack it. He blundered into a much larger force than his two brigades could handle. These Confederates of Jones' brigade brought up four guns that, in Buford's words, "made some excellent practice on the head of my regiments."[22] Despite the well-aimed fire, Buford's men got close enough to temporarily drive off the gunners, but were stopped again by a charge from the 11th Virginia Cavalry as well as two stone fences and the impassable terrain of that part of the mountains. Buford's force was briefly threatened from the north by another large body of Confederates, but they were pushed back into the mountains when Buford's rear troopers caught up with the column. The Confederate artillerists managed to limber up their guns and haul them off.[23]

As his two segments converged upon Upperville, Stuart had two concerns: That the Yankees would still get between the two columns as they converged and that he would have to fight among the houses of Upperville, in which he knew were women and children. He thought he could solve both problems by

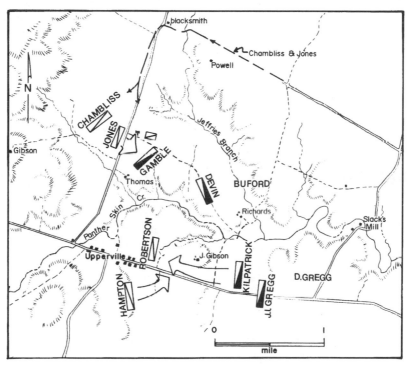

THE BATTLE OF UPPERVILLE

withdrawing Hampton's and Robertson's brigades farther west of the hamlet, which had a number of roads the enemy could use to threaten his flank. West of the town, he could secure his flanks for a while and also buy time for Chambliss and Jones under the support of his artillery, now establishing itself in Ashby's Gap.

But Kilpatrick's leading regiments were pounding into the eastern end of Upperville. Hampton stopped his withdrawal, wheeled about, and drove them back. As Robertson retreated through the village, he was attacked by the rest of Kilpatrick's brigade and Buford's reserve brigade coming up from Millville. The Federals were repulsed initially, but Chambliss' and Jones' brigades were converging on Ashby's Gap and Buford's division was moving on Upperville from the north. The Union attacks pushed the Confederate rear guard back through the town and to the south of it.[24]

About 5:30 P.M., Kilpatrick made a final charge through the town, overrunning a Confederate cannon in the middle of the main street.

Some historians called the battles around Aldie, Middleburg, and Upperville skirmishes, but Stuart's casualties during the fighting amounted to 510. Total losses for the Federals were around 800. Compared to Brandy Station, the losses were about the same, but there both sides had many more troopers engaged.

Stuart, though close at hand, was conspicuously absent from the decision-making at the front lines of the fighting at Aldie, Middleburg, and Upperville. His absence was noticed because the front was where he liked to be, taking hot fire from the enemy just as he expected his men to do. During the recent actions he had issued commands only a few times. His assistant adjutant general, H. B. McClellan, asked him about this. He said he had given all necessary orders to his brigade commanders and wanted them now, after two years of war, to feel the weight of command as well as the joy of whatever honor the field of battle might yield.[25]

Perhaps he was also thinking of his own future. All indications, after the deaths of so many other talented, brave, and efficient Confederate officers, were that he too was likely to fall. A wise commander leaves experienced men behind to fill even the largest gap in the ranks. In war, with sudden death all around, there is no time for a patient executor to sort out the details of a confusing will. There is only the instantaneous change of command and the legacy left by the slain.

In his book *Here Come the Rebels!*, Wilbur S. Nye asserts that this reticence toward direct command from June 17–21 "refutes a common contention that Stuart was always playing to the galleries and at this time was especially eager to neutralize the poor press reports he had received for being surprised at Brandy Station. It increases Stuart's military stature, in showing that he was sufficiently unselfish and wise to build up the skill, experience, and reputation of his subordinates."[26]

The men with Stuart in Northern Virginia were not the only Confederate horsemen in action during mid-June. Brigadier General Alfred Jenkins and his brigade of 1,800 men preceded Lieutenant General Richard S. Ewell's Second Corps into Pennsylvania. Ewell's job was to collect supplies and scout ahead of the advancing infantry. Jenkins was in Chambersburg from June 15 until the 17th, when he retired to Greencastle. By June 22, Jenkins had sent out units to Waynesboro, Fairfield, Welsh Run, Mercersburg, Cove Mountain, McConnellsburg, and then Chambersburg again, gathering in hundreds of thousands of dollars worth of property for the use of the army.[27]

From Carlisle on June 28, Ewell sent Jenkins' men to Mechanicsburg, south of Harrisburg, the capital, then to the outskirts of Harrisburg itself.[28] No doubt, Ewell had been sending information from Jenkins to Lee, since Lee knew where to find Ewell when he needed to recall him on June 28. As well, Lee, by then, was in Pennsylvania himself, and the newspapers had been screaming for a week about the Confederate invasion.

Chambersburg resident Jacob Hoke wrote about Brigadier General J. D. Imboden's large force of cavalry sent to destroy the Baltimore and Ohio Railroad line so the Yankees could not use it to get to his rear.

> Starting at Cumberland, Maryland, he moved eastwardly along the railroad, doing considerable damage to the track, bridges, and depots, as well as the canal boats and locks of the Chesapeake and Ohio Canal, as far down as Martinsburg. . . . While in the cove [Great Cove] he did great damage. The farmers lost all their stock, and Robinson's store at Big Cove Tannery, and Patterson's at Webster Mills, were completely stripped of their contents.[29]

Imboden apparently was in communication with Lee from June 16–21. The commanding general was glad to hear of the destruction of the railroad and encouraged Imboden to continue to guard the left flank of the army as it advanced into Pennsylvania.[30]

On June 21, General Lee issued his General Orders No. 72, pertaining to the collection of supplies for the campaign.

The six points of the orders stated that no private property would be destroyed except by certain officers; how and by whom requisitions upon local authorities would be made; how to handle local people who refused to give up supplies; which detached commands would procure supplies; how to handle people who refused payment for confiscated property; and how to deal with anyone concealing property.[31] In virtually every subsequent order after the Confederates crossed into Maryland, Lee repeated and emphasized the importance of collecting supplies. The supplies were not intended merely to sustain his army during the invasion but also after the campaign. For months after he returned to Virginia, he intended for them to feed, clothe, and supply his army.

CHAPTER FOUR

Orders

*"I have the reputation of being very fond of saying 'no,' but I
have had but one rule of action from the first and that was duty."*
—J. E. B. STUART TO HIS WIFE

arly on June 22, Union Brigadier General Alfred Pleasonton withdrew
his troopers from Upperville. Stuart returned to Rector's Cross Roads to
his former headquarters site.[1]

Mosby, who had again been scouting the area near the Potomac crossings
and in the rear of the Union army, suggested that Stuart could pass through the
center of the Union army and cross the Potomac at Seneca.[2] From their correspondence, it appears that Lee, Lieutenant General James Longstreet, and Stuart may
have already been discussing the practicality of Stuart moving into the Yankee rear.[3]

Charles Marshall, Lee's military secretary, said Stuart met with Lee near
Paris, Virginia, and suggested moving into the rear of the enemy. Marshall said
Longstreet, commander of the First Corps of the Army of Northern Virginia,
thought well of the plan.[4] Mosby's observations may have helped sway Stuart
as to the ease of getting around or through the enemy's army.

On June 22, Lee issued one of the orders to Stuart governing his movements
during the coming campaign. These were his first written orders concerning a
possible route around the enemy's rear:

> General: I have just received your note of 7:45 this morning to
> General Longstreet. I judge the efforts of the enemy yesterday
> were to arrest our progress and ascertain our whereabouts. Perhaps
> he is satisfied. Do you know where he is and what he is doing? I
> fear he will steal a march on us, and get across the Potomac before
> we are aware. If you find that he is moving northward, and that two
> brigades can guard the Blue Ridge and take care of your rear, you can
> move with the other three into Maryland, and take position on General

Ewell's right, place yourself in communication with him, guard his flank, keep him informed of the enemy's movements, and collect all the supplies you can for the use of the army. One column of General Ewell's army will probably move toward the Susquehanna by the Emmitsburg route; another by Chambersburg. Accounts from him last night state that there was no enemy west of Frederick. A cavalry force (about 100) guarded the Monocacy Bridge, which was barricaded. You will, of course, take charge of [A. G.] Jenkins' brigade, and give him necessary instructions. All supplies taken in Maryland must be by authorized staff officers for their respective departments—by no one else. They will be paid for, or receipts for the same given to the owners. I will send you a general order on this subject [No. 72], which I wish you to see is strictly complied with.[5]

On June 22 Lee wrote twice to Ewell, who was commanding the vanguard of the Confederate invasion.

Lee's first letter acknowledges the receipt of an earlier letter and gives Ewell a march route: "I think your best course will be toward the Susquehanna, taking routes by Emmitsburg, Chambersburg, and McConnellsburg." In the same first paragraph he emphasizes, "You must get command of your cavalry [Jenkins], and use it in gathering supplies, obtaining information, and protecting your flanks. If necessary, send a staff officer to remain with General Jenkins. It will depend upon the quantity of supplies obtained in that country whether the rest of the army can follow." Apparently, the continuance of the campaign depended upon finding and gathering sufficient supplies. Lee continues: "Your progress and direction will, of course, depend upon the development of circumstances. If Harrisburg comes within your means, capture it."[6]

At 3:30 P.M. that same day, Lee wrote again to Ewell. Lee virtually repeats his orders to Stuart:

I also directed General Stuart, should the enemy have so far retired from his front as to permit of the departure of a portion of the cavalry, to march with three brigades across the Potomac, and place himself on your right and in communication with you, keep you advised of the movements of the enemy, and assist in collecting supplies for the army. I have not heard from him since. I also directed Imboden [who commanded cavalry detached from Stuart], if opportunity offered, to cross the Potomac, and perform the same offices on your left.[7]

Ewell marched and Jenkins' cavalry preceded him into Pennsylvania.

Stuart had his orders: If he found the Union army was moving northward, he could cross the Potomac and move into Maryland. They read as if the subject had been discussed before. These orders leave no discretion to Stuart. If the enemy is moving northward, then Stuart must move into Maryland.

Lee told Stuart that there was no enemy west of Frederick, Maryland, and that a small cavalry force guarded the Monocacy River bridge. Lee also gave instructions as to taking supplies in Maryland. All these places lie north of the Potomac. Lee gave Stuart specific information on the Union army along the Monocacy and near Frederick because he expected Stuart to enter Maryland.

These orders do not cover other contingencies, such as if the Federal army remained immobile or if it struck southward toward Richmond. If the Union army remained non-threatening, nothing needed to be done except watch it in case it moved. Sending Stuart into Maryland and the rear of the Army of the Potomac would have prevented it from striking toward Richmond for fear of leaving Washington open to attack.

It seemed a good plan—diverting attention from Lee's army, destroying communications between the Federals and their capital, driving a wedge between the Northern army and Richmond, and collecting supplies from a different area of the North than that through which the main army was traveling. Whoever thought of it—Stuart, Lee, Longstreet, or a combination—carefully considered how to disrupt the enemy's operations while protecting their own.

Lee may have wondered when, if Stuart rode around the Union army, he would see Stuart and his men again. Lee knew that even by the nearest route to Emmitsburg, where Ewell's right flank was supposed to be, Stuart would have to ride seventy to eighty linear miles, perhaps more like 100 miles by road. He also knew that this movement would take two (more likely three) days, providing for clashes with enemy cavalry, detours because of weather and washed-out bridges, and the collecting of supplies. Certainly, he did not expect Stuart to reach Emmitsburg before Ewell, who by June 22 was already opposite Shepherdstown and a little more than a day's march from Emmitsburg.

In October 1862, Stuart had made that horse-killing ride of eighty miles in twenty-seven hours on his raid into Pennsylvania,[8] but he was escaping a pursuing enemy. Lee probably was not thinking that Stuart would cover the same distance in a day when any fighting could still be ahead of him.

In fact, Lee knew that the entire Union army was out there, too, with its cavalry, and might impede Stuart. At this point, June 22, when he ordered Stuart to operate in Maryland, he was necessarily ordering him to ride around the Union army, which he thought was still on the west (or south) side of the Potomac. Lee probably expected Stuart to be out of touch for three or four days.

Lee's orders to Stuart went through Longstreet, who had read them since he mentioned them in his next correspondence to Stuart. Longstreet saw what was happening and how Stuart would have to ride around the Union army, regardless of which side of the Potomac the Yankees were on. At 7 P.M. June 22, Longstreet sent a letter to Stuart with Lee's orders:

> General: General Lee has enclosed to me this letter for you [of June 22], to be forwarded to you, provided you can be spared from my front, and provided I think that you can move across the Potomac without disclosing our plans. He speaks of your leaving via Hopewell Gap, and passing by the rear of the enemy. If you can get through by that route, I think that you will be less likely to indicate what our plans are than if you should cross by passing to our rear. I forward the letter of instructions with these suggestions.
>
> Please advise me of the condition of affairs before you leave, and order General Hampton—whom I suppose you will leave here in command—to report to me at Millwood, either by letter or in person, as may be most agreeable to him. . . .
>
> N.B.—I think that your passage of the Potomac by our rear at the present moment will, in a measure, disclose our plans. You had better not leave us, therefore, unless you can take the proposed route in rear of the enemy.[9]

It is clear that Lee had spoken to Longstreet earlier in the day about Stuart riding around the enemy. (The route through Hopewell Gap is not mentioned in Stuart's orders and therefore must have been in Lee's spoken conversation with Longstreet.)

It appears that there could be little question in anyone's mind—then or later—as to what "passing by the rear of the enemy" meant. Regardless of the questions asked later by critics of Stuart's role in the campaign, to Stuart on June 22, there was only one route open if he were to obey Lee's orders: across the Potomac and around the Union army.

Just after he finished the letter to Stuart, Longstreet wrote to Lee, telling him that he had forwarded the letter to Stuart with the addendum that he pass by the enemy's rear if he thought that he may get through. So Lee had not only spoken to Longstreet of Stuart riding around the Union army but he knew that Longstreet had recommended it as a maneuver to deceive the enemy. Longstreet virtually gave Stuart no choice but to either ride around the enemy or disclose Confederate plans.

At this point, Lee and Longstreet were thinking—like Stuart—how best to use light cavalry in an active campaign: with swiftness and surprise, doing what the enemy does not expect, and raiding between him and his base—in this case, Washington. It was exactly the role for which light cavalry was created.

Lee was probably the most intelligent, experienced man in the army; perhaps in either army. He was not a seer, but he could figure time and distance. Lee issued orders and Longstreet backed them up. Everyone communicated with everyone else as to Stuart's course and mission.

At 5 P.M. on June 23, Lee had sent another set of orders to Stuart and passed on some additional information. He wrote, in part:

> General: Your notes of 9 and 10.30 A.M. today have just been received. As regards the purchase of tobacco for your men, supposing that Confederate money will not be taken, I am willing for your commissaries or quartermasters to purchase this tobacco and let the men get it from them, but I can have nothing seized by the men.
>
> If General Hooker's army remains inactive, you can leave two brigades to watch him, and withdraw with the three others, but should he not appear to be moving northward, I think you had better withdraw this side of the mountain to-morrow night, cross at Shepherdstown next day, and move over to Fredericktown.
>
> You will, however, be able to judge whether you can pass around their army without hinderance, doing them all the damage you can, and cross the river east of the mountains. In either case, after crossing the river, you must move on and feel the right of Ewell's troops, collecting information, provisions, &c.
>
> Give instructions to the commander of the brigades left behind, to watch the flank and rear of the army, and (in the event of the enemy leaving their front) retire from the mountains west of the Shenandoah, leaving sufficient pickets to guard the passes, and bringing everything clean along the Valley, closing upon the rear of the army. . . . I think the sooner you cross into Maryland, after tomorrow, the better.[10]

A question about procuring tobacco for his men was certainly not the only thing that Stuart included in his two dispatches sent to Lee on the morning of June 23. No doubt he had answered Lee's questions (asked in Lee's June 22 correspondence) about the whereabouts and intentions of the Union army. It is probably this information—that the Union army was withdrawing from Leesburg and was building a pontoon bridge across the Potomac at Edward's Ferry— that Lee later mentioned to President Jefferson Davis in another June 23 letter.

Whatever information Stuart's notes contained, Lee thought it vital enough to keep it secret in case this dispatch were captured. Stuart, however, understood what Lee was talking about.

Further, Stuart *must* again have mentioned in his correspondence something about crossing the Potomac into Maryland since the restrictions on his men seizing tobacco if Confederate money would not be taken would only apply in Maryland (or Pennsylvania)—not if Stuart's men were moving through Virginia.

The mention of Hooker remaining inactive was one of the most confusing and illogical paragraphs in all of the official correspondence on the Gettysburg campaign. After Lee and Longstreet on June 22 gave Stuart specific orders about crossing the Potomac and riding around the Federal army, now came this; if the enemy remained *inactive,* Stuart could ride around the Union army. His original orders told him that if the enemy were moving northward, he could also in that case ride around him. This now gives him two contingencies upon which he can cross the Potomac and swing around the Yankees. Then he is told if they do not appear to be moving northward, he is to virtually cancel his orders to ride around the Union army.

How can this be reconciled? The first orders (June 22) tell Stuart to move around the enemy if he appeared to be moving northward; the second orders tell Stuart that if the enemy remained inactive, he could "withdraw"—apparently to Maryland—and proceed around the Yankees. They are confusing because of their lack of specificity as to where he should withdraw. However, they are clear in that, when combined with his first orders, they say that in either case Stuart should withdraw the three brigades that he was to take into Maryland.

Then, after being given his orders on how to respond if the enemy remained inactive or moved northward, he was told "but should he not appear to be moving northward," Stuart was to withdraw to "this" side of the mountains—the side Lee was on, the west side—and cross the river at Shepherdstown.

Was there a difference between the enemy remaining "inactive" and his "not moving northward"? There had better have been, because Stuart's orders depended upon which was the case.

The circumstances under which this second set of orders was sent were explained after the war by the man who wrote them, Charles Marshall, Lee's secretary. In Marshall's "Memoirs," published posthumously in 1927, he wrote that after the first letter of June 22 was sent,

> General Lee directed me to repeat it. I remember saying to the
> General that it could hardly be necessary to repeat the order, as General
> Stuart had had the matter fully explained to himself verbally and
> my letter had been very full and explicit. I had retained a copy of my

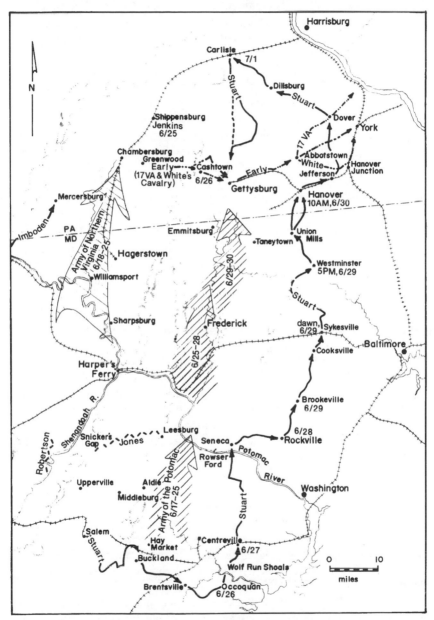

Harrisburg

Carlisle
7/1
Stuart
Dillsburg
Stuart
Dover
17 VA
York
Shippensburg
Jenkins
6/25
Abbotstown
White
Jefferson
Hanover
Junction
Chambersburg
Greenwood
Early
(17 VA & White's
Cavalry)
Cashtown
6/26
Early
Gettysburg
Hanover
10 AM, 6/30
Mercersburg
Union
Mills
Imboden
PA
MD
Emmitsburg
Taneytown
Army of Northern
Virginia
6/18-25
Hagerstown
6/29-30
Westminster
5 PM, 6/29
Williamsport
Stuart
Sharpsburg
Frederick
dawn,
6/29
Sykesville
Baltimore
6/25-28
Cooksville
Harper's
Ferry
Shenandoah R.
Brookeville
6/29
Robertson
Snicker's
Gap
Jones
Leesburg
Seneca
6/28
Rockville
Rowser
Ford
Potomac
Upperville
Aldie
Army of the Potomac
6/17-25
River
Washington
Middleburg
Stuart
Salem
Stuart
Hay
Market
Centreville
0   10
Buckland
6/27
Wolf Run Shoals
miles
Brentsville
6/26
Occoquan

N

Stuart's Route in the Gettysburg Campaign

letter in General Lee's confidential letter book. General Lee said that he felt anxious about the matter and desired to guard against the possibility of error, and desired me to repeat it, which I did, and dispatched the second letter.[11]

It would probably have been better if this second letter had never been written. Sadly, Marshall did not repeat the orders from June 22. The paragraph regarding Stuart's movements in the second letter was unclear, imprecise, and nearly illogical when taken in light of the previous orders. Marshall was apparently reluctant to repeat orders he had just written. One can only wonder whether Marshall's mind was wandering while "repeating" the June 22 orders, since they came out sounding nothing like the original. In fact, if Lee wanted Marshall to repeat the orders of June 22, Marshall failed to do so.

Much was made later by Marshall against Stuart, blaming him for the failure of the entire campaign because Stuart, in Marshall's opinion, disobeyed orders. Marshall even went so far as to say, at that social gathering after the war, that Stuart should have been court-martialed and shot. Lee himself, as Marshall conceded, refused to allow the statement about a proposed court-martial into the official reports.

After the war, Marshall detailed the orders Stuart received and said falsely that they stated that he was to move forward along the army's flank. Marshall said that Stuart was not where he was expected to be and that Stuart had confessed that he had pursued a different course. (This is difficult to believe, considering that Stuart pursued the only course orders allowed.) Marshall added that Lee "did not question the accuracy of the report, but said he could not adopt my conclusions or charge him [Stuart] with the facts as I stated them, unless they should be established by a court-martial."[12]

These statements represented just one of several times over the years that Marshall charged Stuart with disobeying Lee's orders. Others also blamed Stuart to deflect from their own failures or to attempt to make Lee look better. Stuart, of course, was long dead. The charges over the years that Stuart disobeyed orders all seemed to emanate from what many believed was an unimpeachable source: Lee's secretary, Charles Marshall.

During the 1863 summer campaign, Stuart was heedless of what was to be said of him, at least concerning this matter. His conversation with Lee after Upperville, his June 22 orders from Lee, his orders from Longstreet, and his own impending observations in the field dictated his actions.

In the second set of orders, Lee said, "I think the sooner you cross into Maryland, after to-morrow, the better." In other words, do not cross the Potomac before the 25th, but as soon as you can after that. That meant Stuart would have to cover ninety miles from Rector's Cross Roads, across the Potomac to Emmitsburg, Maryland, where he was to meet Ewell. If the Union army appeared not to be moving northward, Stuart would have about forty-five miles to travel to the Shepherdstown crossing point from Rector's Cross Roads and another forty-five miles to Emmitsburg via Frederick.

So, after telling Stuart exactly when he should ride, Lee could not have expected to hear much from him before the 27th at the absolute earliest, if all Stuart did was ride and rest. Realistically, Lee could not have expected to hear from Stuart until the 28th and quite possibly the 29th, allowing for military exigencies. No reasonable man could have expected more from Stuart.

On June 23, Lee wrote to Jefferson Davis:

> Reports of the movements of the enemy east of the Blue Ridge cause me to believe that he is preparing to cross the Potomac. A pontoon bridge is said to be laid at Edwards Ferry, and his army corps that he has advanced to Leesburg and the foot of the mountains, appear to be withdrawing. Their attempts to penetrate the mountains have been successfully repelled by General Stuart with the cavalry. General Stuart last night was within a few miles of Aldie, to which point the enemy had retired.[13]

The next paragraph advised Davis of the movements of Lee's three army corps and the last (and largest) talked about nothing but gathering supplies, a subject weighing heavily upon Lee.

As mentioned earlier, the reports of the movements of the Union army and its preparations to cross the Potomac near Leesburg probably came from Stuart, considering the timing of the letter, Stuart's location, and the fact that Lee went right into discussing Stuart. But more important, it dates the moment when Lee realized that Hooker's army was ready to cross the Potomac: June 23. He mentioned this to Davis because both men were worried that Hooker would not cross the Potomac but instead strike at Richmond. That Hooker was preparing to enter Maryland was actually good news to Lee and Davis.

On the night of June 23, at Stuart's headquarters at Rector's Cross Roads just west of Middleburg, a courier arrived from headquarters. He handed a dispatch marked "confidential" to H. B. McClellan, who determined not to wake Stuart unless the contents were vital. The assistant adjutant general later wrote that it was a lengthy communication from Lee containing the directions upon which Stuart was to act. He took it to the general and read it to him. Many have assumed that these were Lee's orders of June 23. They appear to be, plus a completely different letter.

In his 1885 book *I Rode with Jeb Stuart,* McClellan said, "The letter discussed at considerable length the plan of passing around the enemy's rear. It informed General Stuart that General Early would move upon York, Pa., and that he was desired to place his cavalry as speedily as possible with that, the advance division of Lee's right wing." He continued:

> The letter suggested that, as the roads leading northward from Shepherdstown and Williamsport were already encumbered by the infantry, the artillery, and the transportation of the army, the delay which would necessarily occur in passing by these would, perhaps, be greater than would ensue if General Stuart passed around the enemy's rear. The letter further informed him that, if he chose the latter route, General Early would receive instructions to look out for him and endeavor to communicate with him; and York, Pa., was designated as the point in the vicinity of which he was to expect to hear from Early, and as the possible (if not probable) point of concentration of the army. The whole tenor of the letter gave evidence that the commanding general approved the proposed movement, and thought that it might be productive of the best results, while the responsibility of the decision was placed upon General Stuart himself.[14]

McClellan wrote then that he could not find the original letter and Stuart had not forwarded it with his report. He assumed it had been destroyed during the subsequent marches, but said he had had several occasions since the war to recall what it said and his recollection was confirmed by Stuart's official report.

Perhaps when Lee read Marshall's second set of orders he realized that Marshall, indeed, had not repeated them, for there is much evidence that when Stuart received his dispatch on the night of June 23 that it had been added to considerably. There were a number of points McClellan recalled in the letter that are not mentioned in Lee's preserved and published orders of June 23; they also pop up in a careful examination of Stuart's and Lee's own official reports and other correspondence written after the campaign.

The timing is important. Stuart was at Rector's Cross Roads on the road from Middleburg to Ashby's Gap, about nine miles from the gap. Chiswell Dabney, Stuart's aide-de-camp, said he was sent to Lee with a message from Stuart on June 23. He found Lee, his staff, and Longstreet at a house on the side of the road, "before reaching the foot of the Ridge at Ashby's Gap." [15] Lee and Stuart were, therefore, less than eight miles apart. If Marshall wrote Lee's orders at 5 P.M. on June 23 and Stuart did not receive them until after he had gone to sleep that night, Lee would have had plenty of time to add his own comments to the letter and send it to Stuart.

Had he sent it off right after he dictated the letter, it should have gotten to Stuart well before when McClellan says it was received. Lee and Stuart could not have been more than two or at the very most three hours apart by courier.

Among McClellan's recollected orders of the night of June 23 were several pieces of information not in the published orders of June 23 that appear in the *Official Records:*

- The letter was marked "confidential."
- It was sealed with a seal McClellan had to break.
- It was lengthy, suggesting more than the six paragraphs that were published.
- It told of Early moving on York, Pennsylvania.
- It told Stuart to place his command with Early at York, instead of with Ewell.
- It spoke of accomplishing this "as speedily as possible."
- It informed Stuart that the roads to Shepherdstown and Williamsport were crowded and again recommended moving in the rear of the enemy.
- It informed him that Early would look for him if he chose that course around the Federals.
- It informed Stuart that he should look for Early in York.
- It informed Stuart that York was the probable concentration point of the army.

McClellan recalled what appears to be a different document, or at least a lengthy addition to the orders published in the *Official Records.* Interestingly, the post-battle reports of Lee and Stuart and the memoirs of many participants (including Stuart critics) refer to several points in McClellan's recollected document, particularly the speed with which Stuart was to travel. Memoirs published after 1885 could have used McClellan's work for that piece of information or, if written after the publication of the *Official Records* in 1889, could have used the reports.

It seems that Marshall was not told by Lee to include the subject of speed in his first or second set of orders to Stuart. Apparently Marshall had not heard the information when he wrote Lee's first report in July 1863; the subject does not appear. But it does appear in Lee's second report. (Perhaps by then Marshall had heard from Lee about it.) Therefore, the information that Stuart was to move with rapidity must have come from somewhere other than Lee's published orders.

There is no mention of Early or a destination of York either in the June 22 or 23 published orders to Stuart. In fact, Lee's orders to Ewell on the 22nd mentioned that he would try to get Early's division to Imboden to serve on Ewell's left instead of sending Early ahead or toward Ewell's right. Ewell's right flank was to be covered by Stuart when he arrived. Perhaps Lee changed Early's orders or later found out that Early was on the right and then sent that information on to Stuart in the letter McClellan opened at Rector's Cross Roads.

This correspondence recalled by McClellan is vital because it gave Stuart several more pieces of information. It sent him from the Emmitsburg route farther east toward York and added some distance to the ninety-mile trek originally conceived by Lee and passed on to Stuart. It also mentioned that the roads to the east of the army (but still west of the mountains) were clogging up rapidly with the infantry, artillery, and impedimenta and further bolstered Stuart's impression that Lee wanted him to ride around the Union army because of that. As well, it placed some of the duty of reconnecting with the rest of the army upon Early and placed a tentative destination of the army (or at least the advanced elements of it) much farther east than before mentioned.

This letter made the third time Lee wrote to Stuart about his route around the rear of the Union army. Marshall never mentioned it until years later,[16] nor can reference to it be found in any of the published accounts of Lee's other aides. McClellan may have combined it with other orders in his mind during the fifteen or so years between the end of the war and the writing of his book in the early 1880s. However, there are those other references in Lee's and Stuart's post-battle reports concerning rapid movement and meeting with Early instead of Ewell (in Stuart's report) that make its existence probable. The information McClellan recalled was certainly different from what was in any published orders. That he would have made it up seems unlikely; fabricating such a letter would do more harm than good, since many of the men involved were still alive and could refute it. No one ever did except Marshall. As well, McClellan has historically been considered one of the more accurate historians of the war.[17] Most contemporary historians, including John S. Mosby, one of Stuart's most vehement defenders, never noticed these discrepancies between the published orders and the ones McClellan recalled Stuart receiving on the night of June 23.

The letter itself may never turn up; numerous letters, notes, dispatches, and other documents of the Gettysburg campaign are not extant, but thanks to McClellan, this missing letter's contents have remained.[18]

On June 24, knowing that he would be out of touch with the army for several days, Stuart sent remarkably specific orders to Brigadier General Beverly H. Robertson, whose brigade was working with Grumble Jones' brigade. Robertson was to be in command and Stuart virtually repeated Lee's orders to him, with short, action-filled sentences:

> General: Your own and General Jones' brigades will cover the front of Ashby's and Snicker's Gaps, yourself, as senior officer, being in command.
>
> Your object will be to watch the enemy; deceive him as to our designs, and harass his rear if you find he is retiring. Be always on

the alert; let nothing escape your observation, and miss no opportunity which offers to damage the enemy.

After the enemy has moved beyond your reach, leave sufficient pickets in the mountains, withdraw to the west side of the Shenandoah, place a strong and reliable picket to watch the enemy at Harper's Ferry, cross the Potomac, and follow the army, keeping on its right and rear.

As long as the enemy remains in your front in force, unless otherwise ordered by General R. E. Lee, Lieutenant-General Longstreet, or myself, hold the Gaps with a line of pickets reaching across the Shenandoah by Charlestown to the Potomac.

If, in the contingency mentioned, you withdraw, sweep the Valley clear of what pertains to the army, and cross the Potomac at the different points crossed by it.

You will instruct General Jones from time to time as the movements progress, or events may require, and report anything of importance to Lieutenant-General Longstreet, with whose position you will communicate by relays through Charlestown.

I send instructions for General Jones, which please read. Avail yourself of every means in your power to increase the efficiency of your command, and keep it up to the highest number possible. Particular attention will be paid to shoeing horses, and to marching off of the turnpike.

In case of an advance of the enemy, you will offer such resistance as will be justifiable to check him and discover his intentions and, if possible, you will prevent him from gaining possession of the Gaps.

In case of a move by the enemy upon Warrenton, you will counteract it as much as you can, compatible with previous instructions.

You will have with the two brigades two batteries of horse artillery.[19]

In a postscript, Stuart told him not to change his present line of pickets until daylight of June 25 unless he was compelled to do so.

These instructions could not have been any clearer. In fact, Robertson should have been getting ready to move immediately after receiving this order, which postdates the June 23 information Lee had that the Union army was preparing to cross the Potomac. Robertson should at least have been in motion by June 25, when Hooker's army actually began crossing.

So Stuart rode on June 25, assuming that Robertson, commanding about

3,000 men,[20] would follow Lee, keep on his right flank, and perform all the tasks Stuart would have if he had been there. In addition, Stuart believed that Jenkins' brigade, which was leading Ewell's advance into Pennsylvania and was under his command, contained 3,800 troopers.[21] As well, watching the left flank of the army was Imboden with 2,000 troopers.[22] Stuart left with Lee what he believed were close to 9,000 troopers, most of whom were within a day or two's ride of Lee himself.

Stuart's orders to Robertson were specific because some in the army doubted his efficiency. Along with Jones' unit, Robertson's brigade of North Carolinians had just rejoined Stuart's cavalry on May 23.[23] Some officers thought Robertson had failed in his first big battle afterward, at Brandy Station on June 9.

William W. Blackford, Stuart's engineering officer, was one who blamed Robertson for failing to warn Stuart of the approach from Kelly's Ford of the Union troopers.[24] For some reason, Robertson had been relieved of active duty in September 1862 and sent back to North Carolina to organize and instruct cavalry troops.[25] Though Robertson and Stuart went back and forth in the official reports of Robertson's actions during Brandy Station, it finally ended with Stuart saying that Robertson "intended to do what was right" and that his reports of his actions there appeared to be satisfactory. But a lack of confidence in Robertson apparently dictated Stuart's issuance of such specific orders. As recently as the fighting at Aldie, Middleburg, and Upperville, Stuart began to give freer rein to most of his brigadiers, but to Robertson he gave orders that allowed no interpretation. Early in the war Stuart had commented that he felt "Bev Robertson by far the most troublesome man I have to deal with."[26]

In addition, Stuart knew that Grumble Jones, though subordinate to Robertson, was a fine officer. In spite of his disposition and the animosity between him and Stuart, they had grudging respect for each other.[27] Jones could have been expected, under campaign conditions, to act professionally.

Longstreet, too, apparently knew of Robertson's shortcomings and so assumed that Stuart would leave Wade Hampton, a more competent and aggressive commander, to follow along the right flank of the infantry. Stuart, like any commander, wanted his most competent officers on the most dangerous and important mission, and so gathered the brigades of Hampton, Fitz Lee, and Rooney Lee, the last still under Colonel John R. Chambliss. During the night of June 24, they quietly rendezvoused at Salem Depot on the big southern loop around the mountains made by the Manassas Gap Railroad.

At 1 A.M. June 25, Stuart silently moved out his column of 4,000 to 4,500 men and horses. At least a part of the Union II Corps, under Major General Winfield Scott Hancock, was in Thoroughfare Gap, blocking passage through the Bull Run Mountains. Stuart detoured to the south five miles and passed through Glasscock Gap. Reaching Haymarket, he found that Hancock's corps was passing through, heading north for Gum Springs. Stuart opened with artillery from about 800 yards,[28] scattering the column, only to see it reorganize and advance toward him. He pulled back his artillery and dismounted some men to meet the advance, but the Yankees were more intent on moving northward and protecting their flank than in engaging, so they moved on.[29] Stuart sent Fitz Lee's brigade two miles down the road to Gainesville to find out if he could pass around Hancock's corps there; the hungry horses grazed until Lee returned. The enemy was found to be spread between Centreville, Union Mills, and Wolf Run Shoals on the Occoquan River. As the rain poured down the night of June 25, he notified Lee that Hancock's corps was moving northward. Stuart then pulled back to Buckland for the night as a deception.[30]

Stuart noted in his post-campaign report that at this point he had planned to march west of Centreville, Virginia, but to wait for the enemy to pass would have delayed him. As well, it would have made Stuart sit still, something that grated on him. Seeing that the Union army was moving northward and remembering Lee's orders of June 22, he notified Lee by courier and struck out the next day to cross Bull Run. On June 26, he passed through Brentsville to Wolf Run Shoals, where he again had to halt to graze the horses and gather information on the enemy.

Farther north, on the morning of June 25, Brigadier General Junius Daniel's infantry brigade of Major General Robert Rodes' division began its march for Shippensburg, Pennsylvania, in order to back up Jenkins' brigade of cavalry already there. The Confederates were gathering large quantities of supplies as well as the information that the Union army was not this far north. Jenkins' cavalry was covering every back road and farmhouse in the region ahead of the invading army. By the 27th, it reached Carlisle, Pennsylvania, and the large U.S. Army cavalry barracks there.

Also on June 25, Lee wrote to Davis: "You will see that apprehension for the safety of Washington and their own territory has aroused the Federal Government and people to great exertions."[31] (He may also have been thinking, though he did not write it for security reasons, that once Stuart got between Washington and the Army of the Potomac, there would be even more apprehension.) Lee also said he was voluntarily cutting his lines of communication from Richmond because it took too many men to maintain them.

On June 26, again farther to the north of the main rebel army, Early marched from Greenwood, east of Chambersburg on the road to York via Gettysburg, over South Mountain with fifteen empty wagons to be filled with supplies.[32] With him he took the 17th Virginia Cavalry and Colonel E. V. White's 35th Virginia Cavalry Battalion. The cavalry spread out ahead and on both flanks of the slower-moving infantry, riding along every small road and mountain trail to make sure there were no ambushes ahead. The main column of cavalry led the infantry and smaller groups and individual horsemen scouted the route to flush out any enemy troops. Riders periodically galloped back to Early's main column from around a bend in the dusty road ahead or in from the flanking parties, and reported that there was no sign of Yankees. Daily or even twice a day, riders were sent back to keep Lee informed.[33]

Along the way, Early, headstrong as ever, burned the Caledonia rolling mill, forges, and sawmill owned by Representative Thaddeus Stevens, a Radical Republican leader. Historian Edwin Coddington called Early's conduct, in light of Lee's orders No. 72, "rank insubordination."[34] Other Confederate officers also flouted these and other orders over the next few days.

After leaving the mountains for the rolling hills to the east, Early split his force and approached Gettysburg from the Cashtown and Mummasburg roads. His cavalry told him there were Yankees just outside the town. The Cashtown Road column routed the 26th Pennsylvania Militia before marching into Gettysburg. Early demanded 1,000 pairs of shoes, 500 hats, or $10,000. All he got were horseshoes and nails (which were needed), 2,000 rations in railroad cars, and liquor.[35] Early split his column again, with the two units of cavalry in the lead, and marched the next day toward York.

While the Confederates continued to gather supplies in Pennsylvania, Stuart, still in Virginia, was firmly convinced that the Union army was moving northward. So according to orders, or at least the orders that made sense, and with Longstreet's endorsement, he prepared to cross the Potomac above Great Falls at Rowser's Ford. On the 27th, Stuart crossed the Occoquan and split his column. Fitz Lee he sent to Burke's Station with orders to meet the main column at Fairfax Court House. Near Fairfax Station, Wade Hampton's men encountered Union Cavalry. They promptly dispatched the unit and killed, wounded, and captured a large number of them, securing horses, equipment, and weapons, courtesy of the U.S. government. Once again, near Fairfax Station, Stuart was nearly captured.

Waiting for the column to catch up, he had been letting his horse feed on some oats, captured from the Federal government whose troops had abandoned them as Stuart's men approached. He had taken the bit out of his horse's mouth so the mount could eat. Suddenly a scouting part of Union troopers galloped up at full speed from Fairfax Court House. Throwing himself upon his horse without inserting the bit, Stuart rode off, controlling the horse with halter and leg pressure. The Yankee scouting party soon ran into the main column and turned tail.[36]

Farther north on June 27, Early sent White's Battalion of cavalry to tear up track between Hanover Junction and York and sent the 17th Virginia Cavalry to the mouth of Conewago Creek to burn railroad bridges there. Also by June 27,

Imboden's cavalry brigade had reached Hancock, Maryland, on Ewell's left and was directed to Chambersburg.[37]

Back at Fairfax, Stuart got word from Fitz Lee, who had gone on to Annandale, that the Yankees had left that area for Leesburg while what Stuart called the "locals"—possibly militia—had fallen back to the defenses of Washington. Stuart had been hoping to hear from Mosby, who, under previous arrangement, had gone to scout a crossing of the Potomac for him. But even without Mosby's scouting, Stuart was becoming more and more convinced that he could successfully move around the rear of the Federal army.

They rested a few hours, feasting upon the stores left by the Union army upon its movement northward, then rode to Dranesville in enough time to see the campfires of Union General John Sedgwick's VI Corps still smoldering from their evacuation that morning. Hampton, in advance of the column, was ordered toward Rowser's Ford above Great Falls, east of Dranesville. As his troopers approached the ford, damp darkness was beginning to haunt the tree-lined banks of the Potomac with a ghostly mist. At the ford, a civilian who had just crossed the river told him that, though it was two feet higher than normal, it was fordable by horsemen. Hampton made it across, but realized that artillery caissons could not cross there without soaking their contents. He informed Stuart.

A lower ford was found to be impassable. Stuart was determined not to give up the crossing without a good try. In the darkness, he ordered the caissons unloaded on the Virginia bank and each trooper to carry the primers, powder, and shells across the roiling Potomac. The guns and caissons disappeared beneath the surface and the mile-wide stretch of saddle-deep river bore the column downstream more than once, with the horsemen nearly falling off Rowser's Ford into drowning-depth water. Some bold trooper on the opposite side rode out to lead the men safely into Maryland. In the words of one participant, "No more difficult achievement was accomplished by the cavalry during the war."[38] By 3 A.M. June 28, the rear guard was across and Stuart's three brigades were safely drying off in bivouac in Yankee territory.

CHAPTER FIVE

Around the Yankees Again

"Your paper, as it was intended, is a complete vindication of General Stuart. It shows Gen Lee's authority for the movement of his cavalry, and that those movements were well conducted, rapidly and vigorously executed, that Stuart left more cavalry with us than we actually used—a fact not known to me heretofore—, and that therefore it was peculiarly unjust, not to say cruel, in all who have assailed Stuart, as the cause of the failure of the Campaign."
—JAMES LONGSTREET TO H. B. MCCLELLAN, AUGUST 3, 1878

"The little cavalry that was with the army was kept on the extreme left. Not so much as one trooper was sent us."
—JAMES LONGSTREET, *FROM MANASSAS TO APPOMATTOX*, 1896

O n the morning of June 28, once north of the Potomac, Stuart cut the Chesapeake and Ohio Canal and captured boats loaded with supplies for the Union army. Stuart heard that the day before, Hooker was at Poolesville, Maryland, with his army on its way to Frederick.

Following Lee's and Longstreet's recommendations that he ride around the Union army if it should appear to the moving northward, Stuart marched early on the 28th to meet the leading elements of the Confederate army in York, Pennsylvania. Since the Union army *was* moving, it would be more difficult to get around than if it had remained stationary.

Hampton swung through Darnestown to Rockville; the other brigades took a more direct route. Hampton captured small groups of Yankees while Chambliss had a running fight with and drove off the 2nd New York Cavalry. Entering Rockville after noon, the two brigades found themselves squarely across the main line of communication and supply between Washington and the Army of the Potomac. Miles of telegraph wire were torn down.

Rockville was decidedly pro-Southern and greeted Stuart accordingly. Cooke noticed the women and girls especially, in particular one sixteen-year-old who plucked souvenir hairs from the mane of his horse. Of the affection lavished on Stuart by the ladies, the cousin of his wife thought nothing out of the ordinary and wrote of it freely in 1866.[1]

Shortly after the Confederates occupied Rockville, a huge wagon train approached from the southeast, apparently unaware of the Confederate presence. Finally realizing the trap, the officers tried desperately to turn the eight-mile train around, but Stuart's men captured all but the overturned wagons, which they burned. They got 125 new wagons, loaded with oats, corn, hams, hardtack, bacon, and whiskey, with fresh mules and harness. In light of Lee's repeated orders to gather supplies, Stuart must have been elated.

The Union Quartermaster Corps figured it needed about twenty-five wagons of supplies for each 1,000 men.[2] To the Confederates who were used to skimpy rations anyway, their value practically doubled. Denying the supplies to the Union cause was one thing, but to the Confederates, how many more days of campaigning would this allow? After the campaign, Stuart was blamed for holding on to the wagons because they slowed him up. Actually, he was adhering to one of Lee's most important orders.

Meanwhile, Early arrived in York with the 17th Virginia Cavalry and White's 35th Virginia Battalion of cavalry and again demanded money and shoes. (This shows that he either found no shoes in Gettysburg, or got every pair but still needed more. The search for shoes eventually became an excuse to break Lee's orders for Major General Henry Heth, one of A. P. Hill's division commanders, and arose as one of the most famous fables as to why Gettysburg was fought.) Early demanded 2,000 pairs, and the town actually rounded up 1,500.

So, from June 26 until Early returned to Lee, his advance column had plenty of cavalry with it, certainly enough to spare couriers to and from the commanding general, especially since Lee was at Greenwood near Chambersburg just fifty miles away. The communications were never published, but it is inconceivable that Early did not communicate with his commander while in enemy territory.

Nothing demonstrates the effect of Stuart's movement around the Union army better than the sudden flood of correspondence—sometimes bordering on the incoherent and panic-stricken—that flowed among Harrisburg, Baltimore, and Washington. On no other day of the campaign was there more correspondence, mostly concerning the Confederate cavalry between the Union army and Washington, than on June 28.

One of the first messages came in at 5:30 A.M. from Colonel James A. Hardie of the war office staff to Major General Henry Halleck, the chief of staff in Washington. It simply said that he had conveyed the orders appointing Major

General George Gordon Meade, commander of the V Corps, as head of the Army of the Potomac. Hooker was out.

From Carlisle, Pennsylvania, at 6:15 A.M., came a message reporting that Rodes' Confederates were within two miles of town and were headed for Harrisburg. At 10:20 A.M., word came of the demand for surrender of Mechanicsburg, Pennsylvania, by Jenkins. At 11 A.M., a false report was sent to Major General Alexander Butterfield, chief of staff of the Army of the Potomac, that the main body of rebel cavalry under Stuart had encamped between Williamsport and Hagerstown on the night of June 27 and had begun passing through Hagerstown at dawn on the 28th. At 11:15, Halleck sent two batteries of artillery to Baltimore for its protection.

Suddenly, David Gregg, commanding the 2nd Cavalry Division of the Army of the Potomac, received a message from Pleasonton that a brigade of rebel cavalry had been reported to have crossed the Potomac at Seneca Mills and was heading for the railroad near Baltimore. Gregg was to go after it with two brigades and a battery of artillery. Another message to Gregg came from cavalry headquarters: Edward's Ferry, piled with Union supplies, was unprotected. Gregg was ordered to send a regiment there to protect the stores.

From Gettysburg at 2 P.M. came word that 2,000 Confederate infantry, backed by artillery and cavalry, on June 26 had destroyed the railroad bridge and collected supplies. The force was presumably moving toward York.

From the camp of the Union army headquarters near Frederick, Maryland, on June 28, Brigadier General Rufus Ingalls, chief quartermaster of the Army of the Potomac, requested 10,000 pairs of bootees (shoes) and the same number of socks from General M. C. Meigs, quartermaster general in Washington. The men were wearing out shoe leather in the wet weather and long marches, and Ingalls wished to issue the equipment to the marching men as they passed through the town.

Meigs' reply at 4:05 of the same day referred directly to Stuart's capturing the wagon train and was savage:

> The bootees and socks will be ordered, and will be sent as soon as a safe route and escort can be found. Last fall I gave orders to prevent the sending of wagon trains from this place to Frederick without escort. The situation repeats itself, and gross carelessness and inattention to military rule has this morning cost us 150 wagons and 900 mules, captured by cavalry between this and Rockville. . . .
>
> All the cavalry of the Defenses of Washington was swept off by the army, and we are now insulted by burning wagons 3 miles outside of Tennallytown.

Your communications are now in the hands of General Fitzhugh
Lee's brigade.

Between 5:30 and 6:20 P.M. came several more communications concerning defenses as far north and west as Altoona, Pennsylvania, and another report of thousands of rebels passing through Carlisle. One message at 5:55 from the headquarters of the Department of Washington to Major General Robert C. Schenck, commanding the Middle Department in Baltimore, stands out: "A strong brigade of the enemy's cavalry have crossed the Potomac above Washington, near Poolesville." This, of course, was Stuart.

Meigs telegraphed Ingalls at 10:30 P.M.: "A deserter reports that there are several brigades in all, including Fitzhugh Lee's, and that Stuart commands in person; 6,000 men and seven pieces of artillery."

Union telegraphers must have been exhausted by the end of the day. More messages hummed along the lines, with Federal generals around Baltimore and Washington complaining about the lack of troops to guard the cities and major roads. No one was sure exactly how many Confederates were moving through the area north of Washington, nor where they were headed. Perhaps the most frightening rumor was that Stuart himself was leading thousands of Confederates through the area. With his sagacity, boldness, and vigor, how many men was Stuart himself worth?

Just three days before, Major General S. P. Heintzelman, commanding the Department of Washington, had received confidential correspondence from Brigadier General J. G. Barnard of the Engineers of the Defenses of Washington indicating the state of the forts around the capital:

It was never supposed that the forts alone would protect Washington. Aided by darkness or fog, bodies of cavalry may pass between them, or columns of infantry may, if [aided] by artillery and infantry attacks upon the works themselves, the latter being fully employed otherwise, contrive to pass through. . . .

I understand that not only are there no troops left to man the riflepits and to support the artillerymen of the forts, but that even the number of artillerymen is not up to standard.

The safety of Washington is, therefore, dependent upon Hooker's army, and that army must constantly keep itself between the enemy, and every considerable body of the enemy, and the city. . . .

A considerable body of cavalry might, under such circumstances, dash into and destroy Washington.

Apparently, although Hooker's army had stripped the defenses of Washington and made it vulnerable to attack, there really was no solution to the problem. The panicky communications continued long into the evening of June 28. Staff officers warned that Lee's cavalry was about to cut the road between Baltimore and Washington; that Harpers Ferry was in danger of capture again; that York had formally surrendered to Brigadier General John B. Gordon; that Major General McClellan should take charge of the military situation in Philadelphia; and on and on, from the vital to the ridiculous, much prompted by Stuart's presence between Washington and the Army of the Potomac.

Outside of Rockville, Stuart contemplated a ride on Washington. It would certainly have been his most spectacular feat to date and would have put his name in every newspaper, North and South. But considering the time, he would be faced with a night attack, hazardous with cavalry unless the battleground were well-known. Besides, by then the element of surprise would have been lost. Waiting until morning to attack was out of the question, so, turning north, Stuart passed up the ultimate glory of raiding the enemy's capital, and instead strode before his troopers to cut the Baltimore and Ohio Railroad, another supply line from Washington to the Army of the Potomac.

He paroled nearly 400 prisoners, including many officers, at Brookeville the night of June 28 and the rest at Cooksville the next morning. At 1:00 A.M. June 29, as Stuart rode out of Brookeville, he promptly fell asleep in the saddle, visibly swaying from side to side.[3]

Much has been made of the appearance of the spy James Harrison in the Confederate camps around Chambersburg. A careful analysis of his story is important to Stuart's role in the Gettysburg campaign because many claimed he was doing Stuart's job of informing Lee of enemy whereabouts.

Longstreet hired the spy. In some of his first postwar writings defending himself against attacks that it was he who lost Gettysburg, Longstreet said that Harrison arrived late June 29 with news that five Union army corps were north of the Potomac.[4] He later corrected the date to June 28, blaming a typographical error. To Longstreet, Harrison's story added credence to his own ideas of the probable movement of the enemy and allowed him to mention a note he sent to Lee suggesting the concentration of their army so that the Confederates could engage the enemy on ground of their own choosing.

The other piece of information that Harrison supposedly brought Lee, according to Marshall,[5] was that Meade was in command. Marshall also wrote that Lee told him that Harrison had left the area of Frederick, Maryland, that morning, that the Federals had crossed the Potomac, their advance had reached Frederick, and they had turned west to cut Lee's communications with Virginia through Hagerstown. Marshall also stated that this was the first information Lee had had since leaving Virginia of the movements of the Federal army.

Lieutenant Colonel Arthur Fremantle, the British observer who was traveling with the Confederates, wrote in his diary entry of June 30 from Greenwood, Pennsylvania, that Longstreet told him "he had just received intelligence that Hooker had been disrated, and that Meade was appointed in his place."[6] It adds to the confusion that such an objective observer as Fremantle wrote two days after Harrison supposedly brought word of the command change that Longstreet talked about "just" receiving the information. Still, two days could have been Longstreet's idea of immediacy.

Both of Lee's official reports on the Battle of Gettysburg (July 31, 1863, and January 20, 1864) said that the spy came in on June 28, so Longstreet was probably correct in blaming a typographical error. His wound from the Battle of the Wilderness had crippled him so that writing was painful. A free-lance writer copied and edited his first drafts and they appeared in the *Philadelphia Weekly Times* before Longstreet had had a last look at them.[7] This could account for the errors and Longstreet's rebuttal.

Another typographical—or rather clerical—error possibly placed Harrison in the Confederate camps as early as the night of June 27. Colonel Charles Venable of Lee's staff entered the date and time of a dispatch to Ewell as 7:30 A.M. June 28. In it Lee said that he wrote Ewell "last night" (June 27) giving Ewell the information Harrison supposedly brought in about Hooker crossing the Potomac. That meant that either Harrison arrived on June 27 or Lee already had the information before Harrison arrived on June 28. A note at the bottom of the page, however, stated that the letter was copied by memory. Whether it was dated correctly was later a sticking point as to how important Harrison's information was.

If we accept Longstreet's account, the spy probably walked through the Union lines near Frederick and reached Confederate camps around 10 P.M. June 28. He said that Union advance elements had reached South Mountain and were possibly going to cut Lee's communications with Virginia. After the war, some people made a great deal of the fact that a spy brought Lee this information rather than Stuart. Some even said Lee was surprised that the enemy had crossed the Potomac; this is why the exact date of his arrival is important. One who became one of Stuart's most vehement critics, Charles Marshall, even said Lee was *misled* into thinking that the Union army was still south of the Potomac.[8]

That Lee was surprised is absurd. He had written to Jefferson Davis on June 23 and 25 saying the Federals were preparing to cross the Potomac and he hoped they would do so. He also knew that no Union elements were ahead of him, as far west as Hancock, Maryland, as far north as Harrisburg, or as far east as York. His advance units, which had cavalry with them and were in communication with Lee, would have told him that if they had been present.

He also had to know that the Union army was moving north, since he had not heard from Stuart. Stuart's orders put him in the rear of the Federals if they were northbound. Since Stuart was out of communication, Lee had to figure the Union army was moving northward.[9]

If Lee were confused, it may have been more from the lack of communication from Robertson and Jones. Lee had given Stuart in his orders of June 23 strict instructions for "the commander of the brigades left behind to watch the flank and rear of the army, and, in the event of the enemy leaving their front, to retire from the mountains west of the Shenandoah, leaving sufficient pickets to guard the passes, and to bring in everything clean along the valley, closing upon the rear of the army."

It is unknown whether Lee saw Stuart's orders to Robertson. If he had, he would have been proud of his former student for issuing such clear instructions. It seems unlikely that Stuart would not have submitted them to Lee as well as Longstreet, since Stuart named them both as the others with the authority to order Robertson to withdraw if the enemy remained in his front near the gaps. Not hearing from Robertson would have meant to Lee and Longstreet that the Union army was still in his front, on the south side of the Potomac.

Still, it is inconceivable that Lee could have thought that the Union army would not follow him. One of his goals for the campaign was to draw the Army of the Potomac out of Virginia and perhaps to draw Union troops from other threatened areas of the South to meet the gravest threat yet upon Northern soil.[10] He was not afraid the Union army would follow him; he was afraid it would not.

John Mosby, in his book defending Stuart's actions, also suggested that while Lee was advancing farther away from Richmond, there remained the "bare possibility" that the Union army might turn and take the Confederate capital. If this was on Lee's mind—and losing the nation's capital had been on everyone's mind from the beginning of the war—then Stuart's suggestion of a ride between the Union army and Washington when they met at Paris on June 22 would have calmed Lee's worries.[11]

Nevertheless, Harrison's report, plus Longstreet's endorsement and whatever other information Lee had obtained, seemed to jog Lee into consolidating his army. He had conducted a successful invasion, accomplishing the major goal of collecting supplies for the army for months ahead. He knew that the enemy eventually would approach and it was time to re-group for a withdrawal. If the Federals attacked, it would be against a full army and in a place of Lee's choosing. So, on June 27 (if Venable's dispatch is dated correctly) or June 28 (if Venable meant to write "June 29") Lee ordered Ewell to return to Chambersburg.[12] He also finally sent direct orders for Robertson to follow on June 29.[13]

Stuart rode through the night of June 28–29. In Cooksville, Maryland, he routed a small contingent of Unionists. Just after dawn on June 29, Fitz Lee burned the B&O bridge near Sykesville. The main body of cavalry cut the railroad at Hood's Mill and tried to capture some trains, but the engineers saw the obstructions and chugged back to the safety of Baltimore. Stuart held the railroad almost the whole day, while his advanced column encountered a squadron of the 1st Delaware Cavalry at Westminster. The Federals fought hard but held up Stuart's advance only briefly.

At Westminster, for the first time, Stuart's men found adequate forage but had to stay up most of the night of the 29th gathering it. Westminster was a little more pro-Union than Rockville, though some friends of the rebels did speak guardedly to Stuart, giving him what information they could.

Pushing Fitz Lee's brigade ahead, the Confederates encamped for the night about six miles north of Westminster at the Shriver Farm in Union Mills. During the night, scouts told Stuart that enemy cavalry encamped that night at Littlestown, just a half-dozen miles northwest across the Pennsylvania line.

At this point, even Stuart's loyal adjutant, Henry McClellan, said Stuart should have burned the 125 wagons. They were taking up miles of road and slowing the column down considerably. He also acknowledged that his view was tainted by two decades of reflection. But to Stuart, these were special supplies—rations, fodder, wagons, mules, harness—all in a neat package ready for delivery. As well, no one else was as mindful of Lee's orders to collect supplies. Battles were sure to come and there was Early to meet in York, Pennsylvania, but more than that, there was always the goal of gathering supplies. Abandoning them would be a violation of orders and it would take much more than a little inconvenience to force Stuart to do so.

Farther to the north, with Lee's advance forces, Imboden and his large cavalry force reached Mercersburg while Lee camped in Chambersburg just fifteen miles away.[14]

Early on June 30, Stuart crossed into Pennsylvania, bearing toward Hanover on the way to York. Chambliss took the lead with Lee's brigade riding along some of the minor roads to the left of the main column, between it and where Union forces were last reported in Littlestown. Hampton followed the wagons.

Around 10 A.M., Chambliss' men south of Hanover observed a large body of blue cavalry coming on the road from Littlestown and moving through the town. By noon, most of the column had passed and much of Stuart's cavalry had reached the hills south of Hanover. Some artillery rounds were fired and the 13th Virginia charged the tail of the Yankee column.[15] It turned to the attack.

The 18th Pennsylvania formed several squadrons to the rear, but flee-ing ambulance drivers plowed into the organized lines of horses. The 2nd North Carolina sailed into the supply and ambulance train just as it reached the southwestern outskirts of Hanover.[16] The 18th Pennsylvania was driven into the rear of the column, scattering the Union cavalry in and around the center of town.[17]

Twenty-three-year-old Brigadier General Elon J. Farnsworth, who had received his star just two days before on June 28, formed the 1st West Virginia and 1st Vermont into a line south and southeast of town, covering the roads from those directions.[18] The 5th New York attempted to clear the streets from Chambliss' attack. Without orders, it charged impetuously upon the advancing Confederates, driving them out of the town and upon a large force of rebels in reserve. The reserve fired into the New Yorkers, halting their progress.[19]

Farnsworth himself came up, reformed the unit, and drove the Confederates from the outskirts of town, back along the Westminster road to the protection of their artillery on the hills there.[20]

The 2nd North Carolina took high casualties during its charge and attempted retreat from the streets of Hanover. Nearly half the regiment present for duty were either killed or captured.[21]

Stuart himself had again nearly been captured. Stuart and part of his staff were watching the fight from the town side of a small hill. As the Union cavalry drove the Confederates down the road, Stuart rode up to his engineering officer, William Blackford. It seemed all a game to Stuart. Seeing his men in total confu-sion and being driven by the Yankees, he shouted jovially to his adjutant, "Rally them, Blackford!" as if a mere captain would be able to stop the 100 or so fleeing cavalrymen. Stuart turned and jumped his mare Virginia over a hedge and into a large field of high timothy. Blackford followed.

They saw that they were within feet of about thirty Yankees attempting to flank the retreating Confederates. The troopers called upon Stuart and Black-ford to halt, but they turned and let their horses out across the field, with the enemy cavalrymen chasing and firing their pistols. Suddenly before them was a fifteen-foot-wide ditch that had been concealed by the timothy. Blackford, hitting the ditch an instant before Stuart, looked back to see if the general had made the leap. The magnificent image of Stuart on Virginia, flying over that ditch, remained with Blackford until his dying day. The Union troopers decided not to try the jump and Stuart and Blackford escaped.[22]

The fighting in the town broke down into small affairs. Union artillery was unlimbered on the hills north of Hanover. It was backed up by part of Brigadier General George Armstrong Custer's Michigan troopers. A two-hour artillery duel ensued until 2 P.M., when the Confederates again tested the Union resolve to hold the route Stuart wanted to take. They advanced mounted down the slope of the hill toward Hanover. Some of Custer's men were supplied with the Spencer rifle, which could fire twenty-one rounds per minute,[23] and the Wolverines gave the Confederates hell until they were flanked on the right and the Confederate artillery began to take a toll.[24]

Meanwhile, Hampton had arrived. Southwest of town, the wagons were drawn up in a huge block, ready to be burned if the Yankees came too close. Hampton's men were sent to the right, across the turnpike to Baltimore and north of the road to York. They dislodged the Yankees with good use of sharp-shooters. Backed up by artillery, the Confederates now held the route Stuart wanted to take to meet Early in York. This, not the town, was Stuart's objective.

When the fighting died down in the late afternoon, Stuart saw that the Michigan brigade had moved from in front of his right to his left. This opened the way to York and Stuart ordered Lee around to the right with the wagon train. The rest of his units were a bristling buffer between the Union cavalry and the supplies. It was after dark when Stuart drew off, heading toward the village of Jefferson.

Stuart himself realized after the battle at Hanover that the "wagon train was now a subject of serious embarrassment."[25] He would have burned it then and there, but for Lee's orders. There were those orders. Always those orders.

Nearly 400 horses were captured by Stuart around Hanover and he had gathered up at least 1,000 by the time he reached Dillsburg a few hours later. But they were draft animals, not suited for the swift movement of light cavalry or the Horse Artillery.[26] Prisoners also were becoming a problem; another 400 had been captured since the big parole at Cooksville. As well, exhaustion was becoming a force to be reckoned with. Through the long night the men plodded, tired from the fighting, the short rations and, most of all, the lack of sleep.

On they rode over the dark, undulating roads to Jefferson. At New Salem, Stuart told Cooke to stay behind, wait for Hampton, and direct him on to Dover. Stuart himself rode on with Fitz Lee. Soon enough, Hampton's column arrived. They rode toward Dover, but near dawn, Hampton stopped, rode to a haystack by the side of the road, pulled down some hay, curled up in his cape, and fell instantly asleep. By daylight, however, they had ridden on and entered Dover.

CHAPTER SIX

To Gettysburg

"L'audace, l'audace, toujours l'audace."

—ATTRIBUTED TO NAPOLEON

Stuart reasoned that because of the delay caused by the battle at Hanover, the Confederate advance must have already reached the Susquehanna River. Fitzhugh Lee and the wagons were sent ahead.

By the morning of July 1, the column had reached Dover and Stuart could grant the men a short rest. When Fitz Lee crossed the York-Gettysburg road, he discovered that Jubal Early, the vanguard of the eastern wing of the invasion, had passed that way headed toward York, then had returned, going toward Gettysburg. Stuart first got word at Dover that the Confederates were concentrating near Shippensburg. Early's movement away from York indicated that Stuart was no longer to seek him there and that apparently Lee's plans had changed. Stuart sent a staff member, Major A. R. Venable, to contact Early, then a short time later sent Captain Henry Lee from Fitz Lee's staff on the same errand. After the all-too-brief rest, Stuart's men wearily mounted up and headed toward Dillsburg, moving away from York and toward Shippensburg.

Meanwhile, twenty-five miles to the west, infantry under Major General Henry Heth of A. P. Hill's corps was marching from camps near Cashtown. The day before, Heth had ordered the brigade of Brigadier General J. Johnston Pettigrew to Gettysburg to look for supplies, especially shoes. Pettigrew reported there was a large force of cavalry backed up by some infantry in the area, too large for his men to tangle with. That information was given to Hill, who sent it on to Robert E. Lee the night of June 30. Lee then knew that the Army of the Potomac must be very near. At least he knew that there was enough cavalry, acting like it was backed up by infantry, to discourage Pettigrew from pressing further.

At 5 A.M. July 1, Heth himself took his entire division and a battalion of artillery toward Gettysburg, ostensibly to look for the shoes. Years later, Heth wrote about his conversation with Hill the night before, saying he asked if there were any objection to his going to Gettysburg to find shoes. Heth wrote that Hill replied with the four words that instigated the Battle of Gettysburg: "None in the world." But why would Heth take a whole infantry division, with artillery, into a town he knew was occupied by a fairly large enemy force, just for shoes? He also knew that the Confederate vanguard had swept the area clean five days before.

To help explain why the Battle of Gettysburg began, a number of historians have written that Lee was constantly asking of Stuart's whereabouts until July 2, when he returned. Their reasoning was that had Stuart been with Lee, he would have known more about the Union army's position and could have either avoided the engagement or gained a better position.

A careful study of the writings of those nearest Lee during the campaign shows that the first recorded instance that Lee asked specifically about Stuart was at Chambersburg on June 29. He questioned an aide to Ewell, who was riding through to catch up with his commander. The aide, Lieutenant James P. Smith, said Lee was "surprised and disturbed" that Stuart, as of June 27, was still in Virginia. But Lee must have realized the information was nearly two days old; Stuart could easily ride more than fifty miles in a day and just might have been approaching Ewell at that time. The next documented time Lee expressed concern about Stuart was not until Lee reached Cashtown about noon July 1, several hours after Heth had begun the battle, against specific orders not to bring on a general engagement.

A. L. Long was one of Lee's secretaries and spent time at his side through the campaign. Some of the information Long passed on about Stuart in the campaign in his 1886 work *Memoirs of Robert E. Lee* is misleading and prejudiced, but the first time he mentioned Lee saying anything about Stuart's absence was in Cashtown.[1] Longstreet also was a good observer of Lee, since Lee nearly always set up his headquarters near Longstreet. Longstreet said in his memoirs that on the morning of July 1, as he and Lee rode toward Cashtown, Lee was apparently satisfied with his army's disposition. Longstreet added it was because "he felt safe, depending upon his cavalry coming up in time to meet him there."[2]

They had gotten separated, however, after Longstreet's march route was blocked by Major General Edward Johnson's division of Ewell's corps, which had entered the road before Longstreet's men.[3] Lee rode ahead to Cashtown. Longstreet wrote, "When he rode away from me in the forenoon, he made no mention of his absent cavalry, nor did he indicate that it was not within call. So I was at a loss to understand his nervous condition [after arriving at Gettysburg]."

Longstreet wrote that, as they talked after they both arrived at Gettysburg, he continued to plead for a flank movement (instead of an attack upon the enemy) by saying to Lee, "If he [the enemy] is there to-morrow it will be because he wants you to attack. . . ." Longstreet went on: "Then it was that I heard of the wanderings of the cavalry and the cause of his uneven temper. So vexed was he at the halt of the Imboden cavalry at Hancock, *in the opening of the campaign* [italics Longstreet's], that he was losing sight of Pickett's brigades as a known quantity for battle. His manner suggested to me that a little reflection would be better than further discussion, and right soon he suggested to the commander of the Second Corps to take Cemetery Hill if he thought it practicable, but the subordinate did not care to take upon himself a fight that his chief would not venture to order."[4]

From Longstreet's point of view, Lee was concerned about cavalry—but apparently it was not Stuart or the cavalry with him but Imboden's cavalry. Imboden was not under Stuart's command but under Lee's.

Walter Taylor, Lee's adjutant-general, writing in 1877, mentioned nothing of Lee continually mentioning Stuart's absence. Taylor also gave his opinion of the army's status at that point: "With the exception of the cavalry, the army was well in hand. The absence of that indispensable arm of the service was most seriously felt by Lee."[5] But he blamed the actions of Imboden, Robertson, and Jenkins on Stuart: "No tidings whatever had been received from or of our cavalry under General Stuart since crossing the river; and General Lee was consequently without accurate information of the movements or position of the main Federal army."[6] But the fact that Lee had received no tidings from Stuart after crossing the river told him everything he needed to know: that Stuart was temporarily out of touch and that the cavalry Stuart left with the army was now under Lee's and Longstreet's direct command. The fact that Lee was without accurate information on the movements or position of the Federals at that moment was not Stuart's fault but Robertson's, for not following Stuart's explicit orders of June 24.

Also on Lee's mind was the horrible attrition rate he had seen his corps of young general officers suffer; it was a problem growing acute, with no solution. Considering the close ties between them, it is possible that when Lee mentioned Stuart, he was actually worried about Stuart the man, his former student, frequent house guest and brilliant junior officer, when others assumed he was speaking of the cavalry. In many people's eyes, by this time in the war, the name "J. E. B. Stuart" and "cavalry" were synonymous and virtually interchangeable.

By evening on July 1, Stuart had reached Carlisle, the site of a large U.S. cavalry barracks. Stuart knew it well from a visit there in 1859 to show off his redesign of the saber attachment. Also, Flora Cooke Stuart had lived on the post as a girl while her father, Philip St. George Cooke, was commandant between 1848 and 1852.[7] As well, Fitz Lee and some other officers in the Confederate cavalry column on July 1 had been stationed at the barracks at one time or another.[8]

Stuart's exhausted men rode toward Carlisle on the road from Dillsburg. After

Ewell's advance left Carlisle, Federal troops moved back in under the command of Major General W. F. Smith. With him, Smith had two brigades of infantry, some artillery, and cavalry. Stuart's men were entirely out of rations. He did not want to raid the ponderous wagon train; those supplies were apparently meant for the rest of the army. Besides, food could always be procured in Yankee territory. He planned to get Carlisle to supply his men.

As he approached town, he was told that the militia was waiting in ambush. He demanded the surrender of the town, which was refused. His artillery began to lob shells into town to drive home the point. The re-garrisoned cavalry barracks also refused to surrender. Stuart's bombardment set some of the officer's quarters on fire. Twilight passed into darkness as the barracks buildings burned. The exhaustion of Stuart's men was nearly as complete as it could be. John Esten Cooke recalled that while the artillery boomed, the men fell asleep around the pieces. He himself fell into a sound sleep within ten feet of a rapidly firing battery. A major leaned against a fence a few feet from a howitzer banging away and fell asleep, never even bothering to lie down. Stuart himself saw a man begin to climb a fence, put one leg over the top rail, and balanced thus, pass into unconsciousness from sheer exhaustion.[9]

Twenty-five miles to the south at Gettysburg, Lee's army was reorganizing after a day of victory. They had driven in from three sides on the Union line posted west and north of the town. Union troops retreated to the hills south of Gettysburg, there to await reinforcements. Lee instructed Ewell to carry Culp's Hill "if he found it practicable, but to avoid a general engagement until the arrival of the other divisions of the army."[10] Ewell decided to wait.

Probably about the same time Lee was arriving upon the battlefield—sometime after noon—Major Venable found him and informed him of the whereabouts of Stuart.

In Carlisle after dusk, Stuart received a dispatch from Robert E. Lee telling him of the fighting at Gettysburg. Stuart left Fitz Lee in command at Carlisle and ordered Hampton to continue his ride for at least ten miles that night toward Gettysburg. He also directed some other brigades on their ride southward, then began an all-night ride himself to report to Lee.

Meantime, Lee was using his staff to reconnoiter. Early in the morning of July 2, Captain S. R. Johnston, an engineer on Lee's headquarters staff, and Major J. J. Clarke, one of Longstreet's engineers, had been sent to check the ground on the Confederate right.[11] Strangely, a detachment from Hampton's brigade, about 250 men, had reported to Lee before dawn on July 2 and was given to Longstreet "to explore his ground, watch his flank, and do whatever came to hand." Colonel John L. Black, who was apparently in charge of the detachment, was told to guard the roads in Longstreet's rear.[12]

If this was true—there is no reason to suspect it was not—then it gave Lee and Longstreet *before dawn on July 2* enough cavalry to do any scouting needed as the Union army came up and formed on the ridges and hills less than a mile from them. Why Black's 250 cavalrymen were not used remains a mystery, unless we accept that Lee was getting all the information he thought he needed.

As Lee sat on a log with Hill and Longstreet, he spread a map out upon his knees and began to discuss plans when Clarke and Johnston came up. They said there were no Federals on or around the Round Tops, the two hills at the south end of the Union position on Cemetery Ridge south of Gettysburg. Lee then made his decision to attack up the Emmitsburg Road along the ridge. At dawn the plan was good enough, but by noon the situation had changed.

Perhaps that would have been a good time for Stuart to have been used, but how much more effective would he have been with a large group of cavalry scouting the Confederate right? This force could have tipped off the Yankees as to where Lee's attack was coming. Scouts from Major General John Bell Hood's division of Longstreet's corps had found the area south of Round Top to be unoccupied. They thought the Union rear could be struck from that direction. Instead of relying only on Johnston's and Clarke's dawn reports, which by the minute were growing stale, Lee could have used a heavy skirmish line, a reconnaissance in force, or even Black's cavalry around the Round Tops to locate for certain the enemy's left flank. The first indication that the Federals were before him in force, however, was when Major General Lafayette McLaws' division struck Major General Daniel Sickles' III Corps, which had advanced from the rest of the Union army to the Emmitsburg Road.[13]

The story was repeated over the years that Lee wanted Stuart near him once the Confederates became engaged. Yet he apparently felt that Stuart's role was not with the main army but on its flanks; they were the first places he sent Stuart after he reported in.

At least two Stuart detractors blamed him for Lee not getting the best position at Gettysburg—apparently the one the Union army held—thereby denying him the ability to win.[14] However, there was nothing wrong with Lee's position that maneuvering could not fix. That was Longstreet's point when he and Lee discussed their battle plan on the morning of July 2.

Stuart rode up to Lee during the afternoon of July 2. The reports of his arrival vary. Douglas Southall Freeman wrote that there was no record of their immediate exchange, but merely "tradition" that Lee greeted Stuart by saying, "Well, General Stuart, you are here at last."[15] This account came first from John Thomason, who used Stuart's family for much of his biographical research. To anyone who knew Lee's reserve, this version seems completely in character, with such a comment likely to wither the most headstrong subordinate. But remembering Lee's affection and concern, the words could also have been uttered in intense relief that Stuart was safe. Both versions fit Lee's traits of reserve and compassion.[16]

Another account says that Lee raised his arm and said, "General Stuart, *where have you been?* Not one word from your command has been received by me! Where have you been?" Stuart "wilted," then submitted that he had brought Lee more than 100 wagons and teams. "Yes, general," continued Lee, "but they are an impediment to me now! Let me ask your help. We will not discuss the matter longer."[17]

This account, however dramatic, came from a letter written more than half a century later by former Brigadier General Thomas Munford (a colonel with Stuart's command at Gettysburg) to a Mrs. Charles Hyde of Lookout Mountain, Tennessee. Munford was not even present when Lee and Stuart met, but in the letter he quoted H. B. McClellan, Stuart's assistant adjutant general, who may or may not have been there. Munford said McClellan called the meeting "painful beyond description," apparently re-created the scene described above, and added one more quote attributed to Lee: "I have not heard a word from you for days, and you the eyes and ears of my army."[18]

How accurate could this account be? Although McClellan is considered probably the best and most accurate of the several contemporaries who wrote about Stuart, he would have told Munford about this before his death in 1904, then Munford waited another eleven years before relating it in his letter. In addition, some aspects do not square with what McClellan had put into his book in 1885. McClellan also could not have been a witness. Staff officers, no matter how close to their commanders, did not just ride up to discuss matters with the commanding general. By military protocol, they would have remained at a discreet distance, waiting to be summoned.

There is also some question whether McClellan rode with Stuart or remained behind with the columns. In his richly detailed book, McClellan never mentioned being with Stuart when he arrived at Gettysburg. Nor did Blackford, who also had an eye for detail. Perhaps the answer comes from John Esten Cooke, who accompanied Stuart on that night ride to Gettysburg, one he called "the most severe I ever experienced."

> General Stuart and his staff moving without escort on the Willstown Road, passed over mile after mile asleep in the saddle. At dawn, the General dismounted in a clump of trees by the roadside; said "I am going to sleep two hours;" and wrapping himself in his cape simply leaned against a tree and was immediately asleep. Everybody imitated him, and I was awakened by the voice of one of the couriers,

who informed me that "the General was gone." Such was the fact—Stuart had risen punctually at the end of two hours, stretched himself, mounted, and ridden on *solus,* a wandering Major-General in the heart of Pennsylvania! In the afternoon the cavalry were at Gettysburg.[19]

Some staff members may have caught up with Stuart on his ride to report to Lee. If they had, they probably would not have been close enough to hear the exchange.[20]

Regardless, their meeting represents the first documented time, other than Lee's questioning of his cavalry's whereabouts at Cashtown, that anyone criticized Stuart's role in the campaign, if that is indeed what it was. That it came from Lee gave later critics credence and the seeming tacit acceptance of the most esteemed Confederate.

After his arrival, Lee told Stuart to gather information on the terrain and guard the Confederate left from the unusually vigorous Union cavalry. He established headquarters under a tree on the Heidlersburg Road, about a mile from Gettysburg. To locate the enemy cavalry, he rode out the Gettysburg and Hanover Railroad, which ran parallel to the York Pike, until he was fired upon. Satisfied, he returned to headquarters.[21]

Meanwhile, messengers galloped back to Wade Hampton, still on the road with his brigade from Dover, bringing up the rear. He was told not to bother to go to Carlisle, but to head to Gettysburg instead. Around noon on July 2, he stopped just northwest of Hunterstown, sent out pickets toward the York Pike, and rested his brigade for a couple of hours.[22] Then Stuart ordered his brigade to take position on the left of the infantry at Gettysburg. Just after he got into motion, Hampton's pickets reported a large Union force was headed toward Hunterstown, apparently to descend upon the rear of the main army. Stuart ordered him to check the enemy's movement. The tiny Hunterstown crossroads suddenly was the key to the rear and left flank of the Confederate position four miles down the road at Gettysburg.

As Hampton approached the century-old crossroad town, there was no sight of the enemy. Coming into Hunterstown from the Heidlersburg Road, the column turned right toward Benner's Hill northeast of Gettysburg, which secured the Confederate left. They passed farms whose owners bore Pennsylvania Dutch names that rang strange to the ears of the men from the Carolinas, Georgia, and Mississippi: Wirt, Munich, Brinkerhoff, Stallsmith, Saltzgever. Riding rhythmically, after days without sleep, it all must have begun to take on a dreamlike quality.

A half-hour after passing through Hunterstown, the somnolent column was awakened by sporadic firing behind it. The intensity grew and it became evident that the Yankees had appeared at Hunterstown. Hampton's rear guard had been attacked and was being forced back into the rear of the column.

George A. Custer's Michigan regiments were probably just as tired as Hampton's, having fought at Hanover, then having been a part of Kilpatrick's futile attempts at trying to find Stuart. They had been riding to the northeast of Gettysburg along the inside track to Stuart's arc to Carlisle, to ensure that the Confederates did not turn the Union flank dug in on Culp's Hill. The clandestine, swift-moving flanking maneuver had become the trademark of the Army of Northern Virginia. The last time, it had cost the Union army the Battle of Chancellorsville, just two months before. Only vigilance by the Federal cavalry could prevent it again.

The Union troopers approached Hunterstown about 4:30, led by the 6th Michigan. It pushed the skirmishers of Hampton's rear guard back.[23] About 5 P.M., the regiment rode through Hunterstown and turned southward on a fenced-in road. It halted on the crest of a low ridge just outside the crossroads. Before it was a mounted line of cavalry straddling the road and dismounted skirmishers behind the fences on either side.[24] The Federals attacked and were stopped temporarily, but they fought on as the 7th Michigan came up and deployed into the fields to the left of the road. The fighting was vicious and hand-to-hand in several cases. As the Confederate skirmishers lining the road attempted to pick off blue cavalrymen in the swirl of horses, men, sabers, and pistols, troopers were shot, slashed, and run through. The pressure on the rear guard was more than it could take and the Confederates disappeared in the rising smoke and dust.

Two companies of Cobb's Legion from the main column turned and formed, then charged into the Federals. Two more companies from the legion joined in and began to drive the Federals back. They again came under the fire of the dismounted rebel skirmishers along the road. Assailed on three sides, the pressure was too much, and the Federals wheeled around and retreated to the cover of their guns and reinforcements on the ridge.

Cobb's Legion drove Custer's troopers back along the Gettysburg/Hunterstown road. The newly appointed brigadier general was nearly killed as his horse went down. While attempting to extricate himself from beneath the dead animal, a Confederate rode at him. All his other troopers were gone except for a young man named Norvill F. Churchill,[25] who shot the Confederate and hoisted Custer upon his own horse.

Cavalrymen became intermixed as they swept back up the road toward Hunterstown. From a farmhouse on the left, Federal troopers picked off a large number of Cobb's Legionnaires with their Spencer repeating rifles. A battery of Pennington's artillery upon the ridge finished repulsing the Confederates.

By then, Hampton had turned his entire brigade around and brought it to face Custer's brigade. The Federal artillery opened up, and Hampton sent for artillery support. Two Parrott rifles engaged the Union artillery at dusk and into the night, but outnumbered five to one, the Confederate gunners from Jones' battalion suffered greatly.

By 11 P.M., Kilpatrick's division, of which Custer was a part, had been ordered to Two Taverns on the Baltimore Pike to bolster the battered Union left flank.

CHAPTER SEVEN

The Third of July

"I had rather die than be whipped!"

—J. E. B. STUART

On the morning of July 3, Lee ordered Stuart to ride east out the York Pike to protect the rear of the Confederate left flank northeast and east of Culp's Hill. The move also gave Stuart the opportunity to swing wide around the Union right flank and harass its rear. His orders were verbal; at least no formal record of them exists. Stuart said only that Lee ordered him to move to the left of Ewell. Lee said nothing about Stuart's orders on July 3 in either of his reports. That Stuart would protect the Confederate left is logical; that he should harass the Union rear if the opportunity arose would have been automatic with Stuart.

Hours were spent that morning replenishing the cavalry's ammunition and for some reason, both Stuart and McClellan wrote, Jenkins' brigade only received ten rounds per man. Lieutenant Colonel Vincent Witcher of Jenkins' 34th Virginia Battalion wrote years after the war that this was false. The amount of time they spent in combat proved him correct.[1]

Some historians have suggested that Stuart's movement to the Confederate left was to set up an attack on the Union rear coordinated with Longstreet's major assault—Pickett's Charge—on the afternoon of July 3. From what the participants knew when Lee talked to Stuart, such precise coordination would have been impossible. Even Lee himself did not know exactly when the assault was to begin. There was rarely an "H-hour" synchronization in a Civil War battle. Attacks were made at sunrise or more often coordinated with a signal gun. At Gettysburg, Confederate orders for attacks sometimes contained the fateful words "if practicable." Many officers were given the discretion of developing an attack after an artillery bombardment, if advantage could be gained. This style of command got Lee in trouble more than once at Gettysburg.

Lee left the precise step-off time of the grand assault on July 3 to Longstreet, who left the decision up to Colonel E. P. Alexander. He was in charge of the artillery bombardment to soften up the Union position. When Alexander felt that his artillery had done its job, he was to inform Longstreet, who would order the men forward. So although Lee and Longstreet had planned an afternoon assault for July 3, neither could have told Stuart that it was to step off precisely at 3 P.M.

In addition, an examination of the ground as it appears on war-era maps between the Hanover Road and the Baltimore Pike (which led into the Union right flank) shows it as nearly impassable. Not even farm lanes led from the York Pike to the rear of the Federal army. Cross-country rides were possible but caused straggling. Union cavalry protected the rear of the Union line along some distance of the Baltimore Pike, and so even if Stuart had gained it, he would still have had to fight his way northward into the rear of the Union lines. Still, just the appearance of Confederate cavalry fighting its way up the Baltimore road would have stirred things up greatly and perhaps distracted Meade from Lee's main plan. Very likely, this was what Lee had in mind. If the grand assault were successful, Stuart could increase the panic of the retreating troops, making the victory complete. H. B. McClellan, Stuart's adjutant, said as much in his history and even suggested that Stuart proposed the move.[2]

Stuart led Jenkins' brigade and Chambliss about two-and-one-half miles out on the York Pike to a small road that cut across farm fields toward the Low Dutch Road.[3] Reaching some wooded high ground overlooking the broad, fenced fields of the Rummel, Trostle, and Lott farms, Stuart saw across the undulating land toward the intersection of the Hanover and Low Dutch roads, where he wanted to go. He sent Chambliss and Jenkins' units to the right behind Cress Ridge, to be concealed in the woods while he waited for Hampton to march from Hunterstown[4] and Fitz Lee to move into position farther to the left.

Seeing no Union force in the area but probably suspecting that enemy cavalry was nearby,[5] he ordered an artillery piece to fire several rounds in different directions, to flush out any enemy or, some suggest, to indicate to Robert E. Lee that he was in position. This was perhaps a strange action. He had apparently emphasized a clandestine move to this position and said in his official report that he was trying to move Jenkins' brigade (Jenkins had been wounded on July 2 and the unit was commanded by Colonel M. J. Ferguson[6]) and Chambliss "secretly through the woods to a position, and hoped to effect a surprise upon the enemy's rear." He also expressed regret that Hampton and Lee arrived in the vicinity after noon and moved into the open instead of remaining concealed. This brought the attention of Union troopers to the intersection of the Low Dutch and Hanover roads. Why Stuart fired the four rounds remains a mystery.

While Stuart was on the move, the Federals had not been idle. Gregg's cavalry division returned to the area of the Low Dutch and Hanover roads, near where

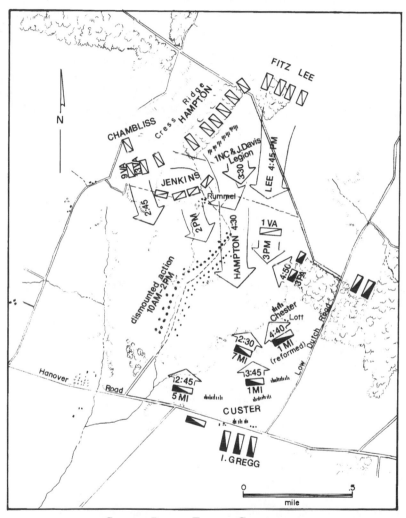

FITZ LEE

Cress Ridge
HAMPTON

CHAMBLISS

1NC & J.Davis
Legion

3:30

LEE 4:45 PM

9VA

N

JENKINS

2:45

2PM

Rummel

HAMPTON 4:30

1 VA

3PM

4:50

3PM

dismounted action
10AM-2PM

Chester
Lott

4:40

2:30

1 MI
(reformed)

7 MI

3:45

1 MI

Low Dutch Road

Hanover

Road

12:45

5 MI

CUSTER

I. GREGG

0   .5
mile

Cavalry Battle East of Gettysburg
July 3, 1863

he had fought the day before, from his position on White Run near the Baltimore Pike. He had been concerned with the Union rear since then. He had already borrowed Custer's Michigan brigade from Kilpatrick's division and had sent it ahead to watch the area from where the Low Dutch Road led to the Baltimore Pike from the Hanover Road. Still worried, Gregg got his own two brigades headed in that direction as well.

Custer reached the Hanover Road around 9 A.M.[7] His line faced toward Gettysburg and straddled the road. Skirmishers from the 1st Michigan were posted along one of the small depressions that drained Rummel's fields toward the south and formed a trickling stream called Little's Run, a tributary of Cress Run. Soon there was commotion on his right flank.[8] Some Confederate artillery and cavalry moved into view—a section of Griffin's battery and some of Jenkins' brigade. If Union troopers had heard the four rounds Stuart ordered earlier, they did not mention them, but the Confederate movement forced Custer to form his brigade into an L-shaped line with the 6th Michigan facing toward Gettysburg and the rest facing roughly north. Between the two arms of the L, he placed four cannon, leaving two other guns on the shorter leg facing down the Hanover Road toward Gettysburg. Custer sent out skirmishers from the 6th Michigan to support those from the 1st Michigan along Little's Run.[9]

Probably to protect the skirmishers as well as the massed Michigan regiments from the artillery, the Federal artillery instigated a short but violent duel. The Union fire was so devastating that the Confederate artillery retired.[10]

Lieutenant Colonel Vincent Witcher's 34th Virginia Battalion—apparently the largest of Jenkins' regiments with 352 men and 20 officers—was ordered by Stuart to dismount and move eastward to the left of the Rummel barn. The battalion was immediately reduced by one-fourth since one man in four was detailed to hold the horses. Witcher remembered that after "passing the barn and fence, we took a position behind another fence which runs almost parallel with one at the barn (my left I remember was just across a drain or hollow, I think a small branch.)" It was about 10 A.M.[11] Witcher's movement to pressure the Union skirmish line signalled the beginning of a phase of dismounted action between Confederate and Federal cavalrymen that would last for several hours and escalate eventually into large-scale mounted fighting.

Witcher gives us one more tidbit of information: "Stewart's [sic] position during the day was near the eastern mouth of the lane, or road." This, of course, would put Stuart just behind the skirmish line at the Rummel farm.[12]

Three more Confederate guns attempted to unlimber to the left of the Union artillery, but the Federals found the range before the Confederates got off a round and chased them away.[13]

About the same time a dismounted squadron of the 9th Virginia from

Chambliss' brigade moved down the slope from where the brigade stood in the woods on Cress Ridge and positioned itself in the barnyard of the Rummel farm extending Witcher's men to the left.[14] They formed a strong picket line guarding the right flank of any column of Confederate cavalrymen that moved along the un-named road that crossed the fields between the York Pike and Low Dutch Road and led to the rear of the Union army.[15]

Around noon, Custer was ordered back to the main Union lines to meet with Kilpatrick nearer the Union left flank. Meantime, Gregg's division had begun arriving on the field. Custer began to draw off but was stopped by Gregg, who had heard from Major General Oliver Otis Howard of the XI Corps that a large body of enemy cavalry was coming his way. Gregg ordered Custer to remain where he was.[16] The additional strength proved helpful.

With Custer's brigade's return, the light Union skirmish line at Little's Run was reinforced at a distance by the 1st and 2nd Battalions of the 5th Michigan, commanded by Major L. S. Trowbridge and Major Noah H. Ferry respectively. For now, the two opposing skirmish lines faced each other, the Confederates along a fence line and the Union troopers along the depression formed by Little's Run.

The other two brigades of David M. Gregg's division arrived on the field. Irvin Gregg's brigade halted south of the Hanover Road about a mile west of Low Dutch Road. It stayed out of action but in a vital reserve position for the rest of the battle. McIntosh's brigade continued to the crossroads, passed Custer, turned north and established itself with pickets along Low Dutch Road north of the Hanover Road. Its pickets pushed out to the Little's Run line to relieve Custer's men and out as far as the un-named road crossing the fields from the Low Dutch Road to the Confederate position.

The fresh Union troopers became a little more aggressive than skirmishers should be, attacking the Confederates at the Rummel farm.[17] Shortly, McIntosh had to send in two squadrons of the 3rd Pennsylvania extending their original picket line to the left. From a strip of woods north of the Lott House, it ran along a fence to Rummel's spring house, then to the left and rear towards the Hanover Road along Little's Run.

The Confederates rolled out a battery of artillery on the wooded knoll behind the Rummel barn, strengthening their skirmish line.[18] The fight was rapidly escalating into a full-scale battle.

Jenkins' Confederates skirmished on and off at the Rummel farm almost five hours, belying the belief that they went into battle with only ten rounds per man. Backing up to Rummel's barn, they began using it as a skirmish outpost and occupied the fence line closer to the barn and along Rummel's lane. They were exhausting their ammunition, however, as were the Yankees. The Confederates reinforced their line and advanced. Firing slacked off and the Yankees tried several times to retire, but each time they were assailed by the Confederates, encouraged by the enemy's withdrawal. The Federals began wondering when their ammunition would be completely expended.[19]

The Confederate guns on the knoll behind Rummel's barn were a section of the Louisiana Guard Artillery. Theodore Dimitry, who was with the detachment, recalled that they became engaged about 2 P.M. He remembered that no other Confederate guns were engaged at the time because he could hear the din of Alexander's guns firing upon Cemetery Ridge in preparation for Longstreet's assault.[20] In fact, the Union horse artillery was far more effective than its Confederate counterpart on Cress Ridge. Some Confederates began using the Rummel barn for sharpshooting, drawing the fire of Union artillery. Shells crashed through the roof and exploded within the confines of the barn almost immediately. The Confederate sharpshooters soon found a less conspicuous roost. Again, the Confederate artillery could do little to stop the Union gunners.[21]

The reinforcements that were sent to Witcher from his own brigade were not going to be enough for the fighting to come. Witcher recalled that "the 16th [Virginia] was a mere skeleton, paper regiment, and the four companies with us did not muster more than 50 men. The 14th [Virginia] had engaged about 100 men."[22]

More dismounted men from Hampton's and Fitz Lee's brigade had bolstered the extended Confederate skirmish line farther to the east, across the crossroad that led to the Low Dutch Road. The rebel skirmish line soon covered the entire front of Stuart's four brigades. Resupplied with ammunition and reinforced, the men from the Rummel barn pressed the dismounted Michigan troopers hard again, firing from their fence line only 150 yards from the Little's Run line.[23] Custer's Michigan troopers' Spencer repeating rifles probably helped them hold back the large force, but their ammunition dwindled rapidly. They were ordered to fall back to their horses about the same time the Confederates began to advance.

Witcher describes the Southerners' attack: "With a wild yell the whole line dashed forward, retook the fence and swept the Federal dismounted men back. Seeing the whole line of dismounted men give way, I moved forward with a view of taking a battery in our front and right."[24] As well, the Confederate skirmishers of the 1st Virginia Cavalry to the left of Witcher advanced. They had gone about three-quarters of a mile when they took a volley from a dismounted group of Federals behind a fence. They drove them back, skirmishing over the three or four hundred yards of farm fields until they saw Lieutenant James Chester's section of two Federal guns unlimber in farmer Lott's orchard. W. A. Morgan, an officer in the 1st Virginia, remembered that they charged the guns and were soon among them, but found no ammunition for them. The dismounted men of the 1st Virginia retired from the guns they took when two squadrons of mounted Yankees charged them.[25]

Chester's men re-took their pieces and poured fire indiscriminately into both the Confederates and their own men, according to Morgan. The Virginians were attacked again by a mounted unit of Union cavalry. The fighting seesawed until Lieutenant Colonel P. M. B. Young, commanding Cobb's Georgia Legion, charged the enemy. Custer's men broke, but they were soon reinforced by a regiment from Gregg's division. Morgan's Virginians reformed on the right of Cobb's Legion, who were now engaged saber to saber with Gregg's men. Morgan's men filled the space between Cobb's right and Chambliss' left. The Michigan men ran out of ammunition and began to fall back.[26]

The 7th Michigan in reserve launched a classic mounted charge across the fields to stop the Confederate advance. Custer himself led the column, at least for a while. Resplendent in his velvet-trimmed suit and scarlet cravat, he called back to his men, "Come on, you Wolverines!"[27] It was around 2:30 or 3 P.M.

One of their comrades, while falling back dismounted, stopped to watch the 7th go in:

> To our astonishment and distress we saw that regiment, apparently without any attempt to change direction, dash itself upon a high stake and rider fence, squadron after squadron, breaking upon the struggling masses in front, like the waves of the sea upon a rocky shore until all were mixed in one confused and tangled mass. The enemy meanwhile had been pouring upon those brave men a deadly fire, and when that regiment retired in some confusion the ground was strewn with the bodies of men and horses.[28]

The 7th, which had dismounted when it reached the Confederate fence line, was compelled to fall back under the stinging rebel fire.

As it did so, the Confederates pressed on dismounted. Two Federal companies managed to mount their horses and make a countercharge.[29] From the stubborn action of the dismounted skirmishers, the battle had progressed to mounted charges against dismounted cavalrymen. The 5th Michigan soon launched yet another charge into the middle of the fray, escalating it even further.

Stuart himself described his reaction to the Union attack:

> The enemy, sending forward a squadron or two, were about to cut off and capture a portion of our dismounted sharpshooters. To prevent this, I ordered forward the nearest cavalry regiment [from Chambliss] quickly to charge this force of cavalry. It was gallantly

done, and about the same time a portion of General Fitz. Lee's command charged on the left, the First Virginia Cavalry, being most conspicuous.[30]

A sergeant from the 1st Virginia reported that a command to his right, apparently one of Hampton's regiments, was ordered to charge, but failed to do so. Another sergeant, E. G. Fishburne, explained:

> A regiment of Hampton's command was ordered and started a charge to protect them [the sharpshooters], but several well directed shots from the enemies [sic] artillery struck the head of their column as they moved out from a skirt of woods and broke them up. Just at this very critical point, whilst the enemy were overriding our dismounted men, the 1st Va. having been countermarched was standing in column of fours with its rear to the line of battle, the command was given us . . . and away we went.[31]

In his official report, Stuart praised their impetuosity. He must have felt a special pride; after all, it was his old regiment, which he trained for combat at the beginning of the war. Despite the exhaustive rides and fights of the preceding weeks, the charge was "not only extraordinary, but irresistible. The enemy's masses vanished before them like grain before the scythe." Unfortunately, it was too much for the underfed and overworked horses, which could not keep up with the demands of combat and faltered. Stuart continued, "Their movement was too rapid to be stopped by couriers, and the enemy perceiving it, were turning upon them with fresh horses. The First North Carolina Cavalry and the Jefferson Davis Legion were sent to their support, and gradually this hand-to-hand fighting involved the greater portion of the command."[32]

Captain William Miller of the 3rd Pennsylvania had a perfect view of the charge from the western edge of some woods north of the Lott farm. He agreed with Stuart. "A more determined and vigorous charge than that made by the 1st Virginia, it has never been my fortune to witness," Miller wrote.[33] He also attributed the 1st Virginia's eventual repulse to weakened horseflesh as well as his flank fire and Union shelling. He also saw the regiment run up against one of those ubiquitous farm fences. By the time the charge lost momentum, the troopers were so near part of the Union artillery that some of the gunners reportedly deserted their pieces.

About this time, on the extreme left of Stuart's line, the 2nd Virginia under Colonel Thomas Munford charged across two fields near Rummel's lane. Half of the regiment was dismounted to tear down Rummel's fence. Shells dropped in on its right and Munford remembered the rapid fire from the Spencers of the Michigan men. While the 2nd Virginia was engaged in the sharp fight at the fence, they saw the Union gunners beyond driven from their guns. Their support troopers charged and were met by Munford's men. Between the mounted action of the 1st Virginia and the dismounted action of the 2nd, it got pretty hot for some Union artillerists.

Chambliss sent back for reinforcements from Fitz Lee. Eventually, Hampton, who was nearer, sent in the 1st North Carolina and the Jefferson Davis Legion. "These two regiments drove back the enemy; but in their eagerness they followed him too far, and encountered his reserve in heavy force," Hampton wrote.[34]

The Confederate regiments had hit the 1st Michigan. Captain A. E. Mathews, who was in the lead squadron of the Yankee unit, remembered first being positioned in a hollow south of the Hanover Road near where it crossed the Low Dutch Road, being able to see almost nothing. Soon the regiment was in motion, crossing the road and riding over piles of rails from fences dismantled by Gregg's men the day before. The men reached the plateau and saw the Confederate column coming directly toward them. About thirty seconds before they would have clashed, Mathews remembered the Confederates faltering:

> We continued our gait and direction while they, becoming a little alarmed at this saucy little atom of insignificance, and to wipe us out [sic], the leaders of their column, which had given up all organization, now dropped down in our front, and their whole column being in full view, the first wavering, at the head of the column, signalled a forlorn hope. The entire length of the column, not by order or detachment, but by individuals, turned back, leaving their leaders to their fate.[35]

Mathews recounted no great collision, as the Confederates generally turned and retreated. He said that they followed the Confederates until they struck "the gap that caused the 'jam' and here the melee occurred." This was apparently where some of the fences had been thrown down. The disorganized, spread-out Confederates were trying to make their way through the narrow spot. Mathews stated that he never worked so hard trying to keep his men moving; he looked behind and saw none of them had followed him. In spite of being virtually surrounded by dismounted Confederates, he was ignored, everyone's attention being on the 2nd squadron of the 1st Michigan, under Captain Alexander, which was riding up to attack the Confederate traffic jam at a place where Mathews thought "no squadron of cavalry in the world dared go."

A large number of Confederates backed out and turned to meet Alexander's charge. Mathews retired from the action while Custer and others gathered in the stragglers and reorganized the unit for additional action.[36] Hampton did not lead his two regiments in their first charge, but was there to rally them when they were driven back:

> Seeing the state of affairs at this juncture, I rode rapidly to the front, to take charge of these two regiments, and, while doing this, to my surprise, I saw the rest of my brigade (excepting the Cobb Legion) and Fitz Lee's brigade charging. In the hand-to-hand fight which ensued, as I was endeavoring to extricate the First North Carolina and the Jeff. Davis Legion, I was wounded, and had to leave the field, after turning over my command to Colonel Baker.[37]

It almost sounds as if Hampton, in command of the brigade, did not quite know what was going on, yet it was explained to him later that the charge had been ordered by a Captain Barker, assistant adjutant general, who supposed that the whole brigade was needed to help Chambliss. Hampton conceded that by looking at the confused mayhem on the broad plains before them, it seemed that nothing less than an entire brigade was needed.

So, suddenly, the rest of Hampton's brigade (except for the Cobb Legion, which was already engaged) began charging the reformed 1st Michigan under Custer. If Hampton was with the 1st North Carolina and the Jefferson Davis Legion, that left the 1st and 2nd South Carolina and the Phillips Legion swinging out from the woods on Cress Ridge into the open plain east of the Rummel buildings. In addition came what was left of Fitz Lee's brigade, the 1st Virginia entering the massive column. Stuart had rallied it personally after its first charge and formed the regiment for the next and larger charge. Though the 3rd Virginia had been formed to support the 1st, it never made it in and remained in reserve with the 4th Virginia.[38]

Records for Munford's 2nd Virginia are sparse, but indicate that it too was held in reserve, making three regiments and possibly more prepared for further action.[39]

From Chambliss' undersized brigade, the 13th Virginia was in the column, as probably was at least part of the 9th, since one squadron had earlier been used as dismounted skirmishers. The regiment was small, however, perhaps no more than eighty men, and there may have been no more than 200 in all of Chambliss' brigade.[40]

The thirty-five men of the 2nd North Carolina also were in the charge. Since the 10th Virginia had earlier been assigned to support the artillery battalion with the 2nd North Carolina, it likely pitched in as well.[41]

Jenkins' brigade (under Ferguson) had been fighting all morning along the Little's Run/Cress Run line and for the most part watched the final charge of the day.

There does not seem to be any record of who ordered the last charge or who commanded it. Stuart did not mention it in his report. Hampton may have assumed command, since his brigade apparently led the column, yet in his post-action account he expressed surprise that while he was rallying the 1st North Carolina and Jefferson Davis Legion, the rest of his brigade and Fitz Lee's unit were charging. He also mentioned that he was wounded rallying the regiments and was not in the final charge. Seeing this, Fitz Lee may have called in his remaining regiments as support, with Chambliss following.

Watching the Confederate column advancing between his dismounted skirmishers at the Little's Run line and his mounted squadrons north of Lott's farm, McIntosh sent his aide, Captain Walter S. Newhall, across the broad field where the Confederate column was approaching from his right, to the men at Little's Run with orders to charge the right flank of the column as it passed. Newhall, fulfilling a staff officer's dream, stayed with the squadrons to participate. His decision set him on a collision course with William B. Harrison of Prince George County, Virginia, color sergeant of the 13th Virginia, with painful results.

From a vantage point to the side, Miller saw the reorganized 1st Michigan and the Confederate column raise their horses from a walk, to a trot, and then to a gallop.

> As the two columns approached each other the pace of each increased, when suddenly a crash, like the falling of timber, betokened the crisis. So sudden and violent was the collision that many of the horses were turned end over end and crushed their riders beneath them. The clashing of sabers, the firing of pistols, the demands for surrender and cries of the combatants now filled the air.[42]

Miller could not stand it anymore, sitting on the sideline, and saw where his small group of Pennsylvanians could charge in at the most opportune time. He turned to his lieutenant, William Brooke-Rawle, and said, "I have been ordered to hold this position, but, if you will back me up in case I am court-martialed for disobedience, I will order a charge." Brooke-Rawle answered that he would do so. As they watched the Confederate column pass, and before Miller, Brooke-Rawle, or anyone could give an order, the restless Pennsylvanians charged. Miller wrote:

> The men fired a volley from their carbines, drew their sabers, sent up a shout, and "sailed in," striking the enemy's left flank about

two-thirds down the column. . . . My command pressed through the Confederate column, cut off the rear portion and drove it back. In the charge my men became somewhat scattered. A portion of them, however, got into Rummel's lane, in front of the farm buildings, and there encountered some of Jenkins' men, who seemed stubborn about leaving.[43]

A. J. Speese, a member of Company H of the 3rd Pennsylvanians, wrote that the Confederates "were not driven like sheep, but retreated in good order to cover their battery. . . . After these Confederates reached Rommell's [sic] lane, they formed in the field beyond, about 200 yards in front of their battery. Seeing our weakness, and that their guns were in no danger from us, they in turn advanced and we were compelled to retreat."[44]

On the other side of the Confederate column from Miller were only sixteen men and five officers, including Captain Newhall. In the melee, he saw the colors of the 13th Virginia and rushed directly for them. A few yards from Sergeant William Harrison, the color bearer, Newhall's attention was distracted by a saber blow at his head, which he parried. He then saw that Harrison, who had noticed him coming, had lowered the staff, aiming the spear point directly at Newhall's face. Unable to react in time, Newhall rode right into the end of the staff, tearing his mouth, mangling his jaw, and knocking him unconscious to the ground among the pounding hooves.

Harrison leapt from his worn-out horse to Newhall's and continued to wield the lance-like staff. He ran Newhall's orderly through the gut; he also dropped into the cauldron of hooves. Despite all attempts to "civilize" warfare, it had moved no more than a spear-length in 4,000 years.[45]

The brigade commander, McIntosh, had mounted together as many men as he could, including musicians, staff members, orderlies, and stragglers, and also charged the Confederate column, which was getting a little ragged. Hampton was carried off with wounds in the thigh and head.[46]

The battle degenerated into small groups fighting one another or two or three men riding to rescue a comrade. A half-hearted, long-range artillery duel rolled across the fields as dusk descended.

Anyone who had not been sabered, shot, unhorsed, or trampled had been lucky. The Confederates retreated more from disorganization than defeat, still ready to countercharge with at least three regiments in reserve. The combatants argued for years just who retained the field and who held the Rummel barn after it was over.[47] One thing was perfectly clear: Darkness was falling and Stuart still had not made it to the rear of the Union army.[48]

CHAPTER EIGHT

Covering the Withdrawal

*"General Stuart was my ideal of a soldier. He was always
cheerful under all circumstances, and always ready for any work,
and always reliable."*
—ROBERT E. LEE TO WADE HAMPTON IN LEXINGTON AFTER THE WAR

O n July 4, Lee had Stuart send Robertson's and Jones' brigades, which were
near Fairfield, to hold the Jack's Mountain passes southwest of Gettysburg for the passage of the rest of the army. Meantime, Stuart's Union
counterpart, Alfred Pleasonton, scattered his brigades in search of Confederate
wagon trains, troops, and lines of communication, all of which they hoped to
harass. Irvin Gregg headed in a wide arc northwestward, ranging from Hunterstown
through Mummasburg toward Cashtown; the rest headed toward Maryland, with
Buford going to Frederick and Kilpatrick to Emmitsburg.[1] Kilpatrick had caught
up with a part of the Confederate wagon train at Monterey Gap near Blue Ridge
Summit and the Maryland line and burned it just before midnight July 4.[2]

Imboden, whose brigade first had guarded the Confederate left flank, had been
busily destroying parts of the Chesapeake and Ohio Canal and demolishing railroad bridges; he did not arrive at Gettysburg until noon July 3. That night, he
was summoned to Lee's headquarters and witnessed Lee's anguish after Pickett's
Charge. Lee instructed Imboden to escort the wagon train of wounded back into
Virginia, one of the most heartbreaking missions Imboden ever undertook.

Imboden told Lee he had 2,100 men and a six-gun battery. Lee promised
him as much artillery as he needed and told him once he got to Williamsport,
Maryland, he would meet with a wagon train of ammunition from Winchester,
Virginia. Lee told Imboden to cross the mountains via the road to Chambersburg,
Pennsylvania, but then to pick the best route from there. He specifically ordered
Imboden not to halt until he reached Williamsport, for fear of Yankee cavalry
capturing the wounded. After crossing the Potomac, Imboden was again ordered
not to halt until reaching Winchester.

Imboden reported nothing later about Lee mentioning his disappointment in Imboden's actions during the invasion. Lee, like he had so many times before, probably had closed the door on those events, summoned his great will, and tackled the immediate problems.

By the morning of July 4, Lee had issued Imboden written orders and an envelope for Jefferson Davis. He also sent Imboden twelve more cannon and a British-made breech-loading Whitworth rifled gun, with a range of nearly five miles. Hampton's and Fitz Lee's brigades were attached to him along with four more guns. All were ordered to protect the rear of the column.

It began to rain in torrents just after noon on July 4, blinding and panicking the mules and horses pulling the wagons in the churned-up fields along the Cashtown Road. Imboden said mere canvas could not hold out the torrents and the wounded suffered even more. Around 4 P.M., the head of the column near Cashtown began its arduous climb over the mountains. It was then that Imboden realized that the train of Lee's wounded stretched for seventeen miles. Imboden himself started out from Cashtown for the head of the column after sunset. As he rode, he suffered perhaps the most horrifying night of his life:

> My orders had been peremptory that there should be no halt for any cause whatever. If an accident should happen to any vehicle, it was immediately to be put out of the road and abandoned. The column moved rapidly, considering the rough roads and the darkness, and from almost every wagon for many miles issued the heart-rending wails of agony. For four hours I hurried forward on my way to the front, and in all that time I was never out of hearing of the groans and cries of the wounded and dying. Scarcely one in a hundred had received adequate surgical aid, owing to the demands on the hard-working surgeons from still worse cases that had to be left behind. Many of the wounded in the wagons had been without food for thirty-six hours. Their torn and bloody clothing, matted and hardened, was rasping the tender, inflamed, and still oozing wounds. Very few of the wagons had even a layer of straw in them, and all were without springs. The road was rough and rocky from the heavy washings of the preceding day. The jolting was enough to have killed strong men, if long exposed to it. From nearly every wagon as the teams trotted on, urged by whip and shout, came such cries and shrieks as these:
>
> "O God! why can't I die?"
>
> "My God! will no one have mercy and kill me?"

Major General James Ewell Brown Stuart, commander of the Confederate Cavalry on the Gettysburg campaign. THE VALENTINE MUSEUM, RICHMOND, VIRGINIA.

General Robert E. Lee, commander of the Confederate Army of Northern Virginia. MASSACHUSETTS COMMANDERY, MILITARY ORDER OF THE LOYAL LEGION, THE U.S. ARMY MILITARY HISTORY INSTITUTE AND THE AMERICANA IMAGE GALLERY.

Lieutenant Colonel Charles Marshall, Lee's military secretary, who wrote Stuart's confusing orders and Lee's contradictory post-campaign reports. He would later accuse Stuart of disobedience. THE VIR-GINIA HISTORICAL SOCIETY, RICHMOND, VIRGINIA.

Lieutenant General James Longstreet, commander of the First Corps, Army of Northern Virginia, who first sanctioned Stuart's ride around the Union Army of the Potomac, then later blamed him for leaving Lee without cavalry. MASSACHUSETTS COMMAN-DERY, MILITARY ORDER OF THE LOYAL LEGION, THE U.S. ARMY MILITARY HISTORY INSTITUTE AND THE AMERI-CANA IMAGE GALLERY.

Colonel John S. Mosby, who scouted the Potomac crossings for Stuart and gathered information on the location of the Union army that helped him decide on the ride around the enemy. Later he would become Stuart's most vehement defender. MASSACHUSETTS COMMANDERY, MILITARY ORDER OF THE LOYAL LEGION, THE U.S. ARMY MILITARY HISTORY INSTITUTE AND THE AMERICANA IMAGE GALLERY.

Major Henry B. McClellan, Stuart's assistant adjutant general, who cited a "lost" order from Lee to Stuart and defended him in his memoirs.
THE VIRGINIA HISTORICAL SOCIETY, RICHMOND, VIRGINIA.

James Harrison, Confederate spy, who Longstreet claimed brought Lee his first information that the Union army had crossed the Potomac. Mosby called the story a "fable."
GETTYSBURG NATIONAL MILITARY PARK.

Brigadier General Beverly H. Robertson, commander of the two brigades Stuart left with Lee. It was his job to accompany the Army of Northern Virginia across the Potomac as it advanced. MASSACHUSETTS COMMANDERY, MILITARY ORDER OF THE LOYAL LEGION, THE U.S. ARMY MILITARY HISTORY INSTITUTE AND THE AMERICANA IMAGE GALLERY.

Brigadier General Fitzhugh Lee, commander of one of the brigades Stuart took around the Army of the Potomac. MASSACHUSETTS COMMANDERY, MILITARY ORDER OF THE LOYAL LEGION, THE U.S. ARMY MILITARY HISTORY INSTITUTE AND THE AMERICANA IMAGE GALLERY.

Brigadier General Wade Hampton, who also commanded one of the brigades Stuart took on his ride around the enemy. Longstreet thought the more efficient Hampton should have been left behind instead of Robertson.

Colonel John R. Chambliss, who commanded the third brigade accompanying Stuart on his ride. MASSACHUSETTS COMMANDERY, MILITARY ORDER OF THE LOYAL LEGION, THE U.S. ARMY MILITARY HISTORY INSTITUTE AND THE AMERICANA IMAGE GALLERY.

Major General Henry Heth, who, contradicting Lee's instructions, precipitated the Battle of Gettysburg. He would later claim that Stuart left Lee's army blind, and that was the main cause of the campaign's failure. LIBRARY OF CONGRESS.

"Stop! Oh! for God's sake, stop just for one minute; take me out and leave me to die on the roadside. . . ."

No help could be rendered any of the sufferers. No heed could be given to any of their appeals. Mercy and duty comply with the prayers of the few. On! On! we *must* move on. The storm continued, and the darkness was appalling. . . . During this one night I realized more of the horrors of war than I had in all the two preceding years.[3]

Hill's corps was first in the line of retreating infantry on the road to Fairfield. Longstreet was in the center of the column and Ewell brought up the rear. The cavalry was positioned so that two brigades under Fitz Lee were on the Cashtown Road and Jenkins' and Chambliss' brigades, under Stuart, headed toward Emmitsburg, thereby guarding both flanks of the army. Jenkins himself was still out of action.[4]

By dawn July 5, Stuart reached Emmitsburg. Louis R. Fortesque, a Union signal officer who had apparently been captured, left in his diary this description:

Arriving at the intersection of the first street [Main Street in Emmitsburg], we were confronted by the cavalry leader of the Army of Virginia, whose headquarters were temporarily established there.

To those who have never had the misfortune of an introduction under such unfavorable conditions, his appearance might have awakened adulatory criticism, particularly by believers in his theory of southern rights. But to us his self-assumption and bombastic exaggeration of dress simply invited contempt. In stature he was six feet, and weighed about one-hundred and ninety pounds. A complexion somewhat ruddy from exposure, with light brown hair, worn rather long, and full flowing beards. His regulation gray uniform was profusely decorated with gold braid, and was topped with a broad-brimmed black felt hat, pinned up at the side with a star from which drooped an extravagantly large ostrich feather. On his left breast was a shield, about two inches in width, which held a chain attached to the handle of a small stiletto, the blade being passed through the button holes of his coat. What the gentleman's object was in adopting this spectacular ornament of decoration, it was difficult to imagine, unless to use as a handy tooth-pick? He may have meant that it should lend an air of ferocity to his appearance; a sort of brigandish style of bearing; if so it was a moderately successful achievement, the 'Bombastis Furioso' standard being courted, as we afterwards observed, by most of the prominent rebel officers.[5]

Stuart realized that the enemy had two possible routes: To the right toward Fairfield, where the massed infantry of Hill or Longstreet could handle any cavalry force; or to the left toward Hagerstown and the wagon train of wounded with Imboden. Stuart rode toward Imboden.

In the meantime, Imboden had reached Greencastle at daybreak.[6] Civilians emerged from their homes with axes and chopped through the spokes of the wagons, disabling some in the streets. Also, a fairly large force from the 6th Pennsylvania Cavalry split, one contingent going to the head of the Confederate column, the other to the rear. The Yankees claimed they destroyed 130 wagons, ran off the horses, and captured two cannon and 200 prisoners. They were driven off by the strong infantry guard and perhaps some cavalry. In the confusion, they lost the prisoners.[7] Though Confederate infantry and cavalry halted the bushwhacking, Union cavalry began to swarm from fields and side roads in small groups, hitting the column where it was unguarded. Imboden himself was nearly captured. He turned two cannon on a party of fifty cavalrymen, but even canister did not stop them. The 18th Virginia came back to help and captured the whole group. Such fighting continued until Imboden's train reached Williamsport on the afternoon of July 5.[8]

Stuart, at about the same time, was continuing southward toward Frederick on the Old Frederick Road heading toward Cooperstown (now Creagerstown) and halted the column for an hour in the tiny Moravian village of Graceham to water and feed the weary horses.[9] They took up the march again, riding through Harbaugh's Valley, passing Zion Church, and continuing through the Catoctin Mountains.[10]

Meantime, while descending Catoctin Mountain, Stuart divided his command to ensure that at least one column would get through, sending Jenkins' brigade (under Ferguson) toward Smithtown (now Smithburg) and accompanying Chambliss himself toward Leitersburg. At the western end of the pass in the Catoctins, Stuart and Chambliss ran into the enemy. Fighting dismounted, the Confederates forced the passage, only to come under artillery fire from batteries posted on three hills and backed up by three cavalry brigades.

Also hearing firing from the direction in which he had sent Ferguson, Stuart sent a message to him to come the way he had already cleared. Stuart's artillery soon drove the pesky Union battery from its position. A civilian told him that the cavalry he had just engaged was Kilpatrick, who had bragged about capturing thousands of prisoners and 400 or 500 wagons. Stuart later learned that Kilpatrick only had about forty wagons with him and that much of Ewell's wagon train had already cleared the mountains. He also was told of a rumor that Grumble Jones had been captured.

At nightfall on July 5, Stuart informed Lee of the cavalry's movements and actions up to that point. At daylight in Leitersburg, Stuart realized that Kilpatrick had headed toward Boonsboro and so pursued, adding to his force Jones' brigade, which had just come up from Fairfield without its commander. The previous day, Jones was separated from his command but connected with a portion of the wagon train that escaped toward Williamsport. Later, despite the rumor of his capture and much to Stuart's relief, Jones rode in from Williamsport and rejoined his command. He brought the news that Imboden and the wagon train of wounded had finally reached Williamsport.

After Stuart's column arrived in Cavetown, Jones was sent out the Boonsboro road a few miles, covering Hagerstown against attack from the east. Chambliss and Robertson were thrown together because of recent attrition. They formed a "very small command"[11] and were ordered from Leitersburg to Hagerstown along with Alfred Iverson's brigade of infantry from Robert Rodes' division in Ewell's corps. Stuart accompanied Jenkins' brigade via Chewsville toward Hagerstown and once there learned of the approach of the enemy.

While Stuart rode, a large body of Union cavalry was approaching Hagerstown from the south and was preparing to engage Chambliss. Stuart sent Ferguson riding ahead to reinforce him. When Ferguson arrived, he found that the Yankees under Kilpatrick had already driven Chambliss' undersized brigade through Hagerstown and held the town. Swinging east, Ferguson attacked. Jones came up on his left and opened with artillery. Some of Iverson's North Carolinians, decimated on the first day at Gettysburg, held the north end of Hagerstown along with Robertson and some of Chambliss' men, now rallying with the infantry support.

Stuart realized that the Yankees' objective was Williamsport, southwest of Hagerstown. There the Confederate wagons were parked at the foot of a hill near the Potomac, unable to cross because of the recent rain.

Since Imboden's arrival, Williamsport had become a vast hospital, the surgeons finally having time to attend to the long-suffering wounded. They were scattered through the village. If the Confederates were driven from Hagerstown, then Williamsport, they would have to abandon not only their nearest Potomac crossing but their suffering comrades as well. Conveying that to his outnumbered force, Stuart attacked vigorously through Hagerstown. The Confederates drove the Yankees first toward Sharpsburg, but they turned again toward Williamsport. As his own firing subsided on the southern outskirts of Hagerstown, Stuart heard artillery fire coming from Williamsport. Buford's division had ridden in from Boonsboro and was within a half-mile of the Confederate wagon park.[12]

In spite of the arduous trip from Gettysburg, Imboden organized his combat units and even ordered the teamsters to collect the weapons of the wounded and fall in line. Groups were sent to the right to help hold the flank resting on the Potomac, another to the left to the Hagerstown Road, and a third out in front as skirmishers. Imboden placed his artillery on the hills that hid Williamsport and dismounted his own command in the center of the line.[13]

The artillery opened up about 1:30 P.M., discouraging Buford from advancing. Ammunition ran low at one point, but some had just arrived from Winchester, as Lee had promised. Knowing that Buford could not see that he had no reserves behind the hills, Imboden sent his entire line forward about 100 yards ahead of his artillery on the Hagerstown side of town, had it stand in full view of the Yankees for a while, then withdrew methodically behind the hills. He then sent the men rushing to the other side of town to his right flank, where he actually expected the attack after his show of strength. The ruse worked. The Union attack was spirited, but with the aid of the teamsters and artillery, it was driven back.[14]

Meanwhile, at Hagerstown, with nearly all of his cavalry concentrated, Stuart ordered Chambliss directly down the road to pursue the enemy while Ferguson and two of Robertson's regiments drove down the left of the road, keeping parallel with Ferguson and hoping to swing to attack the enemy's flank if the opportunity arose.

Chambliss' unit had been whittled to only a few hundred men, yet it charged with vigor, supported by part of the Horse Artillery, with the 9th and 13th Virginia regiments particularly attracting Stuart's attention. The Yankees rallied on a hill among fences and rocks, backed up by their artillery, while the attempted Confederate flank attack bogged down, held up by obstacles and terrain.

Ferguson dismounted and advanced against the Federals, who began to withdraw. A mounted charge by the Confederates helped move them along and a countercharge was repulsed. A saber charge down the road turned the Union retreat into a rout.

Though the Yankees were still advancing near Williamsport, Stuart's victory at Hagerstown put him nearly in the Union rear and compelled the Yankees to retreat back toward Downsville shortly after sunset. Meantime, Buford was reorganizing his attack upon Williamsport when suddenly the Confederates counterattacked. Fitz Lee had advanced down the road from Greencastle, Pennsylvania, with 3,000 fresh men.[15] As the battle heated up, Buford urged Kilpatrick to hook up with his right flank and support him. The tenuous connection was finally made just before dark, when Kilpatrick's troopers gave way and retreated to the right behind Buford's men with Confederates hot on their heels. This and the growing Confederate force in his front at Williamsport and to his right as Stuart approached forced Buford to retire back toward Boonsboro after dark.[16]

Stuart's victories at Hagerstown and Williamsport on July 6 were paramount. One of the major goals of the campaign had been the gathering of supplies. Had the wagons been destroyed, the campaign would have been an unmitigated failure on all counts. Stuart and Lee knew it; Buford's and especially Kilpatrick's reports clearly show this. Neither was ever happy to report a failure—especially Kilpatrick, who sometimes adjusted the facts to make himself look better—yet Buford acknowledged, "The expedition had for its object the destruction of the enemy's trains, supposed to be at Williamsport. This, I regret to say, was not accomplished." [17] Kilpatrick's admission, considering the source, was even more astounding, although he softened it by adding a fact that his division had nothing to do with: "We failed in destroying the large trains parked at Williamsport but forced the enemy to burn a large train northwest of Hagerstown." [18] Stuart reported no such destruction but noted that sixty wagons had been lost near Mercersburg, Pennsylvania. Stuart was upset enough about it later to request an inquiry on the matter. [19]

On July 7, Stuart posted his cavalry in advanced defensive positions and placed W. T. Wofford's infantry brigade, on loan from Longstreet's corps, at Downsville with Ferguson in advance of it. Robertson's small unit was sent where there was the least threat, north of Hagerstown. Jones was placed to his right across the Cavetown Road. By that morning the main army's rear guard had arrived in Hagerstown. [20]

On July 8, Stuart sent his cavalry toward Boonsboro via different roads, hoping by his aggressive advance to cover for the main army, now concentrated at Williamsport. It still was unable to cross because the river was still rising.

From Beaver Creek Bridge to the north edge of Boonsboro, Jones' brigade fought dismounted, the heavy rains having turned the earth into mush too soft to carry a mounted man. The Confederate cavalry pushed the Yankees slowly through the town and into Turner's Pass in South Mountain. Ferguson's arrival along the Williamsport road from the northwest took the Union troopers in the left flank. That, combined with the Horse Artillery's fire driving Northern batteries from the hills behind Boonsboro, forced the Yankees back up the mountain and into Turner's Pass. [21]

Stuart soon learned that ammunition was running short and that the enemy was being heavily reinforced with infantry and artillery. [22] Though he wanted to hold Boonsboro, the Yankee artillery commanded the town from Turner's Pass, so he began a slow retreat north on the old National Road toward Funkstown.

To Stuart on July 9, Robert E. Lee wrote about the enemy capturing some wagons in Clear Spring Valley, probably referring to the disaster at Cunningham Crossroads. [23] Lee again expressed his displeasure with one of his cavalry commanders—Imboden—and also leads us to believe that Stuart may have suggested a raid back into Pennsylvania, to capture Chambersburg, some thirty miles away: "Imboden's cavalry is on that side. They are unsteady and I fear inefficient. I think it more important to clear them away than to take Chambersburg. I doubt whether a shoe could be found there. They are all hidden or carried off."[24]

On July 10, Stuart snatched a moment to write to his wife, Flora, from near Hagerstown: "Upon the eve of another battle I write today to say God has mercifully spared me through many dangers and bloody fields. My Cavalry has nobly sustained its reputation and done better and harder fighting than it ever has since the war. . . . We got the better of the fight at Gettysburg but retired because the position we took could not be held. We now have a fresh supply of ammunition and will give battle again. May God grant us victory."[25]

That day, the Federals advanced on the road from Boonsboro. Although Grumble Jones' brigade was still to the north on the Cavetown Road, Stuart had some infantry to cover Funkstown, behind which, along Antietam Creek, the main army was forming. He placed his dismounted cavalry on the flanks of the foot soldiers. His line stretched from Antietam Creek on his right to the Smithburg Road on the left. The Union advance began at 8 A.M. and pushed the Confederate skirmishers back. Right to left were Merritt's reserve brigade, Gamble's brigade straddling the National Pike, and Devin's brigade, dismounted and advancing up the pike toward Stuart's line. They were backed by artillery.[26] George T. Anderson's brigade of Confederate infantry under Colonel White counterattacked, moving the Federals out of the fields, but White's men could not drive the main Union force from the woods. The fighting lasted until 3 P.M. and ended only when the Yankees' ammunition gave out. Funkstown, seemingly just another skirmish on the Confederate retreat, ended with a total of nearly 500 casualties.[27]

The attack alerted Stuart to the weakness of his position at Funkstown, so in darkness he withdrew his troops back behind the Antietam.[28]

July 11 was a day of relative inactivity, except for Fitz Lee's movement from Downsville to just west of Hagerstown, where the left flank of the main army lay on the National Road. He was later joined by Chambliss. Robert E. Lee continued concentrating his forces.

On July 12, Lee wrote to Stuart concerning the placement of his cavalry and the need to coordinate his actions with those of Longstreet. "Keep your eye over the field, use your good judgement, and give assistance where necessary," Lee advised.[29] Apparently, with the enemy at his front and the swollen Potomac at his back, Lee leaned heavily on Stuart's judgment.

Early on July 12, the Federals advanced by several roads toward Hagerstown. The effect was to compact Lee's army even more toward the possible Potomac crossings at Williamsport and Falling Waters and to push Stuart back along the National Road to the fortified outposts along Conococheague Creek. But by this

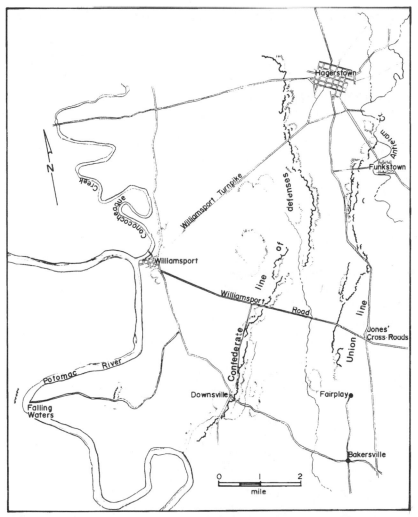

Confederate Defenses at the Potomac Crossings

time, Lee's infantry had had time to entrench itself into one of the more formidable positions of the war.

H. B. McClellan related an incident during this time that reminded him of just how heavy a burden Stuart carried throughout the campaign. There was still fighting to do in case the Potomac did not recede enough for Lee to cross. As well, the enemy could always cross the Potomac below the Confederates and be waiting on the other side when they attempted a crossing.

No one on the cavalry staff, including Stuart, had had much to eat. In Hagerstown, the daughter of a Southern sympathizer provided one meal a day, about nightfall, for Stuart's staff.

After a full day of fighting, the general and his staff returned to the house for supper about 9 P.M. Stuart promptly fell asleep on the sofa and could not be roused at first when dinner was ready. McClellan led him to the table, where he picked at the food. His hostess, concerned, asked whether he would prefer a hard-boiled egg. "Yes," Stuart replied, "I'll take four or five." She brought the eggs. Stuart, eyes wide open, cracked one, ate it, and, as if sleepwalking, rose from the table. Everyone went into the parlor and McClellan began to play the piano. Ironically, he played and sang, "If you want to have a good time, jine the cavalry." This seemed to rouse Stuart and he joined in on the chorus, finally conscious of his surroundings. He remembered nothing of the meal, the eggs, or his discourtesy to his hostess. He apologized profusely, embarrassed that his iron resolve had finally melted.

Though the term "sleep deprivation" would not be heard for a long time, that was what Stuart's cavalry was experiencing. McClellan related one more incident from the night of July 11 or 12. McClellan, Stuart, and a courier had stopped at a toll house on a turnpike into Hagerstown after Stuart had been dictating orders from horseback. As McClellan wrote, Stuart crossed his arms on a table, put his head down, and fell fast asleep. The dispatches done, McClellan awoke the general to review them. In one of the last dispatches, Stuart erased the names of two places and scratched in "Shepherdstown" and "Aldie," towns that suddenly floated into his woozy mind. They had been passed and fought over weeks earlier and had no relevance to current matters.[30]

Yet, during the same period, on July 13 from near Hagerstown, Stuart wrote a bubbly letter to his wife. He first told her that he was all right and then ran down a list of purchases he made of clothing and other items she had apparently requested. "I had a grand time in Pennsylvania and we return without defeat, to recuperate and reinforce, when, no doubt the role will be re-enacted. I shelled Carlisle and burned the barracks. I crossed near Dranesville and went close to Georgetown and Washington, cutting four important railroads, joining our army in time for the battle of Gettysburg, with 900 prisoners and 200 wagons and splendid teams."[31]

Did Stuart stretch the truth for Flora's sake? Probably not in his estimation of the campaign. In spite of virtual total exhaustion, his spirits remained high. He felt that he had accomplished his missions so far. Although he sometimes left the field in Federal possession, by denying the Union cavalry access to the main Confederate army, Stuart had succeeded overwhelmingly.

In the letter, Stuart gave his vision of a grand strategy and one of Lee's accomplished objectives: "We must invade again—it is the only path to peace. . . . General Lee's maneuvering the Yankees out of Virginia is the grandest piece of strategy ever heard of." His admiration for the commander cannot be hidden.

Finally, in almost an aside, he talked of his troopers: "My cavalry is the finest body of men *on the planet.*"[32]

Though Meade's superiors urged him to destroy the Confederate army with its back to the river, he was cautious. For this, he drew the impatience of Lincoln as well as criticism from numerous historians. Neither Lincoln nor the historians were at Williamsport. By the time the entire Army of the Potomac reached the area, it had been reinforced, somewhat mitigating the losses suffered at Gettysburg. However, the replacements were mostly untried newcomers to the army.[33] Also, along with numerous experienced brigadiers shot down at Gettysburg, who could replace Winfield Scott Hancock of the II Corps, wounded on July 3, or John Reynolds of the I Corps, killed on July 1?

The final consolidated Confederate position consisted of some of the most formidable fortifications seen to this date in the war. Lee's right flank was held by Longstreet's corps and rested upon a hill a half-mile from a big northern curve in the Potomac a mile south of Downsville. His left, held by Ewell's men, was protected by Conococheague Creek, north of Williamsport, as well as by Stuart's massed cavalry between Hagerstown and the Conococheague. Hill's corps held the center. The works were situated on a line of almost uninterrupted ridges about eight miles long and contained a six-foot wide parapet studded with gun emplacements. Artillery was positioned to lay down a latticework of projectiles, making the fields before it a killing ground. The defenses were completed by late morning on July 12.[34]

Meade, an engineer like Lee, had been impressed before with Lee's fortification skills. He also knew Lee's fighting ability and how dangerous his army could be on the defensive.

Secretary of War Edwin Stanton, Major General Henry Halleck, the chief of staff, and Lincoln all wanted Meade to attack. But they were in Washington, not standing before Lee's lines. In fact Lee expressed a desire to receive an attack in a letter to Davis on July 12. He stated that if it were not for the Federal reinforcements and his own tenuous supply situation, "I should be willing to await his attack."[35] That alone was reason enough for Meade to hold off.

On the morning of July 13, Meade and Brigadier General A. A. Humphreys, his new chief of staff, rode out into the misty rain to inspect the opposing lines. When they returned, Meade ordered Humphreys to draw up orders for his corps commanders to begin reconnaissances in force for the next morning.[36] At 4:15 P.M., Lee gave Stuart his role in the re-crossing of the Potomac. "I know it to be a difficult as well as delicate operation to cover this army and then withdraw your command with safety, but I rely upon your good judgement, energy, and boldness to accomplish it, and trust that you may be as successful as you have been on former occasions."[37] The cavalrymen were given the unenviable task of manning the trenches and parapets as the foot soldiers pulled out to cross the river. Fitz Lee's brigade took the place of Longstreet's men on the right; Hampton's brigade filled in for Hill in the center and stretched his men to occupy the left, as well, where Ewell's men had pulled out.[38] The cavalrymen were being asked to take the place of 50,000 foot soldiers. But Stuart knew that in the dark, the Federals would not know how many troops were in the trenches. The cavalry could mount and swiftly move from one part of the line to another, depending on the threat.

That night, Lee's pontoon bridges spanned the Potomac at a village, Falling Waters, named for the falls that still cascade on the south bank. Although it continued to rain through the night, the river had fallen to a safe level at Williamsport. By 11 A.M. July 14, all but two Confederate divisions had made it into Virginia.

Shortly after daylight, part of the cavalry had begun to follow Ewell's corps across the river. Stuart had told Fitz Lee to cross at Falling Waters, the nearest point to him, if the infantry had cleared the bridges. If the bridges were still in use, Lee was to ride to Williamsport and ford.

When Fitz Lee was ready to withdraw, Longstreet's men had not yet cleared the bridges, so, sending two squadrons to protect Longstreet's rear, Lee and the rest of his brigade moved up to Williamsport. In the mist and rain of early daylight, the two squadrons mistook the rear of Longstreet's command for the rear of the army. Two of A. P. Hill's divisions, Heth's and Pender's, were still in the hills a little less than a mile and a half from Falling Waters, waiting for their trains and artillery to cross and for the cavalry that was to follow them.

Finally, about 11 A.M., Heth was told to send Pender's division after Anderson's, which was already across the river, and, leaving one brigade as a rear guard, to follow on. During the preparations, Heth noticed in the open area below his position a small group of cavalrymen who galloped out of some woods, stopped, and faced about, as if expecting an attack. They then galloped to within 175 yards of Heth's men. Generals Heth and J. Johnston Pettigrew as well as Heth's staff assumed by their behavior that they were Confederates.[39]

Heth took a look through his field glasses and realized they were Yankees. He ordered his men to open fire.

It was too late. The commanding Union officer ordered a charge. The Confederate infantry was caught with unloaded weapons and fought with clubbed muskets. Almost all the attackers were killed or captured, but not until Pettigrew, one of the most refined and intelligent men in the Army of Northern Virginia, had been mortally wounded by a pistol shot.[40]

Shortly afterward, a much larger body of dismounted cavalry, backed by artillery, advanced against Heth's line. This attack was repulsed by Brockenbrough's brigade. More troops appeared on Heth's left flank and in his front. It began to look as if Lee's rear guard would be sacrificed. Heth recalled some of Pender's brigades from the river crossing as well as the artillery he had earlier sent across. Instead of the artillery, Heth received orders to pull out as rapidly as he could. He formed a strong battle line to shield his withdrawing men and put them across the river a brigade at a time. The last crossed about midnight, just as the bridges were being cut loose.[41]

The rear-guard was over.

Part Three

THE CONTROVERSY

CHAPTER NINE

Stuart under Attack

"The Battle of Gettysburg in its results was a great victory for the Federal cause, but Lee's army did not feel at all like a beaten one. There was no rout or confusion; not even a pursuit to remind us that our invasion had come to an end, and all the silly stuff we read in the Northern accounts of 'flying rebels' and 'shattered army' are pure fictions prepared for the Northern market."[1]

—W. W. BLACKFORD

"Nothing is more erroneous than the idea that the Southern army was 'demoralized' by the result of the bloody action of these three memorable days. Their nerve was unshaken, their confidence in Lee and themselves unimpaired. Longstreet said truly that he desired nothing better than for General Meade to attack his position—that his men would have given the Federal troops a reception such as they had given Pickett. The stubborn resolution of the Army of Northern Virginia was thus unbroken—but the game was played for the time. The army was moving back, slow and defiant, to the Potomac."[2]

—JOHN ESTEN COOKE

S afely across the Potomac River, full of fight and hope and feeling that they still had not been whipped, the men of the Army of Northern Virginia needed no excuses for their role at the great battle just fought.

Casualties had been horrendous. Some of the high-ranking officers eventually asked why they had to fight at Gettysburg, on the offensive. Some blamed others and at least one blamed Lee.

Though a battle had been lost, the fruits of the campaign were clear: supplies to last, hopefully, through the winter, gathered by troops who spread to the very city line of the capital of one of the largest and most productive Northern states; relief for the farmers of Virginia from having to feed both armies for the summer of 1863; disruption of any thought of a summer campaign by the Federals in the Eastern theater; world recognition as the Confederate invasion carried on through most of the summer, occupying the largest Union army in the East so as to render it incapable of anything more than a minor invasion for the rest of the year.

The invasion had physical width and depth, too: From Imboden's actions near Hancock, Maryland, to Stuart's rattling the gates of Washington and Baltimore, the Confederate army covered and scoured an area encompassing 6,500 square miles. No one seriously thought that this one invasion could have won the war for the Confederacy—at least not in the same way the North was planning to win it. A big victory at Gettysburg would have meant only that the Union army would have fallen back on Washington and the Confederates would have been free to continue the invasion, if they could. Perhaps then, the war would have ended through negotiation. Then again, perhaps Lee, with his lenient invasion policies, would have never been able to force the North into hating war so much that even defeat was preferable. He was no Sherman.

So even if the battle was considered a loss, the campaign could be considered a success, for the Confederate army had accomplished much. Lee was the first to accept blame for the tactical defeat at Gettysburg. But he also realized, even before it had re-crossed the Potomac, that his army was still an effective fighting force. "Though reduced in numbers by the hardships & battles through which it has passed since leaving the Rappahannock," Lee wrote Davis on July 8, "its condition is good and its confidence is unimpaired."[3] Lee also assured Davis that he was not in the least discouraged. On July 12, he wrote, "Had the late unexpected rise [in the Potomac] not occurred there would have been no cause for anxiety. . . . Everything would have been accomplished that could have been reasonably expected. The Army of the Potomac had been thrown north of the river, the forces invading the coasts of North Carolina and Virginia had been diminished, their plan of the present campaign broken up, and, before new arrangements could have been made for its resumption, the summer would have been ended."[4]

The rank and file were immediately disappointed when Lee broke off at Gettysburg and began heading toward the mountains. They expected to fight again, probably within a day or two and perhaps a little farther north. The Hollywood image, in which everyone immediately after the battle heard the death knell of the Confederacy, is not true. There were twenty-two months more of fighting in the East and, tragically, a lot more dying before it was all over.

Years after the battle and the war, regardless of the immediate success of the summer campaign of 1863, Gettysburg was seen as the watershed battle, after which the war became one slow, prolonged retreat for the Confederates.

Although they had made enough mistakes in enough other battles to lose the war, the loss of Gettysburg seemed to require blaming someone.

Lee was untouchable. Though he wished to shoulder all the blame, no one would allow him to. Writers sometimes grew absurd, practically doing backflips on the page to avoid any hint that Lee had erred.

In his postwar writings, Longstreet made the mistake of suggesting that Lee at Gettysburg had lost his "superb equipoise." This comment and statements defending himself from criticism seemed meant to build up his role in the battle while inadvertently pulling down Lee's. This, plus the fact that Longstreet had become a Republican, spelled doom for Lee's "Old War Horse."

Over the years, Longstreet was blamed for everything from disobeying orders during Pickett's Charge to dragging his feet in getting to the battlefield. He was accused of sulkiness for not wishing to make the grand assault on July 3. He was called insubordinate for arguing his case against Lee for maneuver instead of attack on the night of July 1. "If the enemy is there to-morrow," said Lee after the first day's fighting, "we must attack him." "If he is there," replied Longstreet, "it will be because he is anxious that we should attack him—a good reason, in my judgement, for not doing so."[5]

It got very bad for Longstreet when some of Lee's other subordinates, particularly Generals Jubal Early and William N. Pendleton, held that Longstreet had been ordered to attack at sunrise July 2. This was totally false—no such orders were ever given, as Walter Taylor and others of Lee's staff testified in correspondence with Longstreet—but it stuck and is still waggled around by the unsophisticated as a "reason" for Lee's defeat at Gettysburg.

Longstreet, naturally, rose to defend himself in print. In 1877 and 1878 Longstreet published articles in the *Philadelphia Weekly News* and later as reprints in *Annals of the War* called "Lee in Pennsylvania" and "The Mistakes of Gettysburg." Much later, in 1896, Longstreet published *Manassas to Appomattox*, about how he saw the war. Unfortunately, Longstreet had been stung badly by other former Confederates and in defending himself he fired a scattergun of blame, sometimes hitting others, drawing them and then their defenders into the controversy. Though often Longstreet's criticism was inadvertent, ex-Confederates remained sensitive and responded vehemently. Still, through the obviously defensive arguments, many small, accurate historical details can be gleaned from Longstreet's articles and book that reflect on Stuart's role in the campaign.

Stuart was mortally wounded at Yellow Tavern just north of Richmond on May 11, 1864, and died the next day in the city. The controversy over his role in the Gettysburg campaign had already begun, however, almost immediately after he left Lee on his ride around the Union army. At least that is what some of his critics would have us believe.

After the war, others, hungering for a scapegoat to defend Lee or to screen their own inadequacies at Gettysburg, quickly landed on and attempted to devour Stuart. Sadly, the criticism even now is based on a few original premises laid out aggressively as either apologia or scapegoating.

Some took Lee's original comments about Stuart (or "the cavalry") and to Stuart as proof that whatever disaster Gettysburg proved to be, it forever was Stuart's fault. Indeed, the earliest documented criticism of Stuart's role in the campaign came from Lee himself.[6] From Cashtown, about 10 A.M. July 1, came the first documented time that Lee made comments about Stuart that could be taken negatively.[7] This was according to R. H. Anderson, as quoted in Longstreet's article "Lee in Pennsylvania" written in 1877 and published in the *Philadelphia Weekly Times* (and later in *Annals of the War* in 1879).[8] Looking more closely, however, they can be considered not so much criticism as concern. Lee specifically talks, according to Anderson, of Stuart, not necessarily of the cavalry:

> I cannot think of what has become of Stuart; I ought to have heard from him long before now. He may have met with disaster, but I hope not.

Lee made the statement to Anderson after he had heard cannon fire coming from the east as he was crossing the mountains. He had given instructions not to bring on a general engagement and so was perplexed and concerned at just what this prolonged firing meant. At this point in his statement, if it has come down to us verbatim, Lee was talking about Stuart himself.

Lee's genuine affections for his younger subordinate are evident in both his official correspondence and especially in his private letters to his wife, who was also concerned about the young man whom she had hosted at her home at West Point and to whom she had once sent flowers. Especially after Jackson's death just a month and a half before, Lee was concerned for Stuart, off on a dangerous mission, for both personal and professional reasons. Later, others took Anderson's recollection as an indictment of Stuart's absence with his cavalry, but taken at face value, it may not necessarily be that.

Anderson recounted the rest of Lee's comments:

> In the absence of reports from him, I am in ignorance as to what we have in front of us here.

Even if that is exactly what Lee said, it is not entirely true. Lee knew from Harrison, Longstreet's scout, that the Union army had been across the Potomac for at least four days now. Actually it had crossed on June 25, and Harrison may have told Lee that, too. It is inconceivable that Lee thought the Union army was not following him; that is what he wanted. As well, on the night before, A. P. Hill said he had sent him the information gleaned by Pettigrew—that there was cavalry in his front and the sounds of infantry drums behind them at Gettysburg. This had been enough to discourage Pettigrew, with an entire brigade, from pushing too far into the town.[9] Lee also had the information he had sent to Jefferson Davis on June 23 that he had reports that the Union army was preparing to cross the Potomac.

Anderson had Lee continue, sounding more like he was thinking aloud than speaking to a subordinate:

> It may be the whole Federal army, or it may be only a detachment.
> If it is the whole Federal force we must fight a battle here; if we do not
> gain a victory, those defiles and gorges through which we passed this
> morning will shelter us from disaster.

It sounded like Lee was already forming contingency plans, with or without cavalry or a scout to ride ahead and tell him what he was hearing.

Part of the problem that emerges when reading authors attempting to blame Stuart for Gettysburg is that they make Lee sound foolish, as if he were totally ignorant of what had been happening around him the last several days and even of his own orders. The lowliest private knew the Army of the Potomac would be on the move and protective of its territory once the Confederates crossed the Potomac. No one could say that Lee would not have known it, too.

In addition, by the time Lee made this statement, he had been trying for at least two (possibly three) days to concentrate his army. Because of the orders he had issued, he knew that Ewell should have either been approaching Gettysburg or Lee at Cashtown at that very moment.[10] The firing from Gettysburg could have been Ewell running into the Yankees that Lee was told Pettigrew had seen the night before; it could have been elements of Hill's corps moving to Gettysburg from Cashtown. If both cases were true, then they would have been assailing any Union force there from two sides, which was tactically sound. If Ewell were marching to Cashtown and Hill's forces were fighting, Lee knew that they could always break off the engagement and return to Cashtown, where the rest of the army awaited. Lee may have been anxious on the morning of July 1, but he had all the information he needed to understand the reason for the firing in his front, except personal observation. Once he got to Gettysburg in the afternoon, he watched his army driving the Yankees from their positions, which must have pleased him.

Interestingly enough, Longstreet, nearly two decades later, printed the full text of Anderson's letter in his book *From Manassas to Appomattox*.[11] Even more interesting are Longstreet's specific comments on Lee and the cavalry:

> When he [Lee] rode away from me in the forenoon [of July 1, when they parted at Cashtown] he made no mention of his absent cavalry, nor did he indicate that it was not within his call. So I was at a loss to understand his nervous condition.[12]

Later in the day, on the battlefield, Lee was contemplating what to do next. Longstreet said:

> Then it was that I heard of the wanderings of the cavalry and the cause of his uneven temper. So vexed was he at the halt of the Imboden cavalry at Hancock, *in the opening of the campaign* [Longstreet's italics], that he was losing sight of Pickett's brigades as a known quantity for battle.[13]

This is very important, since Longstreet nearly continuously rode with Lee during the campaign. Longstreet, of all people, certainly knew whether Lee was worried or his plans were upset by Stuart's absence.

It also is possible that at times, when he talked about not having information from his cavalry, Lee was wondering of the whereabouts of other cavalry commanders—Robertson, Jones, Imboden, or Jenkins. He knew that Stuart was incommunicado and in great danger. The other cavalry officers were supposed to keep in touch with him.

Even then, an analysis of Lee's communications shows that he *was* in touch with at least some elements of his cavalry virtually daily. Stuart was in contact with Lee on June 22–23 when Lee gave Stuart his orders. Lee wrote that he received information from Stuart twice, at 9 and 10:30 A.M., June 23.[14]

On June 23, Lee also communicated with Imboden, thanking him for sending along livestock, and urging him to continue to gather supplies.[15] This was also the day Lee wrote Davis of the Yankees' preparations to cross the Potomac.[16]

On June 24, Stuart ordered Robertson to report anything of importance to Longstreet via relays through Charles Town. He had no reason to believe Robertson would disobey a direct order to keep in touch with Lee's second in command.

Stuart also said that he sent a courier to Lee on June 25, telling him that the Union army was crossing the Potomac. (Marshall said the messenger never arrived, but Mosby disputed this, since he was travelling within Confederate lines.)

Mosby wrote that on June 26, couriers from the 12th Virginia Cavalry, detached from Jones' brigade and picketing the Potomac west of the Blue Ridge from Harpers Ferry to Shepherdstown, were sent frequently to Lee. Although conspicuously not mentioning Robertson, Mosby says—and most agreed—that there was not a more vigilant outpost officer in the army than old Grumble Jones, whose brigade was on picket in Loudoun County, Virginia, near Leesburg. Mosby found it inconceivable that Jones, if not Robertson, would not have communicated with Lee any valuable information such as the crossing of the Potomac by the Federals.[17]

There is no evidence in the official records that any of Lee's cavalry communicated with him on June 27. Mosby, however, in his book and private writings said that most of the cavalry outposts were in daily contact with Lee.

On the evening of June 28 (if we accept the theory that Venable misdated the June 29 dispatch to read "June 28"), Lee wrote to Ewell that he knew that the Union army had crossed the Potomac and was headed to Frederick, Maryland, via Middletown, Maryland.

At 7 A.M. June 30, Imboden wrote to Lee and Lee responded from Greenwood on July 1. He told Imboden to relieve Pickett at Chambersburg, then move to Greenwood on July 2. He said to "turn off everybody belonging to the army on the road to Gettysburg."

It was revealing that as of early July 1, Lee apparently had no need of cavalry and told Imboden not to rush. He said almost leisurely, "You will at the same time have an opportunity of organizing your troops, refreshing them for a day or two, and getting everything prepared for active operations in the field, for which you will be speedily wanted."[18] He did not order Imboden to him to help find the enemy probably because he had received Hill's message regarding Pettigrew's encounter with the enemy the night before.

Also, before dawn on July 2, the 250 cavalrymen from Hampton's brigade reported to Lee. They were given to Longstreet and told "to explore his ground, watch his flank, and do whatever came to hand." They were relegated to guarding the roads in Longstreet's rear.[19] Even when he had cavalry in hand, Lee did not seem to need it.

That Lee needed cavalry or information before he spoke to Anderson between 10 A.M. and noon July 1 at Cashtown is not evident in any of the extant communications between Lee and his other generals, even his cavalry officers. He may have needed a few cavalrymen right at that moment on July 1, to ride ahead and tell him who had gotten into a fight when he had issued orders against it. In fact, Lee did it himself.

Two of the documents used for years to impugn Stuart's role in the campaign were Lee's official reports published in the *Official Records*. They should have resolved all the arguments. Unfortunately, they only added to the confusion.

Lee's official reports were written by Colonel Charles Marshall, Lee's military secretary, after he had collected the reports from other officers. Although eventually approved and signed by Lee, the reports still reflect some of Marshall's bias against Stuart. Lee's reports, dated July 31, 1863, and January 1864, were not as definitive as possible. At least one Stuart defender claimed that he believed Lee did not even read the final drafts before signing them.

The first report should have been the freshest, but it was often sketchy. Marshall acknowledged in the report that not all subordinates had submitted their reports when he wrote it and that this report was an "outline" of recent operations. Checking the dates on the campaign reports, almost half came in after Marshall wrote Lee's first account.

Lee's reports did not castigate or overemphasize the role of the cavalry over any other branch. Marshall did misinterpret what some of Lee's orders were to the cavalry when making the reports. Comparing Lee's original orders to Stuart with the final report showed these discrepancies. Unfortunately, many writers chose to ignore what Lee ordered Stuart to do and used instead what Marshall reported he was supposed to do.

For example, in Lee's July 31 report, Marshall summarized Stuart's orders like this:

> [On June 17] General Stuart was left to guard the passes of the mountains and observe the movements of the enemy, whom he was instructed to harass and impede as much as possible, should he attempt to cross the Potomac. In that event, General Stuart was directed to move into Maryland, crossing the Potomac east or west of the Blue Ridge, as, in his judgment, should be best, and take position on the right of our column as it advanced.[20]

This only referred to Stuart's orders of June 22, which included only that he should move into Maryland and ride on to Ewell's right.[21] These orders implied that Stuart would be going into Maryland and necessarily around the Union army whether it was south or north of the Potomac. Nothing was said about crossing the Potomac east or west of the Blue Ridge.

Marshall mixed in Stuart's orders of June 23, which allowed him to judge only whether he could pass around the Union army without hindrance. There was no judgment involved, however, when Lee told Stuart where to cross the river in the June 23 orders: "If General Hooker's army remains inactive, you can leave two brigades to watch him, and withdraw with the three others, but should he not appear to be moving northward, I think you had better withdraw this side of the mountain to-morrow night, cross at Shepherdstown next day, and move on to Fredericktown." Shepherdstown is west of the mountains. Lee's orders left no discretion to Stuart as to where to cross if he found the enemy not moving northward.

Lee may have caught this in the first report, because by the time Marshall composed the second in January 1864, he wrote:

> General Stuart was directed to hold the mountain passes with part of his command as long as the enemy remained south of the Potomac, and, with the remainder, to cross into Maryland, and place himself on the right of General Ewell. Upon the suggestion of the former officer that he could damage the enemy and delay his passage of the river by getting in his rear, he was authorized to do so, and it was left up to his discretion whether to enter Maryland east or west of the Blue Ridge; but he was instructed to lose no time in placing his command on the right of our column as soon as he should perceive the enemy moving northward.[22]

More information emerged from this account. It was Stuart's suggestion, advanced after the fighting at Upperville on June 22, that he get in the rear of the enemy; and he was authorized to do so. (This we also know from Lee's and Longstreet's orders.) But Marshall repeated his mistake about the discretion left to Stuart about where to cross the Potomac. In Lee's orders, the only judgment was in whether to pass around the rear of the enemy and that depended on Union movements. As well, a speed factor was inserted for the first time: Stuart was to "lose no time" in reaching Ewell. There was no mention of how quickly Stuart should move in any of Lee's published orders. So where did this emphasis on speed or rapidity of movement come from? Perhaps by the time Marshall wrote Lee's second report, he had heard it from Lee. It was a main point in McClellan's "missing dispatch" from Lee to Stuart.

In his first report, Marshall said that no word had been received by June 27 that the enemy had crossed the Potomac, "and the absence of cavalry rendered it impossible to obtain accurate information." The three brigades under Stuart were not needed for this; it was Robertson's job. Also, other cavalry and advanced infantry units had been in virtual daily communication with Lee; a detached company of cavalry could have done it; and one spy, Harrison, apparently did it and reported to Lee the next day that the Union army had crossed, information that Lee had suspected from June 23.

Later on in this first report, Marshall said:

> General Stuart continued to follow the movements of the Federal

Army south of the Potomac after our own had entered Maryland, and, in his efforts to impede its progress, advanced as far eastward as Fairfax Courthouse. Finding himself unable to delay the enemy materially, he crossed the river at Seneca, and marched through Westminster to Carlisle, where he arrived after General Ewell had left for Gettysburg. By the route he pursued, the Federal Army was interposed between his command and our main body, preventing any communication with him until his arrival at Carlisle. The march toward Gettysburg was conducted more slowly than it would have been had the movements of the Federal Army been known.[23]

This paragraph, seemingly innocuous, was later used by Marshall and others to prove that Stuart had blundered into a position where he could not fulfill Lee's orders. If Stuart had been authorized to go around the Union army, how else could he have done it but by putting it between him and the main body of the Army of Northern Virginia?

Marshall also implied in the first report that Stuart and the lack of information on the enemy were the cause for the slow march to Gettysburg. He also implied that Gettysburg was an objective. It seemed as if Lee caught that in his editing, too, because in the second report Marshall wrote nothing about Gettysburg being an objective and substituted the real reason for the slow march: "The weather being inclement, the march was conducted with a view to the comfort of the troops."[24]

Another reason for the slow march was because Lee spent time in Chambersburg, Pennsylvania, which his troops used as a depot to send supplies from Pennsylvania back into Virginia. The Confederates also were destroying much public property. This took time, and Chambersburg, at the northern access to the Shenandoah Valley, was a good place for Lee to establish himself.

In the remainder of the first report, the only things Marshall wrote about Stuart were the news of his arriving at Carlisle on July 1 and his driving off of enemy cavalry on July 6 during the retreat.

In his second report, Marshall said that the absence of cavalry made it "impossible to ascertain the enemy's intentions."[25] By military logic, Union intentions certainly would have included following and watching the invaders.

Marshall had received Stuart's report by August 20, 1863. After reading it and including what may have been Lee's corrections from the July report, Marshall wrote in the second report:

The movements of the army preceding the battle of Gettysburg
had been much embarrassed by the absence of cavalry. As soon as it

was known that the enemy had crossed into Maryland, orders were sent to the brigades of [B. H.] Robertson and [William E.] Jones, which had been left to guard the passes of the Blue Ridge, to rejoin the army without delay, and it was expected that General Stuart, with the remainder of the command would soon arrive. In the exercise of discretion given him when Longstreet and Hill marched into Maryland, General Stuart determined to pass around the rear of the Federal Army with three brigades and cross the Potomac between it and Washington, believing that he would be able, by that route, to place himself on our right flank in time to keep us properly advised of the enemy's movements.[26]

Marshall then narrated Stuart's movements, again mentioning the circumstances of the Union army "interposing itself" between Stuart and the main army throughout his movement northward. If Stuart's objective had been to connect with Lee and the main body, this would have mattered; but Stuart was ordered to connect with Ewell or Early, whom he knew were farther north, not west. Marshall's implication was clear: Stuart's misjudgment somehow affected Lee's campaign.

Many writers took Marshall's words as Lee's, since they were over Lee's signature. Lee certainly read them, but there were key phrases left in both reports that writers and historians seized upon as irrefutable evidence of Lee's indictment of Stuart. Mosby often took issue with former Confederates who used Marshall's words as Lee's. He even wrote that he did not believe Lee ever read the reports.

Lee's aversion to army paperwork was well known. Walter Taylor, Lee's adjutant general, wrote in 1877, "He had a great dislike to reviewing army communications: this was so thoroughly appreciated by me that I would never present a paper for his action, unless it was of decided importance, and of a nature to demand his judgement and decision."[27] The editor of Marshall's papers repeated this story,[28] so perhaps Mosby had a point.

Still, it is unlikely that Lee failed to read any of either report. It is possible that he read the first one, corrected some of Marshall's prejudices, read and edited at least the first half of the second report, and perhaps made minor revisions in the last half.

Some changes in the second report softened Marshall's prejudices against Stuart; perhaps these reflected Lee's editing. The first half of the second report showed these, but the apparent indictment of Stuart came in the second half. Lee did not edit out the part that said Confederate movements into the North were embarrassed by the absence of cavalry.

Why did Lee leave this in? Probably because Marshall, in the very next sentence, began to talk about Robertson and Jones, whose absence *did* embarrass Lee's movements. Lee was known for his subtle way of castigating officers who failed him. Perhaps this was his way of doing so.

There was another brother officer who blamed Stuart for the defeat at Gettysburg by using Lee's alleged statements. Perhaps his indictments were the most long-lasting, because variations recur and resurface in Civil War literature and films. Yet a careful analysis of the writings of Major General Henry Heth, and the words he put into Lee's mouth, show how much can be relegated to fiction masquerading as fact about the battle.

The accounts of Lee constantly fretting about his cavalry that pop up even in contemporary histories came mainly from Heth's article "Causes of Lee's Defeat at Gettysburg," published in the *Southern Historical Society Papers* in July 1877. The papers were the voice of the society, which was mostly made up of former Confederates and had been organized in 1869 to gather and preserve the scattered records of the South and the war period. Organized in New Orleans, the society stagnated under its original leadership. It was revitalized in 1873 and moved to Richmond under the guidance of Jubal Early, back from his self-imposed exile in Canada.

Most writers over the years that the papers were published recollected events to the best of their knowledge; some, like Heth, only added to the confusion by advancing opinions for their own purposes. In his article (which answered questions posed by the Comte de Paris for his upcoming book), the former division commander in Hill's corps first listed all the "whethers" that were popular at the time: whether Stonewall Jackson's presence would have made a difference; whether Longstreet's delays made a difference; whether the attacks were uncoordinated; whether Pickett's Charge should have been made at all. He says they all "sink into insignificance" compared with what he thought was the "*great cause* which brought about the failure of the Pennsylvania Campaign."

Conjuring up for his support the rest of the several hundred officers in the army—whether they agreed or not—"in the opinion of almost all the officers of the Army of Northern Virginia, [the reason for defeat] can be expressed in five words—*the absence of our cavalry.*"[29]

The drama of his italics notwithstanding, it was an incredible statement, unfortunately for Heth, "full of sound and fury, signifying nothing." He had already contradicted himself, having just a few lines above his statement quoted Lee from immediately after the campaign: "And sir, we did whip them at Gettysburg, and it will be seen for the next six months that *that army* will be as quiet as a sucking dove."

Heth then hyperbolized the parable about how a giant can be beaten by a pygmy if you first put out the giant's eyes. This gave the impression that Stuart left Lee blind, without any cavalry whatsoever. This is clearly misleading and false.

Heth went on to fictionalize Lee's orders to Stuart, not once mentioning Lee's real instructions to ride around the rear of the enemy: "Before Ewell crossed the Potomac General Lee wrote to General Stuart, commanding the cavalry, in substance, as follows." Then he placed in quotation marks, as if it were a direct statement from Lee, his idea of Lee's orders. That is, that Stuart was told that after Longstreet had left the gaps in the mountains, Stuart was to hold them and protect Longstreet's crossing of the Potomac; that Stuart was to follow Longstreet, throw himself on the right flank of the army, watch the enemy, give Lee all the information he could gather, and collect supplies. Lee's orders to Stuart on June 22–23 bear little resemblance to this, which, by amazing coincidence, fits right into Heth's argument that Stuart was disobedient. Heth reflected much of Marshall's reports, which may be where he got his ideas.[30]

Heth brought Stuart's cavalry to the battlefield *late in the evening of July second*" and said, "So far as deriving any assistance from his cavalry . . . it might as well have had no existence." He did a remarkable job of trivializing Stuart's threatening of Washington, the capture of the wagon trains, the disruption of communications and supplies in the rear of the Union army, the battles at Rockville, Westminster, Hanover, and Hunterstown, and the immobilizing of two Yankee brigades, artillery, and cavalry in Lee's rear at Carlisle.

Worse, he stretched an iota of truth in trying to convince his readers how desperate Lee was for his cavalry. Without naming a single one, he went on to say that:

> Every officer who conversed with General Lee for several days previous to the Battle of Gettysburg, well remembers having heard such expressions as these: "Can you tell me where General Stuart is?" "Where on earth is my cavalry?" "What is the enemy going to do?" "If the enemy does not find us, we must try and find him, in the absence of our cavalry, as best we can!"[31]

Strangely enough, of all the staff and combat officers around Lee, only one gave a specific date or quote where he asked about his cavalry or about Stuart, until Longstreet told Anderson's story from the morning of July 1.[32]

Walter Taylor also wrote nothing of any harping on Stuart's whereabouts. He said the absence of the cavalry was "seriously felt" by Lee, but then included the common misinterpretations of Lee's orders to Stuart. Writing in his book in 1877, Taylor never once quoted Lee directly or mentioned Lee's asking daily about his cavalry:

> With the exception of the cavalry, the army was well in hand. The absence of that indispensable arm of the service was most seriously felt by General Lee. He had directed General Stuart to use his discretion as to where and when to cross the river—that is, he was to cross east of the mountains, or retire through the mountain-passes into the Valley and cross in the immediate rear of the infantry, as the movements of the enemy and his own judgement should determine—but he was to maintain communication with the main column, and especially directed to keep the commanding general informed of the movements of the Federal army.[33]

Taylor misinterpreted Lee's orders as to what Stuart was to do. In no written orders was he "especially directed to keep the commanding general informed of the movements of the Federal army." That was left up to the cavalry Stuart left behind.

Colonel A. L. Long, military secretary and biographer of Lee, wrote in his 1886 biography of Lee that once Lee and his staff reached Cashtown he "now exhibited a degree of anxiety and impatience, and expressed regret at the absence of cavalry. He said that he had been kept in the dark ever since crossing the Potomac, and intimated that Stuart's disappearance had materially hampered the movements and disorganized the plans of the campaign."[34] Long would have seen Lee frequently during the campaign. Yet, it was when they were at Cashtown on July 1 that Long first said that Lee "intimates" anything about Stuart's absence. Long's statement that Lee had been kept in the dark since crossing the Potomac is questionable; it certainly does not fit with the published records of cavalry communications with Lee between June 23 and July 1. Long also did not quote Lee personally, but used information heard from somewhere else—perhaps Longstreet's article of years before.

Even Marshall, who was with Lee daily, mentioned nothing specific about Lee's wondering continually about Stuart. The closest he came was to mention that Lee was apprehensive about whether the Union army had followed them north. While Lee was at Chambersburg between June 27 and June 29, Marshall "heard General Lee express this apprehension [that the Union army had not followed him] more than once while we lay at Chambersburg, and the apprehension was due entirely to his hearing nothing from Stuart."[35]

If Marshall had said Lee's apprehension was caused by not hearing from his cavalry—instead of "Stuart"—it would be more correct. By June 27, it was no longer Stuart's responsibility to inform Lee of the movements of the Union army, but Robertson's.

So, in spite of what Heth wrote about "every" officer, he named none and only one can be found among those who were with Lee daily that said he asked about Stuart before 10 A.M. July 1, at the earliest. Later, however, some of the officers with points to prove forced themselves to dovetail into Heth's claim.

Yet, in fairness, Heth's story has some believable elements. The question must be asked whether Lee was expressing concern about Stuart the individual or about his arm of the service. Were Lee's comments about Stuart confused by others with his lack of specific, immediate intelligence on July 1?

Heth may have sought to cast blame on Stuart to cover his own actions, which, in direct conflict with Lee's orders, brought on the Battle of Gettysburg. Heth wrote that Lee intended to strike the enemy at "the very first available opportunity that offered." After all the careful planning before and during the campaign, Heth threw it out the window and asserted Lee did not act out of strategic or tactical consideration but because suddenly he "was the most aggressive man in his army." How could any of Lee's former officers dared to have disputed this just seven years after the death of Lee, one of the most beloved men in the South at that time, without drawing wrath upon himself?

Heth's argument went on to say that the Battle of Gettysburg "was the result purely of *an accident*," and then manfully admitted, "for which I am probably, more than any one else, accountable." Heth thereby made himself merely Lee's alter ego. He went on to tell the fabulous shoe story, that the cause of the battle was barefoot Confederates looking for shoes. It so easily ties it all together and appeals to all. But Heth had to know that Confederate advanced forces had gone through the area days before, picking it clean.

In his later years, Heth wrote two versions of his conversation with his commander, A. P. Hill, the night before going into Gettysburg looking for nonexistent shoes. In 1877, in his *Southern Historical Society Papers* article, he had himself tell Hill what General Pettigrew had just told him about Yankee forces near Gettysburg. Heth had Hill reply, "The only force at Gettysburg is cavalry, probably a detachment of observation. I am just from General Lee, and the information he has from his scouts corroborates that I have received from mine—that is, the enemy are still at Middleburg, and have not yet struck their tents." Heth then asked if there were no objections to his going on to Gettysburg to find shoes, to which Hill replied, "None in the world."

Pettigrew, who was standing there, was incredulous. He called in Lieutenant Louis G. Young, one of his scouts. Young said the troops he had seen were seasoned, not just the militia that had been driven from Gettysburg by Early a few days before. Hill only said that if it were the Army of the Potomac, it was all right, because that is right where he wanted it to be.

Pettigrew even went to Brigadier General James J. Archer, who led the march the next day, and told him what he had discovered toward Gettysburg, describing the terrain, roads, and the enemy's threatening presence. Archer heard him but, like Hill, refused to believe it.[36]

In his *Memoirs* in 1897, Heth wrote that neither he nor Hill believed, in spite of what Pettigrew and Young had just told them, that there was infantry in Gettysburg or even a significant cavalry force. This is a repeat of the 1877 story, putting words in the mouth of the dead Hill that sanctioned Heth's march to Gettysburg. In 1897, he had Hill answer, in response to his question about going to Gettysburg, "Do so."[37] Not only do the stories make Hill look bad, ignoring fresh intelligence for stale, but they contradict Hill's and Heth's own official reports on the matter.

Hill's report of the battle, submitted in November 1863, said that there was a force in Gettysburg, principally cavalry, but in unknown numbers, calling for caution.[38] He mentioned nothing about shoes or about scouts telling him of the alleged Union position in Middleburg. He did say he sent word to Lee of Pettigrew's information on the Union cavalry.

Heth's report of the battle, dated September 13, 1863, said, "On reaching the suburbs of Gettysburg, General Pettigrew found a large force of cavalry near the town, supported by an infantry force." Heth mentioned Pettigrew going into town "for army supplies (shoes especially)" but never again mentioned shoes as his reason for going into Gettysburg. He did say that he "was ordered to move at 5 A.M. in the direction of Gettysburg. On nearing Gettysburg, it was evident that the enemy was in the vicinity of the town in some force."[39] This could not have been a surprise, however, after Pettigrew's report of the same thing the night before.

The closer Heth got to Gettysburg, the clearer it became that more Union troops were being brought up. After feeling out the enemy with two brigades, and according to Lee's expressed wishes not to bring on a general engagement, Heth should have backed off. He said in the report that because of the lack of his own cavalry, he was ignorant of what force was before him, but later realized that it was cavalry, infantry, and artillery. Precisely because of the lack of Confederate cavalry, he should have disengaged. Mosby later wrote, "The absence of cavalry (if they had no cavalry) was no reason for Heth's going there [to Gettysburg] on a raid; it might have been a good reason for his staying in camp."[40]

In *Four Years with General Lee,* Taylor wrote, "Instructions had been sent to General Heth to ascertain what force was at Gettysburg, and, if he found infantry opposed to him, to report the fact immediately, without forcing an engagement."[41] It sounded as if Lee issued those orders directly to Heth, but it could have gotten back to Taylor that Hill had done so. Either way, they would have gone through Hill. Nevertheless, Hill, Heth, and Pettigrew all knew of Lee's orders not to force an engagement. Only Pettigrew obeyed them.

No wonder Lee looked and acted anxious when he crossed the mountains and heard firing. At that particular moment, it would have been helpful to have a few cavalrymen. Instead, Lee rode ahead to investigate himself. By the time he got to Gettysburg, Heth and Hill had gotten him entangled in a large battle that, fortunately, they were winning. That made Lee change his attitude. He then plunged into battle.

Could Stuart have brought Hill or Heth any more information than they had gotten from Pettigrew? Would Hill or Heth have listened any more closely to Stuart than they did to Lee?

Addressing Heth's dramatic claim that "the failure to crush the Federal army in Pennsylvania can be expressed in five words—the absence of our cavalry," Mosby retorted, "I would rather say it was due to the presence of Heth."[42]

Sadly, Heth's information, including his indictment of Stuart, went on to the Comte de Paris and became part of his history. Mosby considered Heth's story, which the Comte de Paris believed, to be the origin of the Comte's criticism of Stuart. It has also led to countless other criticisms.

The questionnaire sent by the Comte de Paris also gave Jubal Early an opportunity in the *Southern Historical Society Papers* to manipulate answers and mix them skillfully with Longstreet's articles from the *Philadelphia Weekly* in order to make Longstreet look bad. Early defended Stuart's role in the Gettysburg campaign, according to at least one historian, in order to align Stuart with Lee. This supposedly was an attempt to eliminate one more scapegoat so that the full blame for Gettysburg could drop on Longstreet.[43]

Early wrote:

> I have never thought that our failure at Gettysburg was due to the absence of Stuart's cavalry, though I can well understand the perplexity and annoyance it caused General Lee before the enemy was found. He was found, however, without the aid of cavalry, and when found, though by accident, he furnished us the opportunity to strike him a fatal blow. When Hooker was crossing the Potomac at Edward's Ferry, it was simply impossible for Stuart to cross that stream between that point and Harper's Ferry, as Hooker was keeping up his communications with that place, and the interval was narrow. Stuart's only alternatives, therefore, were to cross west of the Blue Ridge, at

Shepherdstown or Williamsport, or east of Hooker's Crossing. He selected the latter in accordance with the discretion given him; and it is doubtful whether the former would have enabled him to fulfill General Lee's expectations.

Early then described the position of all the Union corps. They effectively covered the area between below Harpers Ferry and Middletown, Maryland, seizing the gaps in South Mountain. He continued:

> It is difficult, therefore, to perceive of what more avail in ascertaining and reporting the movements of the Federal army Stuart's cavalry could have been if it had moved on the west of South Mountain, than individual scouts employed for that purpose, while it is very certain that his movement on the other flank greatly perplexed and bewildered the Federal commanders, and compelled them to move slower. It is not improbable, however, that it would have been better for him to hurry on, and not meddle with the wagon train he captured—but, then the temptation was so great to a poor Confederate.[44]

Regardless of his motives, Early brought up a good point: As the Potomac River and the Blue Ridge converge at Harpers Ferry, the space between them narrows. Not only would it have been more difficult for three extra brigades of cavalry to operate in an ever-shrinking field, but such a mass would have been wasted there, where a small force could gather all the information Lee needed. This point also was made by Lee in the sealed dispatch Stuart received on June 23, according to H. B. McClellan.

A final question is, why did Lee not have a cavalry escort attached to his headquarters? Meade and each of his corps commanders but two had several companies or more of cavalry accompanying them. Ewell had a company of cavalry with his headquarters.[45] Lee disliked a large staff, but a few troopers at his disposal could have supplied all the information Stuart and his three brigades could have provided after the fighting along the Blue Ridge. A cavalry escort could have investigated the firing he heard early on July 1.

Apparently, Lee felt no need to have cavalry attached to him. Until he heard Heth's guns echoing from the east, Lee was calm, poised, and in no hurry to get specifically to Gettysburg.[46] He was getting as much information as he thought he needed; Confederate cavalry was roaming all around. Union cavalry division commander John Buford wrote as much to both Pleasonton and the I Corps commander, Major General John F. Reynolds, on June 30.[47]

Several other former Confederates also answered the questions posed by the Comte de Paris in the same issue of the *Southern Historical Society Papers.* Never mentioning Stuart or his cavalry were Colonel William Allen (on April 26, 1877) and E. P. Alexander (on March 17, 1877), both of whom were with Lee and the main Confederate army on its summer 1863 invasion. Confederate General John B. Hood, who also marched with the main Confederate army on the campaign, in a letter to Longstreet dated June 28, 1875, as well said nothing about needing cavalry; he used his "picked Texas scouts" for reconnaissance.[48]

Though the Comte de Paris asked several specific questions, none on cavalry, some respondents could not help but include "the absence of cavalry" as a cause for Lee's defeat at Gettysburg. On March 5, 1877, Fitzhugh Lee listed this as the main reason for the overall failure of the 1863 summer campaign. He wrote that it was "evident that General Stuart was ordered to give information of the enemy's crossing the Potomac, or why did General Lee loiter after crossing his army and wait to hear from him? Without orders it was his duty to do so as commander of his cavalry." It is not known for sure why Lee loitered; because of the hot weather or possibly to allow his advanced forces more time to gather supplies, which was the main reason for the invasion anyway. That he halted to wait for word from Stuart is mere speculation on Fitz Lee's part, since Robert E. Lee knew where Stuart would be according to his orders. Stuart was not "without orders," so that part of Fitz Lee's statement may be ignored.

Fitz Lee went on to give some revealing information about Stuart and the Federal crossing of the river:

> Knowing as I do Stuart's strict attention to forwarding all species of information, I am bound to believe he did not fail to send the notice of this important fact. It may have miscarried. It has been charged that Stuart disobeyed orders in crossing his command at a lower point on the Potomac than that at which the Federals crossed, and making the circuit which interposed the army of the enemy between his command and the force of General Lee. I deny that.

Fitz Lee was right in that Stuart sent information—Stuart said in his official report that he sent a courier to Lee on June 25. He also talked about the discretion given Stuart, but took the quote from Robert E. Lee's report, written by Marshall.

Cadmus Wilcox, a brigade commander in Hill's corps, wrote in the March 26, 1877, issue of the *Southern Historical Society Papers:*

> He [Stuart] was instructed to place his command on the right of our army as soon as the Federals should cross the river and move

north, and ordered to lose no time in doing so, and he was expected to give notice as soon as Hooker crossed the Potomac. As no report had been made it was believed that Hooker was still in Virginia, and, under this impression, orders were issued to move on Harrisburg. . . .

Without his cavalry, General Lee could not divine the purpose of the enemy, but he determined, with the view of guarding his communications with Virginia and to check the advance west, to concentrate his forces east of the mountains. . . .

Had the cavalry been with the army Hill would have known the condition of affairs in his front [on July 1] and would have pushed Buford back and reached Gettysburg before the [Federals'] First and Eleventh Corps moved from their camp at Emmettsburg [sic].

All these "revelations" about Stuart's absence began to sound much alike, probably because the writers were using Lee's official report put together by Marshall.

A. L. Long, the one-time staff officer of Lee's, wrote in April 1877, answering the Comte de Paris' questionnaire:

While preparing for his campaign in Pennsylvania General Lee carefully considered every contingency that could mar success, except the possibility of tactical blunders of those who had always maintained his confidence by a prompt and intelligent execution of instructions. When, however, he had crossed the Potomac, the absence of his cavalry, caused by the fatal blunder of Stuart, which separated it from the army at the most critical time, obliged him to grope his way in the dark, and precipitated him, by the want of timely notice, into a premature engagement with the enemy.[49]

Long, even though on Lee's staff, apparently had not read Lee's orders to Stuart when he wrote this. As was shown earlier, it was Heth who, after he knew the enemy was in Gettysburg, began the fight and continued it in spite of orders not to bring on a general engagement. And Stuart's "fatal blunder"—as Long called it—was that he was following Lee's orders.

Walter Taylor, also formerly of Lee's staff, in an undated "memorandum" appearing in the same issue of the *Southern Historical Society Papers* (and so written before July 1877) wrote:

The first great disadvantage experienced by General Lee was the unexpected absence of his cavalry. Certain discretionary power had to be left with General Stuart as to where he would cross the Potomac. It was arranged that the movements of the enemy and his own judgement should determine this, but he was to connect at once with General Lee, keep on his flank, and advise him of the enemy's movements.

Taylor apparently confused Lee's orders with Marshall's report. Stuart was not to "connect at once with General Lee, keep on his flank, and advise him of the enemy's movements." It was Ewell (or Early) that Stuart was supposed to contact, either in Emmitsburg or farther north and east. Taylor continued:

> After crossing the river General Stuart consumed some time in pursuing and capturing a train of wagons, and when he turned to join the main column of the army, he found that General Hooker had interposed between him and General Lee, and so was compelled to make the circuit of the Federal army.

Stuart was ordered to gather supplies, and the Union army wagon train at the time was a godsend; he never turned to join the main army not because the Federals interposed, but because his orders told him that once across the river he was to go to Ewell's right. Taylor made it sound, by his misinterpretation of Lee's orders, that Stuart disobeyed them, a very serious charge considering Taylor's station in the army.

Taylor published another article in the *Southern Historical Society Papers* that is nearly a verbatim copy of the Gettysburg section of his book, *Four Years with General Lee.* Once again, he implied that Stuart was to keep Lee informed of the movements of the enemy—a clear impossibility if Stuart was incommunicado on the other side of the Federal army. The most unfortunate part about Taylor and Long writing either without reading Lee's orders to Stuart or misinterpreting them (willfully or inadvertently) was that, because of their positions on Lee's staff, their words were taken as documented evidence. Others would pick up on their statements, including the Comte de Paris and numerous readers of the *Southern Historical Society Papers,* and believe they had the key to Lee's defeat at Gettysburg.

CHAPTER TEN

Mosby Parries

"Upon the suggestion . . . that he [Stuart] could damage the enemy and delay his passage of the river by getting in his rear, he was authorized to do so."
—CHARLES MARSHALL IN R. E. LEE'S SECOND REPORT
OF THE GETTYSBURG CAMPAIGN

In December 1877, in the *Philadelphia Weekly Times,* John S. Mosby began to defend Stuart. He wrote that he had submitted a plan to Stuart on June 23, 1863, to cross the Bull Run Mountains through Glasscock's Gap and cut through Hooker's army in Loudoun and Fairfax counties in order to cross the Potomac at Seneca Ford. Since Stuart's role in the Gettysburg campaign was beginning to be questioned by this time, Mosby's admission was courageous and also probably true. Why would he intentionally draw attention to himself for a plan that others were attacking? Probably because Mosby insisted upon the truth being told.[1]

Lee's and Longstreet's orders to Stuart around June 22–25 showed that Mosby's suggestion on June 23 came after Stuart had already thought of it and discussed it with Lee. Mosby no doubt solidified in Stuart's mind the idea of riding around the enemy. Mosby's article in the *Weekly Times* allied him with Stuart and forthcoming articles and books showed what a powerful advocate Mosby was.

From 1877–79, Longstreet became embroiled with defending himself in print. This included an analysis of Stuart's role. Sadly, Longstreet used Lee's first official report to represent Lee's orders to Stuart. They were not orders, of course, and represented more of Marshall's opinion than Lee would allow in the second report.

Longstreet wrote that Lee had lost his "superb equipoise" because of Stuart's absence.[2] "General Stuart should not have been permitted to leave the general line of march, thus forcing us to march blindfolded into the enemy's country; to this may be attributed, in my opinion, the change of policy of the campaign." (Longstreet was referring to his claiming that Lee had told him he wanted to conduct a campaign that strategically was offensive but tactically defensive.) Perhaps the oddest thing about Longstreet's statement—Mosby caught it—was that he condemned Stuart for doing what Longstreet himself saw the value in, and encouraged, if not ordered, in his letter to Stuart on June 22. Others picked up that Longstreet seemed to condemn Lee for permitting Stuart discretion. This also gave ammunition to Longstreet's critics over the years.

Embroiling himself further, Longstreet quoted a letter Lee allegedly wrote to him in January 1864 in which he deplored not taking Longstreet's advice at Gettysburg. Later, Longstreet wrote about Lee's sudden decision to attack after the successes of July 1: "I cannot see, as has been claimed, why the absence of General Lee's cavalry should have justified his attack on the enemy. On the contrary, while they may have perplexed him, I hold that it was additional reason for his not hazarding an attack. At the time the attack was ordered, we were fearful that our cavalry had been destroyed."[3]

In 1880, Stuart's aide, Henry B. McClellan, gave a speech that was reprinted in the *Southern Historical Society Papers.*[4] McClellan first described the letter he received from Lee containing orders to Stuart on June 23. He gave several pieces of vital, previously overlooked data; the letter informed Stuart that Early would move upon York, Pennsylvania, and that Stuart should ride as quickly as possible to meet him. It told Stuart that the roads north from Williamsport and Shepherdstown were clogged with Confederate troops and in order to lessen the delay, Stuart should pass around the enemy's rear.

This is the letter McClellan indicated in his 1885 memoir that was subsequently lost. Again, it does not seem to be the same letter that appears in the *Official Records* as Lee's second order, dated June 23. McClellan has just too much information in it, including adding that this letter "further informed him [Stuart] that if he chose the latter route General Early would receive instructions to look out for him, and endeavor to communicate with him; and York, Pennsylvania, was designated as the point in the vicinity of which he was expected to hear from Early, and as the possible, if not probable, point of concentration of the army."[5] None of this appears in Stuart's published orders.

McClellan said that the tenor of the letter approved of Stuart's movement around the enemy and that the decision was up to Stuart.

Early wrote that the only communication he received from Lee was through Ewell on the night of June 29, along with verbal instructions to rejoin the rest of the army on the west side of South Mountain.[6] Perhaps that courier of Stuart's who Marshall claimed did not get through on June 25 rode to tell Lee that the Union army was crossing the Potomac and that Stuart was riding around the Union army. According to McClellan's recollection, Lee would have sent Early information, if Stuart rode around the Union army, to communicate with and meet him. Records show Lee never sent any such communication to Early and Early marched to York, then back to the army, never looking for Stuart.[7] Evidently Marshall was right: Stuart's courier never arrived.

McClellan repeated that Stuart left Jones', Robertson's, and Jenkins' cavalry with Lee and was "certainly justified in considering it sufficient to fulfill every duty which might be required by the commanding General from the cavalry." McClellan narrated a short version of the cavalry's trials moving through Maryland and Pennsylvania and said that, in spite of the information Stuart had that Early was going to communicate with him, he had heard nothing for six days, except what he had read in Northern newspapers. "From these he learned that General Early was in York, Pennsylvania; and every other item of news which he could gain led him to think that General Lee's plans were being carried out as originally proposed, and that the concentration of our army would take place in the vicinity of York, Pennsylvania, or at some point north of it on the Susquehanna." Next, McClellan wrote:

> He [Stuart] was now within striking distance of York, and anxiously expected, in accordance with General Lee's letter of instructions, that he would receive some word from Early. But for some reason, which will probably never be explained, the order to endeavor to communicate with Stuart had never reached General Early, nor did he have any knowledge whatever of Stuart's proposed movement around the enemy's rear.[8]

That Early never received word from Lee to watch for Stuart can probably be traced back to that missing courier. Yet, one would think that with three more days before he was to cross the Potomac, Stuart would have communicated with Lee again about the enemy's movements. Perhaps Stuart was relying on Robertson and Jones to report. They obviously did not.

With what he knew of the orders and the final letter Lee sent to Stuart, McClellan wanted the blame to fall on Lee, where it belonged. He still assumed that critics would refer to Lee's orders, not the reports, and see that Stuart was merely doing as he was told.

McClellan also suggested that critics must show how Stuart's presence with the army would have helped win the battle or made the campaign successful. The point here was interesting. Those who wanted to blame Stuart's absence for the loss

of Gettysburg forgot that Lee was winning the battle before Stuart arrived. After
Stuart showed up, Lee fought one more day and retreated. The logic was that it was
not Stuart's absence that cost the battle, but his presence, which clearly is absurd.

McClellan said that Robertson and Jones, both experienced, senior officers,
were left with full instructions. McClellan wrote and laid to rest a major argument
as to whose fault it was that Lee moved blind (if one is to concede that point):

> There can be no reasonable ground for supposing that this com-
> mand [Robertson and Jones], which was in daily and almost hourly
> communication with the commanding General, could not have
> learned everything concerning the enemy's movements which Stuart
> could have discovered in the same place; and had these brigades
> been moved northward on the 26th of June, they would have reached
> such position on the 28th as to have stopped Buford's march, and
> would have so occupied him as to have prevented him from reach-
> ing Gettysburg on the 30th.[9]

Many of these same points were developed more fully in McClellan's 1885
memoirs. He conceded that the sealed letter from Lee to Stuart he delivered on the
night of June 23 had been lost. McClellan regretted this but assured readers[10] "I
have many times had occasion to recall its contents." It is unfortunate the letter
has never been found because it makes McClellan sound as if he made it up to
defend Stuart.[11] McClellan, however, was too highly regarded a historian to invent
something, especially with so many of Stuart's critics still alive to assail him.
Some of Stuart's most vehement critics who were still to publish or speak about
his role in the campaign and who had been on Lee's staff never mentioned
McClellan's third set of orders. Neither A. L. Long in his 1886 memoirs nor
Walter Taylor, who would revise his 1877 memoir in 1906, denied the existence
of McClellan's lengthy, sealed letter. Nor did either of them confirm its existence. Only Charles Marshall, who spoke in 1896 to the Confederate Veteran
Association in Washington, said that the dispatch could not be found among
Lee's papers, and the one to which Stuart refers in his report must be the one of
5 P.M. June 23.

In a sort of backhanded confirmation of the letter, Mosby suggested in his
private papers that McClellan in 1885, "under some influence had suppressed
such conclusive evidence in Stuart's favor," which Mosby began to suspect
sometime after June 1887.[12] (Mosby was not referring to the "lengthy" communication; it seems that even he did not realize it was a different one from the published June 23 letter.) Why, if McClellan possibly suppressed evidence in Stuart's

favor, would he have to invent a letter in his favor? Unfortunately, Mosby never said exactly what he believed McClellan suppressed.

McClellan acknowledged that Stuart's ride around the Union army had been much discussed and that most writers, Union and Confederate, believed it was a strategic mistake. McClellan discounted the allegation that Stuart disobeyed orders, but built his case upon the contention that Stuart could not have exceeded his orders because he was given discretion. A careful reading of Stuart's orders shows what little discretion he was given; not nearly as much as many writers, including one of his most solid defenders, would have posterity believe.

Nevertheless, McClellan's work represents one of the more accurate studies of the 1863 cavalry campaigns. He pointed out that Stuart left a sufficient—if not superior—force of cavalry, compared with the force he took away, for any of Lee's needs.

In summing up his segment on the results of Stuart's movement around the Union army, McClellan may have hit on an important point:

> It was not the want of cavalry that General Lee bewailed, for he had enough of it had it been properly used. It was the absence of Stuart himself that he felt so keenly; for on him he had learned to rely to such an extent that it seemed as if his cavalry were concentrated in one person, and from him alone could information be expected.[13]

He also gave an outstanding account of the cavalry fighting east of Gettysburg on July 3 as well as the cavalry battles during the retreat. McClellan wrapped up his book with the fall and winter of 1863–64 and the sad springtime when Stuart was mortally wounded at Yellow Tavern. Douglas Southall Freeman, notably antagonistic to Stuart in some of his works, called McClellan a careful biographer.[14]

In 1886, A. L. Long began building a case against Stuart in his biography of Lee. In May, before the Gettysburg campaign, Long wrote that Lee's "plans of operation were fully matured, and with such precision that the exact locality at which a conflict with the enemy was expected to take place was indicated on his map. This locality was the town of Gettysburg, the scene of the subsequent great battle."[15]

Long continued:

> At the period mentioned he called the writer into his tent, headquarters then being near Fredericksburg. On entering I found that he had a map spread on the table before him, which he seemed to have been earnestly consulting. He advised me of his designated plan of

operations, which we discussed together and commented upon the probable result. He traced on the map the proposed route of the army and its destination in Pennsylvania, while in his quietly effective manner he made clear to me his plans for the campaign.[16]

The fact that Lee pointed to the map and chose Gettysburg did two things for Long's argument. First, it added to Lee's reputation. Not only was he a great and tragic military leader, but like a seer, he had superhuman powers. No one in the South after the war argued with that.

More important for Long's argument, it made Gettysburg the destination of the Army of Northern Virginia. In building his case, Long intimated that if Gettysburg was where Lee wanted to fight, anyone who subverted this goal was culpable in the defeat there. By not helping Lee reach Gettysburg, Stuart was to blame.

Looking at maps available to him in May 1863, however, Lee could not possibly have detected the minute features that made Gettysburg a fine battlefield for the army that got there first. He could have seen that several roads converged there, but that could be said of other towns in that area. Gettysburg was no place special until the armies got there. But in order to blame Stuart, Long had to convince his readers that Lee was trying to get to Gettysburg and that it was Stuart's fault that he failed to get there before the Union army did.

Long spent several pages saying how Lee's movements northward were "embarrassed" by Stuart moving around the Union army. He ignored the fact, as Marshall did, that Lee knew where Stuart would be if he had not heard from him and that if that were the case, according to his own orders, the enemy would be inactive or moving northward.

Finally, Long mentioned that it was at Cashtown that Lee "expressed regret at the absence of cavalry. He said that he had been kept in the dark ever since crossing the Potomac, and intimated that Stuart's disappearance had materially hampered the movements and disorganized the plans of the campaign."[17]

In the very next paragraph, Long said that Lee's suspense was broken by a messenger from Hill saying that he was engaged against two corps and needed reinforcements. Anderson's division, he wrote, which had just reached Cashtown, was hurried forward and Lee and staff followed immediately.[18]

Finally Long got to the purpose of his argument, a great lesson for future generals on harmonizing the various branches of an army:

This battle was precipitated by the absence of information which could only be obtained by an active cavalry force. General Lee had previously considered the possibility of engaging the enemy in the vicinity of Gettysburg, but the time and position were to have

been of his own selection. This could have been easily effected had
not the cavalry been severed from its proper place with the army.[19]

For Long's argument, it was important for Lee to have chosen the Gettysburg
area a month and a half before. If this were true, why did Lee not tell Stuart? It
certainly would have made everyone's job easier.

On the evening of July 1, in the orchard where Lee's tents were pitched,
Long had Lee frankly solicit him as to whether the army should attack without
cavalry. Long replied:

> It would be best not to wait for Stuart. It is uncertain where he
> is or when he will arrive. At present only two or three corps of the
> enemy's are up, and it seems best to attack them before they can be
> greatly strengthened by reinforcements. The cavalry had better be
> left to take care of itself.[20]

Finally, in a reply to the Comte de Paris' history, Long seemed to ignore one
of the more successful operations of the invasion: "It must be borne in mind
that in entering Pennsylvania without his cavalry General Lee was unable to
accumulate supplies." On the contrary, and in spite of Lee's restrictive policies
for gathering supplies, an overabundance had been accumulated.[21]

During the winter of 1886–87, Longstreet wrote an article for *Century Magazine* (later reprinted in *Battles & Leaders*) in which he stated that by June 30,
1863, "We then found ourselves in a very unusual condition: we were almost in
the immediate presence of the enemy with our cavalry gone. Stuart was undertaking another wild ride around the Federal army."[22]

Mosby was not going to let Longstreet get away with that. At the time, he
was in Washington, settling accounts as consul to Hong Kong. When Longstreet's
article and Long's book appeared, he went to the War Department archives and
examined the Confederate records on Gettysburg, which had not been published
yet. He discovered two things. First he found Lee's orders to Stuart and Longstreet's
endorsement of his ride around the Federal army. Second, in speaking with the
archivist, he discovered that H. B. McClellan had spent several days at the
archives and had had access to the same documents but never used them in his
book, *I Rode with Jeb Stuart*.[23]

In May or June 1887, *Century* published Mosby's rebuttal. Mosby reminded
Long and Longstreet that Stuart left Lee with more cavalry than he took away
and stated that both implied that Stuart disobeyed orders. He then included
Longstreet's endorsement letter for the "wild ride" in his article.

Using the same information from the archives, Mosby also indicted Robertson, who had been ordered by Stuart to "report anything of importance" to Longstreet. Mosby related how Robertson retired to the mountain gaps and remained there until the afternoon of June 29, when he was finally called in by Lee instead of reporting to Lee himself after Hooker had crossed the Potomac. Mosby blamed Robertson for Lee believing that Hooker was still in Virginia. "As Stuart had been ordered to Ewell on the Susquehanna," Mosby concluded, "it could not have been expected that he should also watch Hooker on the Potomac."[24]

Robertson responded in a following article that his role should not be impugned because Stuart's orders "were exactly obeyed by me, to his entire satisfaction as well as to that of General R. E. Lee." This seems impossible. He never mentioned not following the Confederate army once the Federals crossed the Potomac, which is what he was ordered to do. Robertson essentially said that because he was not censured by Stuart or Lee after the campaign, he did the right thing.[25]

In 1894, Fitz Lee wrote a biography of his uncle titled simply, *General Lee*. In the section dealing with the Gettysburg campaign he used Stuart's orders from Lee and Longstreet, and went on to show how Stuart followed those orders. He made a statement that probably only one related to Robert E. Lee by blood could get away with: "This officer [Stuart] has been unjustly criticized for not being in front of Lee's army at Gettysburg, but Lee and Longstreet must be held responsible for his route. Lee crossed the Potomac west of the Blue Ridge, Hooker east of it, and Stuart between him and Washington."[26]

Though the general tone of the Gettysburg segment was sympathetic to Stuart, he perpetuated the assumption that while at Chambersburg, Robert E. Lee still believed—because he had not heard from Stuart—that the Union army was in Virginia.[27] Again, a writer used the post-battle reports rather than the orders to determine what Stuart was supposed to do.

On January 19, 1896, Marshall spoke before the Confederate Veteran Association of Washington. The remarks, published in the *Southern Historical Society Papers,* represented one of the most scathing attacks upon Stuart's role in the Gettysburg campaign. Though he began by saying he deplored historians who used hindsight, Marshall proceeded to mix orders (given before the battle) with the two reports of the battle and campaign that he himself subsequently wrote. Marshall began by using Lee's second report of the campaign rather than the actual orders Lee gave Stuart, which were available to the general public by then.[28] It was a confused and misleading speech, broadening Stuart's discretion as to where he could cross the Potomac and erroneously saying that he was to join the main column instead of Ewell's advance forces after he crossed.

Marshall continued by then quoting verbatim the orders out of the *Official*

Records, which said that Stuart, if he found the enemy moving northward, was to move into Maryland and take position on Ewell's right. By directly quoting Stuart's orders, he destroyed his own previous point.

But he proceeded to completely misinterpret them:

> The letter of General Lee to General Stuart, however, shows that when it was written General Lee expected that General Stuart would pass with all his cavalry, except two brigades, to the west of the Blue Ridge, and cross the Potomac on that side of the mountains.

How did Marshall conclude that Stuart was to pass west of the mountains when he was supposed to cross the Potomac if the enemy was moving northward?

Marshall reviewed Longstreet's letter to Stuart suggesting that Stuart not leave the army unless he pursued a route around the enemy's rear, then condemned it because "it does not notice the positive instruction contained in General Lee's letter to General Stuart, should the latter cross the Potomac, to place himself as speedily as possible, after the enemy begun [sic] to move northward, upon General Ewell's right." Longstreet's June 22 letter mentioned nothing about speed of movement because instructions to move "speedily" or to "lose no time" appeared only in Marshall's report, not in Lee's orders, which Longstreet was commenting upon. Marshall, in essence, was castigating Longstreet for not having read instructions inserted by Marshall some seven months later in Lee's January 1864 report.

Marshall then quoted Lee's letter of instructions written at 5 P.M. on June 23 to Stuart—Stuart's second set of orders on the subject—and said that they were the last directions to Stuart. Marshall began to develop the theme that by Lee's directive, Stuart was "unconditionally" ordered to move on and feel the right flank of Ewell's troops. He was not to leave the Confederate army *"unless he could pass around the Federal army without hindrance"* (italics Marshall's). His next sentence concluded, "Under this instruction, General Stuart was practically instructed not to cross the Potomac east of the Federal army, and thus interpose that army between himself and General Ewell." Marshall then quoted Stuart's report, in which Stuart mentioned a communication or possibly more than one communication from Lee:

> The commanding general wrote me, authorizing this move [around the Union rear], if I deemed it practicable, and also what instructions should be given the officer in command of the two brigades left in front of the army. [This refers to Lee's June 23 order.] He also notified me that one column would move via Gettysburg,

the other by Carlisle, towards the Susquehanna, and directed me, after crossing, to proceed with all dispatch to join the right (Early) in Pennsylvania.

Marshall then said to his audience, "There is no such letter as is mentioned by General Stuart contained in the book, in which are found copies of all the other letters of General Lee to him, which I have cited, and it is inconsistent with the other letters I have quoted on the same subject." That may be so, but it is remarkably consistent with the letter described by McClellan that he opened at Rector's Cross Roads, the one he searched for diligently and could not find when he was writing his book.

Although Marshall claimed that the only letter Stuart referred to is the one of 5 P.M. June 23, that seems impossible, since the information in the letter that Stuart mentioned in his report appeared in no other published dispatch of the time period. And yet there were enough references to his moving quickly in numerous post-battle reports and articles that there must be some other source for that information.

Unfortunately, the existence of McClellan's missing "lengthy letter" still cannot be confirmed by physical evidence.

That Marshall may have been going to extremes to indict Stuart is evident in a letter among Mosby's correspondence. In it may also be found more evidence of McClellan's missing last dispatch from Lee to Stuart. To former Confederate Major General Lunsford L. Lomax on February 19, 1896 (a month after Marshall's speech), Mosby wrote:

> Very glad to get your letter. [Senator] John Daniel writes me that Marshall acknowledged to him that there is one unpublished dispatch. I suspect what it is. If you will read Longstreet's letter to Stuart (June 23) you will see that he had just received one from General Lee suggesting that Stuart should go via Hopewell Gap in rear of the enemy. This letter of General Lee is not among the records.[29]

Mosby thought the missing dispatch was one from Lee to Longstreet. Though that one is missing too, he was mistaken. The missing dispatch Marshall referred to is the one McClellan was looking for, the "lengthy" letter with the additional information in it about Early and moving speedily, a dispatch of far more importance to Marshall's case than the one to Longstreet. But Mosby then continued with something quite shocking:

> In the spring of 1887 I was writing on this subject and found

Longstreet's letter and wrote to Charles Marshall asking about General Lee's letter. His answer was to the effect that he did not have it. He then went on to say that the letter of June 23, 5 P.M. from General Lee to Stuart was revoked by a subsequent one written that night by him in which General Lee ordered Stuart to ride on the right of his column. . . . General Lee admits [in his report] that he authorized Stuart to go the route he took and that he ordered him to go on Ewell's flank which shows that the instructions of June 23rd had not been revoked. Colonel Charlie had no more to say. Now if what he wrote me was true he ought to have stated it in his address. He did nothing of the kind. He writes this dispatch to Stuart, does not say a word about its having been revoked which shows that he knew that it had never been.[30]

Why did Marshall try to suggest to Mosby that he had written a letter revoking Stuart's orders to ride around the Union army? There can be only one answer: to prove that Stuart directly disobeyed Lee's orders. He could not prove it any other way.

It is difficult to believe that a man of Marshall's stature and reputation attempted something like this. The suggestion that he wrote a letter revoking Stuart's marching orders never appeared in any of his published correspondence. Perhaps it was too great a stretch, after Marshall realized it would not fly with Mosby, to attempt to publish it. But the information must shade the image of one of Lee's most trusted staff members and indicate the contempt, for whatever reason, in which he held Stuart.

Narrating Stuart's march northward, Marshall condemned Stuart for fighting the subsequent battles because they "consumed much more time, the consequences of the loss of which will be presently described." The battles were not all Stuart's fault—the Yankees had something to do with their being fought.

Marshall stated, "The movement of General Stuart, as will be perceived, left the army which had passed into Maryland with no cavalry, except the brigade of Jenkins' and White's battalion, which accompanied General Ewell." Marshall did not mention that Stuart left Robertson and Jones with explicit instructions on what to do as the Confederates moved into Maryland and Pennsylvania. Marshall also claimed that the army could not look for supplies because of Stuart's absence, possibly taking this theme from A. L. Long.

He talked about Lee's confidence in Stuart:

> He [Lee] had not heard from him [Stuart] since the army left Virginia, and was confident from that fact, in view of the positive

orders that Stuart had received, that General Hooker's army had not yet crossed the Potomac. He remained at Chambersburg from the 27th to the 29th, and repeatedly observed while there that the enemy's army must still be in Virginia, as he had heard nothing from Stuart.[31]

This is ground covered before. How could Lee believe that the Union army would not follow after his army had been roaming and raiding all the way into Pennsylvania, and Pennsylvania's governor had been calling for troops since mid-June? Marshall wrote the very orders to Stuart to go around the enemy if he appeared to be moving northward; *not* hearing from Stuart gave Lee the information he needed. And, by June 28, Lee had received confirmation from Harrison and other sources of what he certainly must have expected.

Marshall said that Lee began to grow apprehensive that the Union army might move against Richmond, and that "apprehension was due entirely to his hearing nothing from General Stuart." Lee, however, had been concerned about a Federal move on Richmond as early as June 13[32] and in several subsequent communications before Stuart even left him.[33]

Stuart's swinging south of the Union army, in essence between the Federals and Washington, would also place him between the Federals and Richmond. Lee's apprehension of the Yankees moving toward Richmond would have been greater if Stuart were merely following along on his right flank.

Marshall had not mentioned to his audience that by the time Lee was in Chambersburg, it was no longer Stuart's job to inform Lee of the Union army's movement north of the Potomac. Marshall's statement would have been correct if he had said that Lee's apprehension was due entirely to his hearing nothing from General Robertson.

Marshall re-told the story of Harrison the spy, saying that he brought the first information that the Union army had left Virginia, ignoring Lee's June 23 letter informing Jefferson Davis that the Federals were preparing to cross the Potomac. He concluded narrating Stuart's role:

> You will thus see that the movement to Gettysburg was the result of the want of information, which the cavalry alone could obtain for us, and that General Lee was compelled to march through the mountains from Chambersburg eastward without the slightest knowledge of the enemy's movements, except that brought by the scout.[34]

Marshall, in his staff position, should have known about the June 30 communication Hill sent Lee about what Pettigrew found in Gettysburg, but he failed to convey that to his audience. (He should have known about other bits and pieces of communication that were flowing to Lee's headquarters from various sources from June 25 through July 1, after Stuart went incommunicado, but did not mention any of these either.)

He concluded his speech by saying that all Confederate troops could have been at Gettysburg on the first day, apparently if only Stuart had been at Lee's side. This implied, along with A. L. Long and some others, that Gettysburg was where Lee was headed. He continued:

> It has been my object to correct the impression that has pre-vailed to some extent that the movement of the cavalry was made by General Lee's orders, and that at a critical moment of the campaign he crossed the Potomac river and moved into Pennsylvania, send-ing the entire cavalry force of his army upon a useless raid.

How Marshall could have said that the cavalry moved without Lee's orders after previously including the orders in his speech defies common sense. Marshall pointed to the fact that Stuart, as soon as he started on his movement, ran into Hancock's corps, and so should have turned around then and there. He empha-sized "if he [Stuart] thinks he can get through" in Longstreet's letter to Lee (which Stuart never saw) over the several orders Lee gave Stuart on June 22 23. In other words, Marshall vilified Stuart for not disobeying several orders from Lee at the very outset of his movement.

Mosby took great offense. Writing from San Francisco just nine days after the speech, he called it a "Jesuitical attack on Stuart by Colonel Charles Marshall, all a lie. It looks like I shall be at war forever."[35]

In the letter to Lomax of February 19, 1896,[36] in which Mosby destroyed Marshall's tale of writing orders revoking Stuart's march, Mosby wrote of the letter Marshall had sent to him after the spring of 1887:

> He [Marshall] also said that when Stuart handed him his report of the Gettysburg campaign he (Stuart) explained to him why he (Stuart) had disobeyed General Lee's orders. I sent the letter to both General Payne and W. A. Stuart (J. E. B.'s brother) to read. I replied to Marshall that I did not mean to impeach his veracity but his memory, that Stuart in his report says he acted in accordance with Lee's orders and that he could never make me believe that Stuart volunteered to tell him that his report was false.[37]

Mosby shattered Marshall's claim that Stuart had "confessed" to disobedi-ence of orders with common sense after Marshall told of Stuart's alleged statement during the infamous Baltimore dinner party in February 1887. Sadly, Marshall's story of Stuart's "confession" emerged again in Marshall's memoirs.[38]

In 1896, Longstreet re-entered the conflict over the Gettysburg campaign in his memoirs, *From Manassas to Appomattox*. While the Gettysburg segment was aimed primarily at clearing Longstreet for not obeying the bogus "sunrise attack order," Stuart somehow got dragged into it. Longstreet was even more uncomplimentary than he had been earlier.

Longstreet cited "the general plan" of the campaign for his assuming that the cavalry was to operate with the First Corps, that Stuart was ordered to follow its withdrawal to the west of the Blue Ridge, cross at Shepherdstown, and ride to Baltimore. Then Longstreet inserted, "He [Stuart] claimed that General Lee had given him authority to cross east of the Blue Ridge." Longstreet continued:

> It seems that General Lee so far modified the plan of march north as to authorize his cavalry chief to cross the Potomac with part of his command east of the Blue Ridge, and to change the march of the Third Corps by Hagerstown and Chambersburg. The point at which the cavalry force should cross the river was not determined between the Confederate commander and his chief of cavalry, there being doubt whether the crossing could better be made at Point of Rocks, between the Union army and the Blue Ridge, or between that army and Washington City. That question was left open, and I was ordered to choose between the two points named at the moment that my command took up its line of march.[39]

Longstreet mentioned Stuart's orders sent through him from Lee on June 22, "to be forwarded, provided the cavalry could be spared from my front and could make the ride without disclosing our plans, expressing his preference for the ride through Hopewell Gap east of the Union army." None of this appears in Lee's written and published orders to Stuart of June 22. This apparently was the information Longstreet said Lee spoke of in Longstreet's cover letter of June 22 (the letter Mosby thought Marshall was writing of as missing). It was this information that caused Longstreet to write a postscript in his cover letter to Stuart, "You had better not leave us, therefore, unless you can take the route in rear of the enemy." This has been quoted as his authorization to Stuart to make the raid.

It was also this additional information from Lee that made Longstreet suggest to Stuart the ride via Hopewell Gap rather than Point of Rocks. Longstreet wrote in his book, "The crossing at Point of Rocks was not only hazardous, but more likely to indicate our plans than any move that could be made, leaving the ride through Hopewell Gap the only route for the raiding party."

Longstreet referred back to the general plan that Stuart should ride on the right of his column until they got to Shepherdstown, ignoring the fact that the situation had changed because of Lee's and Stuart's discussion after Upperville. Several letters also subsequently had passed from Stuart to Lee, which Longstreet may not have known about. By the time he wrote his book, however, Longstreet's assumption that Stuart would leave Hampton in command of the remaining two brigades of cavalry had become an order.[40]

Longstreet continued: "These orders, emanating properly from the commander of the rear column of the army [Longstreet] should not have been questioned, but they were treated with contumely. He [Stuart] assigned General Robertson to command the cavalry that was left on the mountain, without orders to report at my headquarters."

Contrary to what Longstreet wrote, his entire letter of June 22 represented merely an endorsement of Lee's orders to Stuart, not orders from himself. His cover letter said, "I forward the letter of instructions [Lee's] *with these suggestions*" (author's italics). These did not constitute orders. Finally, referring to Stuart's raid, Longstreet wrote, "If General Stuart could have claimed authority of my orders for his action, he could not have failed to do so in his official account." Stuart never claimed that Longstreet ordered him on his ride; Longstreet merely suggested it, as an endorsement of Lee's order. Stuart knew what he was doing according to his orders, and from whom those orders emanated. They came from Lee and not Longstreet, though they were endorsed—and rightfully as a good plan— by Longstreet. For reasons of his own, after three decades Longstreet changed a simple, correct endorsement of a good plan into a confusing, misinterpreted defense against a ridiculous charge made against him by others. He sadly summed up his argument by writing, "So our plans, adopted after deep study, were suddenly given over to gratify the youthful cavalryman's wish for a nomadic ride."

Through the rest of the narrative on the battle, Longstreet continued to throw jibes at Stuart: "[We were] without a cavalryman to ride and report the trouble," "[On the night of June 30] cavalry not in sight or hearing, except Jenkins' brigade and a small detachment." Yet, he conceded that in the forenoon of July 1, when Lee left him, "he made no mention of his absent cavalry, nor did he indicate that it was not within call."

In 1898, Mosby used the research for some articles he had been writing for the *Boston Herald* to produce his book, *Mosby's War Reminiscences and Stuart's Cavalry Campaigns*. He was particularly harsh on Beverly Robertson. Mosby began developing several themes that would permeate his writings; Robertson waiting in the Blue Ridge passes until ordered up by Lee was one of them. In light of Stuart's orders, which Mosby then published, Robertson's behavior was a mystery. Clearly, Robertson was not where Lee had wanted him; Lee had to send back for him. Mosby practically charged Robertson with disobedience. After seeing Stuart's orders to Robertson, it was clear that "he does not appear to have been in the least governed by them." And when Robertson finally did move, Mosby pointed out, he followed on Lee's left flank instead of his right. "Gen. Lee's right flank was thus left exposed to the enemy's cavalry, but fortunately they had nearly all been sent in search of Stuart." Had Robertson advanced with Lee with his 3,000 troopers and two batteries of artillery, the Union advance into Pennsylvania would have slowed; when the time came, Gettysburg could easily have been occupied before the Union army got there.[41] (Mosby was apparently trying to patronize the "Gettysburg as a destination" crowd.)

Another theme Mosby began to develop was that of Longstreet's and Hill's "premature" marches from Berryville on June 24. After warning Stuart on June 22 to pass in the rear of the enemy rather than to the right, lest the movements disclose Lee's plans, Mosby said that Longstreet and Hill then marched in plain view of Union signalmen, who telegraphed the news. This set the Union army in motion, which put Hancock's corps in front of Stuart, delaying him. "If the corps of Longstreet and Hill had delayed a single day in leaving Berryville, Stuart would have landed on the north bank of the Potomac on the night of June 25,"[42] Mosby wrote. This theme also re-emerged in Mosby's next book.

Mosby considered Stuart's ride an integral part of Lee's invasion plan and that Lee not only authorized it but helped conceive it.

> He [Lee] would not have committed the blunder of marching all his infantry into Pennsylvania knowing that all his cavalry was in Virginia. He must, therefore, have expected for Stuart to cross the Potomac on the same day [as Longstreet and Hill] to the *east* of the Ridge; which he would have done but for Hancock's movement. Some have contended that his anxious inquiries for Stuart when he got to Chambersburg prove that he did not know which way he had gone. They only show that he did not know where Stuart was *at that time* (Mosby's italics).[43]

A final theme Mosby advanced was that Lee's reports were misinterpreted as to the references to Stuart, not the *cavalry.* In some cases, Lee "uses *Stuart's* name not in a personal sense, but descriptive of his cavalry corps. . . . Clearly Gen. Lee did not intend to involve himself in the contradiction of saying that he expected Stuart *personally* to perform at the same time the double duty of watching Hooker along the Potomac and guarding Ewell's flank on the Susquehanna."[44] Stuart and the cavalry were, to Mosby, to Lee, to the army, and eventually to most of the South, synonymous. Though there was glory in it, there also was much blame caused by such confusion, but Stuart had become the saber of the Confederacy.

In 1905 G. Moxley Sorrel, adjutant general and chief of staff to General Longstreet, published his memoirs of the war, *Recollections of a Confederate Staff Officer.* He summed up his view of the role of Stuart's cavalry: "One can build many theories [about the reasons for the loss of Gettysburg], but theories only will they be; besides, my opinion is already given that the loss of the campaign was due to the absence of Stuart's cavalry."[45]

Sorrel also made a curious statement that "it now appears that Stuart left the army with his fine command and started on his too fascinating raid in violation of Lee's orders, which failed to reach him. All doubt had passed from Lee's mind and he had ordered Stuart to keep with him." Could Sorrel be talking about Marshall's fictional orders revoking Stuart's march mentioned in Mosby's letters? Nevertheless, Sorrel's illogic popped out directly: How could Stuart be blamed for violating orders he never received?

Sorrel then conceded, "It is not to be supposed that no cavalry whatever was left with the army," but then adds ironically, "Stuart's defenders have taken pains to point that out. There was a squadron or two, here and there, a regiment at one place, and a brigade under an efficient commander left in the rear. But these separate little commands amounted to nothing. It was the great body of that splendid horse under their leader Stuart that Lee wanted." Sorrel's estimation of the cavalry at Lee's beck and call was sadly underestimated: there were two brigades under Robertson, Imboden's brigade, Jenkins' brigade, White's battalion, and the 250 horsemen of Hampton's brigade sent to Longstreet before dawn on July 2. Sorrel here, purposefully or inadvertently, misled the reader, but not as much as when he attempted to describe Stuart's horse-killing, sleepless ride from Seneca to Carlisle to Gettysburg, and the battles fought and won between. Sorrel wrote that: "Stuart was on a useless, showy parade almost under the guns of the Washington forts, and his horse, laurel-wreathed, bore the gay rider on amid songs and stories." Of Stuart's fighting from June 17 to the end of the campaign, Sorrel flippantly remarks, "He met some opposition, of course, and had a share of fighting in Ashby's Gap and the plain on the east."[46] This, and only this, of the wicked fighting at Aldie, and Middleburg, and Upperville, at Haymarket, and the saddle-deep; swift-water crossing of the Potomac; of Rockville and the Westminster fight; of the day-long battle at Hanover and the long night's march to Carlisle; of Hampton's combat at Hunterstown and of the huge battle east of Gettysburg. It was clear what Sorrel was trying to do by trivializing these things, and it was also unfair.

Mosby emerged more and more through the years as Stuart's greatest defender. In addition to his admiration and affection for Stuart, Mosby desired truth and fairness to the man and history. His work *Stuart's Cavalry in the Gettysburg Campaign* was a refutation built by the astute lawyer he was. Mosby knew many of the men who attacked Stuart and so was particularly vicious when he caught one of them in a lie.

Mosby began his military career as a private, then organized and led a band of partisans officially recognized by the Confederacy as the 43rd Virginia Cavalry Battalion. He was a full colonel at war's end. His independence and guerrilla tactics drew the wrath of the Union leadership, which put a price on his head. He was wounded and nearly taken prisoner a number of times. Mosby ranged over a large segment of Virginia from the mountains east to Fairfax County so freely with his hit-run-and-vanish tactics that it began to be called "Mosby's Confederacy."

After the war, he practiced law in Virginia but could never avoid public attention. In 1870, he and George Pickett visited Lee in Richmond. As they left, Pickett muttered something about "that old man" who had had his division massacred at Gettysburg. Mosby replied tartly, "Well, it made you immortal," and walked off. Perhaps because he had seen Lee virtually at the end of Lee's life, Mosby could acknowledge his admiration for the man, but could not concede to the blind adulation that arose as a "fashionable cult." Mosby mostly disliked the irrationality of considering Lee infallible.[47]

In 1894, he passed up an opportunity to go to Richmond to see some old war comrades because "I don't think that I have the stomach to stand the oratorical nonsense."[48] Myths were being made in the South about the "late unpleasantries" and Mosby wanted nothing to do with them.

Some called *Stuart's Cavalry in the Gettysburg Campaign* emotional apologia, but Mosby logically documented it as if he were defending a client in court. Former Union Major General Daniel Sickles was delighted by it.[49] The director of the United States War College, Major Eben Swift, wrote Mosby, thanking him for the contribution to military history.[50]

Major Charles F. Winter of the Department of Militia and Defence in Ottawa, Ontario, wrote Mosby that his "book throws a great deal of light upon what I as a British student thought obscure about Chancellorsville and Gettysburg. I am so pleased to know the real reason of the meeting at Gettysburg."[51]

Nearly the first third of *Stuart's Cavalry in the Gettysburg Campaign* dealt with Chancellorsville and Stuart's role as a commander of Jackson's corps, and the Battle of Brandy Station. Mosby then picked up the narrative of the summer campaign. His explanation of the Confederate plan of invasion generally agreed with Longstreet's, in that the cavalry rode along the right flank, securing the gaps and remaining behind the advanced forces of Ewell to deceive the enemy into thinking the entire Confederate army was still along the Rappahannock. Mosby wrote that Stuart's ability to determine enemy intentions while screening his own army were unsurpassed: "[The Union commanders'] ignorance of the whereabouts of Lee's army shows how well Stuart, with a curtain of cavalry, had screened its operations. Hooker was evidently greatly surprised when he heard of the collision at Aldie. Pleasonton had expected to stay one night there; he stayed a week. Hooker came to a halt."[52]

Mosby began his defense of Stuart after June 25 by assailing A. L. Long of Lee's staff. Long, of course, had said Lee pointed to a map while still encamped at Fredericksburg in May 1863 and picked Gettysburg as the site of the great battle to come. Mosby questioned that if Gettysburg were Lee's destination, then why, once he got to Hagerstown, Maryland, did he not march directly there? As late as June 19, Ewell still had not been ordered by Lee into Pennsylvania. This, to Mosby, did not sound like a man heading for Gettysburg.

Mosby pointed out a letter written on that same day, June 19, from Lee to Jefferson Davis concerning the Union army: "Indications seem to be that his main body is proceeding towards the Potomac, whether on Harper's Ferry or to cross the river east of it is not yet known." To Mosby, it was proof that Lee was expecting the Union army to cross the Potomac as early as June 19. That it eventually did cross could not have surprised Lee, and those who would later say how surprised he was on June 28 upon hearing the Union army had crossed were mistaken. He pointed out that Lee repeated his knowledge of the Union army's movement toward the Potomac twice more in correspondence to Davis by June 23.

Mosby then chronicled the Confederate movements north of the Potomac and pointed out that first Brigadier General John B. Gordon's brigade of Jubal Early's division was sent to Gettysburg, then Early himself met Gordon there. If, as Long based his argument, Lee was heading to Gettysburg specifically to wage battle, why did he not have Gordon or Early hold the place? Mosby wrote that Long's story was fiction.[53]

Long and others also blamed Stuart for Lee not reaching Cemetery Ridge, Cemetery Hill, and the Round Tops before Meade did, condemning him to a poorer position. Mosby wrote that even if Lee had gained that high ground, it would not have protected his line of communication from the Blue Ridge or his line of retreat to the Potomac. He then referred to Meade's communications to Washington during the battle in which Meade said he intended to fall back to Pipe Creek in Maryland as a defensive position. Mosby said this showed that not even Meade thought Gettysburg was the perfect place to fight. The disproving that Gettysburg was Lee's objective continued throughout Mosby's book.[54]

From his legal background, Mosby drew the phrase "due diligence," assuming that the Confederate generals during their march north used every means available to discover Union positions and movements.[55] He wrote that "it was not necessary to send out scouts and signal officers to the top of the [South] mountain; by the 26th, Hooker's troops were occupying the Passes and in plain view."[56] He reminded readers that Grumble Jones' brigade had been on picket duty in Loudoun County, Virginia, specifically to observe the enemy and Hooker's troops marched up the Potomac where he could see them. Mosby, as Jones' former adjutant, vouched for Jones' reputation as the best outpost officer in the army; that he did not send a message to Lee was inconceivable to Mosby. And, if Lee ever wanted to know where the Union army was, all he had to do was send one of his couriers over the mountain to look. Those who said Lee was anxious or panicky upon hearing the enemy had crossed the Potomac made him sound incompetent.[57]

Rather, Mosby thought Lee knew that the Union army was just beyond the mountains on June 26, that "he would not in fact have advanced into Pennsylvania if he had not known it. He left the gaps open to Hooker to pass. He must have calculated that Hooker might cross the mountain and get in his rear: I think he wanted Hooker to do it. He would have turned and finished Hooker."[58]

That Lee would allow the enemy to cut off his avenue of retreat is a wild thought; yet, where is it written that an invading army had to retreat back along its advance route? An attempted attack upon Lee's rear might not have been such a good idea for the North; it would have left the path to Washington open along the east side of the mountains. Lee knew well of the North's fear for the safety of Washington; he wrote to Davis about it several times. Once he knew the Yankees were following and that Richmond was safe (on June 26, according to Mosby), Lee continued his advance into Pennsylvania.

Mosby then began to develop a main theme of his book: Harrison, the spy, and whether his information affected the campaign as much as Lee's staff officers and Longstreet would like us to believe.

It was their contention that the spy came in on the night of June 28 and gave Lee the information that the Union army had crossed the Potomac (and possibly the information that Meade now commanded). Lee, in a panic, ordered his troops to concentrate upon Cashtown or Gettysburg. Their point was that without Stuart, Lee had to rely on a single spy for his first information on the approach of the enemy.

Mosby referred to the letter sent from Lee in Chambersburg to General Ewell marked 7:30 A.M. and dated June 28, 1863: "I wrote you *last night* [Mosby's italics], stating that General Hooker was reported to have crossed the Potomac and is advancing by way of Middletown, the head of his column being at that point in Frederick County." He stated that if Lee had this information on the night of June 27, then the story of the spy and his importance to the army's concentration was a fable.

Mosby additionally documented the date of the letter from General Lee's letter-book, at that time in the possession of one-time Lee staff member W. Gordon McCabe, an early biographer of Lee. The order was in the handwriting of Colonel Charles Venable, staff officer. As Mosby told it, "The hour and the minute of the day on which it was written are noted; General Lee understood the importance of dates in military dispatches. It must have been copied soon after the original was written as its place in the letter-book is in due succession of dates and pages. No doubt the dispatch was sent off in haste as it partly countermanded orders of the night before."[59] According to the accompanying letter from McCabe, it was entered in Lee's letter-book immediately after Lee's letter to Jefferson Davis from Williamsport on June 25, and immediately before the one from Lee to Imboden, July 1.

Later, in an article in the *Southern Historical Society Papers,* Mosby's arguments on several issues in the book were assailed. The date of this letter was questioned by General Edward Johnson's aide-de-camp Randolph Harrison McKim. His argument was based upon the note at the top of the orders that said, "From memory—sketch of a letter." Obviously, because the orders were to go out quickly, Colonel Venable did not have a chance to copy them immediately into Lee's letter-book.

In the end, after building his argument on the supposition that the letter had been written on June 29, McKim proved nothing in error with Mosby's times of twenty-four hours before. The only way McKim's suppositions become important is if one accepted Longstreet's, Long's, Marshall's, and Taylor's suggestions that Harrison's arrival was the first time Lee knew of the whereabouts of the Union army; Mosby, of course, said this was untrue and proved it by citing Lee's correspondence to Davis on June 23, and the fact that his other cavalry was in touch with Lee about Hooker's crossing on June 25.

McKim concluded his argument by calling up Lee's great and unimpeachable reputation:

> Either Colonel Venable in writing the letter from memory made
> a mistake in dating it the 28th, or General Lee and General Longstreet,
> and General Long and Colonel Marshall and Colonel Taylor were
> all mistaken in the belief that the change in plans of the campaign
> was due to the arrival of a scout on the night of the 28th. Which is
> the more likely supposition?[60]

With the exception of Lee, all the above had a reputation to defend. McKim's strange final argument was exactly Mosby's point: Longstreet, Long, Marshall, and Taylor, each for his own reasons, *were* wrong in their supposition.

Mosby did not doubt that a spy came into camp and brought the news that Meade was in command of the Federal army, but, he writes, "It was after Lee left Chambersburg, and on the 30th, at Greenwood, when the army was on march to Cashtown." Whether it was the 30th or the 28th did not really matter to Mosby; all that mattered was that Lee had begun the concentration of his army *before* the spy brought in his information, because it proved that Lee already had the information about the Union army from Stuart and others. There was nothing sudden or panic-stricken about it.

Mosby then turned to Hill and Heth, denouncing them for disobeying Lee's orders by precipitating a battle when none was desired.

> There have been complaints, but no one has proved that Lee did anything, or left anything undone, for want of information that cavalry could have brought him. In fact he did know all that cavalry could tell him. Longstreet says the spy [Harrison] told him *more*. [Mosby's italics.] The two generals who precipitated the battle are responsible for the disaster; they attempted to shift the blame on Stuart because his absence on the first day gave color to the charge, and had the assistance of certain staff officers at headquarters.[61]

Mosby wrote that if part of Lee's cavalry was absent, nearly all of Meade's was absent, in pursuit of Stuart, and used Union reports and correspondence to prove his point.

Mosby referred to that other "missing" courier, sent on the morning of June 25 with the information that Hooker's army was marching to the Potomac: "The courier traveled inside our lines and could not have been intercepted. General Lee must have received the letter about Williamsport the next day [June 26] as there was a line of relay couriers to his headquarters. It is therefore a reflection on General Lee to suppose that he was surprised when he heard that Hooker had crossed the Potomac."[62]

Of Stuart's role in the entire campaign, Mosby wrote, "He was not conducting a raid, or an independent expedition of cavalry, but was assigned to perform a part of a combined movement of the whole army." Stuart met with Lee, Mosby wrote, on June 21 in Ashby's Gap. Mosby expressed the thought that Lee may have selected Jones' and Robertson's brigades as the ones to stay behind. Mosby reminded his readers that along with Longstreet, three of Lee's staff members said that Stuart disobeyed orders, even though Lee's orders, in their handwriting, said otherwise.

Of the wagon trains, Mosby wrote, "None of Stuart's critics can show any bad results from his carrying the trains along with him."[63] Indeed, the train was supposed to have slowed him up, but he missed Early by only a few hours. That could be blamed on any one of the battles Stuart had to fight when the Yankees got in his way.

Mosby backed off on the charge he had made against Robertson in his first *Philadelphia Weekly Times* articles, and began, in his book, laying the full blame for the unwanted battle upon Heth and Hill. Because of information from the *Official Records* that he had not seen before, and from a re-examination of Heth's reply to it, Mosby concluded that, as Heth wrote in his reply, "General Lee was in daily communications with Robertson and knew exactly where he was. . . . Some days as many as three couriers were sent by General Lee to General Robertson." Mosby also decided, reading Stuart's orders to Robertson, that Robertson was to hold the gaps in the mountains as long as the enemy remained in his front, unless otherwise ordered by Lee and Longstreet. Heth said just the opposite, that Jones and Robertson were to stay in the gaps waiting for further orders after the Union army crossed the Potomac.

That couriers went from Lee to Robertson daily meant that Lee knew that Robertson knew the Union army had crossed the Potomac by the 26th.[64] Lee also had the means to order Robertson to remain in the gaps or to follow Longstreet. To Mosby, that put the blame on Lee and Longstreet for not having cavalry, but also said that Lee knew that the enemy had crossed into Maryland and could not have been surprised by any report of that fact later in the campaign.

"Blame" is too strong a word for Lee and Longstreet. The supposition that they needed cavalry came first from the section of Lee's (Marshall's) second report in which Lee apparently made only minor revisions. Such a supposition is not supported except by others who have quoted from the second report. It does not appear in the first report; only near the end of the second. If Lee communicated with Robertson thrice daily and did not call him up until June 29, he probably did not need him until then because he was getting all the information he needed. If, on the morning of July 1, he needed cavalry to tell him what the firing at Gettysburg meant, it was not Stuart's fault or Robertson's but Heth's and Hill's.

Yet why, after the Federals had crossed the Potomac, did Robertson remain in Virginia? Mosby figured he had been ordered to stay by Lee or Longstreet. Since neither ever said Robertson disobeyed their orders, this may have been the case. Mosby said of Robertson's remaining behind, "I can see no damage that resulted from it, as the myth of General Lee having been surprised by meeting the enemy at Gettysburg has been exploded."[65]

Mosby cited two other sources who testified that daily communications were kept up between Lee and Robertson, making it virtually impossible for anyone to still believe that Lee was kept in the dark about the enemy's crossing the Potomac. He concluded that Lee's reports were erroneous more in implication than fact. He maintained that Lee, like so many other harried, high-ranking officials, trusted his subordinates and signed the reports without reading them. It will probably never be known. But the reports in many instances did not correspond with the orders given to Stuart. As was mentioned before, Lee possibly read the first report, edited[66] it in the places obvious in the second report, then edited lightly the rest of the second report, leaving in the part that his army was "embarrassed" by the lack of cavalry for his own reasons—perhaps in reference to Imboden or Robertson.

In either case, beyond Marshall's prejudices, Mosby emphasized what he considered the real culprit in the matter: "The Confederate War Department immediately published Lee's report in the newspapers but suppressed Stuart's." The reason was to assuage public opinion about the whys and hows of the defeat. "After reading the report the public did not wait to hear the other side—it never does—but jumped to the conclusion that Stuart had gone off without authority with all the cavalry on a raid around Hooker's army; and that General Lee having no cavalry, was left like a giant with his eyes put out."[67] The public also had to wait until 1889 for the mass publication of Lee's orders in the *Official Records* before it could examine the differences between Stuart's orders and the reports. The orders should have been published first, to be compared with Stuart's actions in the reports. But from July 31, 1863, what Stuart was supposed to do and what others said he was supposed to do were reversed. Public criticism of Stuart began on that date.

Mosby continued to remind readers that most historians had not compared the two reports to each other or to the orders as issued. The discrepancies were numerous. Among other things, Mosby saw that Lee's report did not mention that Stuart left behind two brigades of cavalry when he rode away, with instructions to do everything that Stuart had been blamed for not doing. Mosby saw concealment and careful subterfuge in the works of Lee's staff members. By concealing much of the orders and using the post-battle reports of Marshall, Lee's staff rallied around their leader and refused to allow anyone to place blame where Lee himself placed it: upon himself. An adoring South went along with them and Stuart suffered for it. To post-war Southerners, there were several causes of the defeat—Longstreet, Stuart, fate, or God in His infinite wisdom—but not Lee.

The point of the entire complaint against Stuart in Marshall's report was that the cavalry was absent during the invasion; "if such was the case, General Lee was responsible for the absence of the cavalry with Stuart," Mosby wrote. Reading Lee's orders, it can be seen that Stuart followed them; reading Stuart's orders to Robertson and Jones, it can be seen that they were supposed to be in communication with Lee. If Lee needed cavalry, he could have had it anytime; if he did not, it was his fault.

After his book came out, Mosby continued corresponding with others concerning Stuart's role in the campaign and his critics. He pointed out that the Comte de Paris' history of the campaign relied on Heth's version as well as that of G. Moxley Sorrel of Longstreet's staff, who in his 1905 book backed up his former boss. Mosby also said he thought the Harrison story was a fable.

Mosby's arguments benefited from his sharp legal talents, but his contention that Lee never read either of his reports done by Marshall is refuted by the obvious editing and apparent changes in the second report. Mosby also missed the evidence that there were additional orders sent from Lee to Stuart that McClellan wrote about and of which there is evidence in Stuart's and Marshall's reports.

Mosby's book drew a critical article from Colonel T. M. R. Talcott, Lee's one-time aide-de-camp.[68] He began by quoting a letter from Colonel Walter H. Taylor of Lee's staff, who said that he did not attach much importance to Mosby's statements, then repeated the same misunderstanding of Stuart's orders that Taylor did in his 1877 book: that Stuart was to keep in touch with the main army, that Stuart was to inform Lee of the movements of the enemy, and that Lee was "greatly embarrassed" at not hearing from Stuart.

Talcott attacked the assumption that Lee never read the two reports; it was indeed the weakest point of Mosby's argument. He also attacked Mosby's contention that Lee had two brigades of cavalry with him, since they stayed behind after the Federals crossed the Potomac. Talcott seemed to suddenly realize that this was either Robertson's or Lee's fault and so abruptly wrote, "If they [the two brigades] were not available because of failure to obey orders, Stuart must have erred in the selection of the officer whose duty it was to carry them out."

Talcott then proceeded to examine both of Lee's reports, with regards to the cavalry's actions side-by-side. This method revealed little except evidence of Lee's editing of Charles Marshall's assumptions. Talcott's arguments rested on the predication—like so many before him—that Stuart was to keep in touch with Lee constantly, and with the Federal army between them he could not. Talcott then attempted to rally the Lee supporters against Mosby: "From the above quotations it would appear that Col. Mosby holds General Lee responsible for the failure at Gettysburg."

Mosby replied to Talcott's article in the January 30, 1910, issue of the Richmond *Times-Dispatch*. It eventually found its way into the *Southern Historical Society Papers*.[69] He discredited Taylor's letter, defying him to point out one word in Lee's orders that said anything about Stuart keeping in touch with the main army or keeping Lee informed of the enemy's movements. Mosby also mentioned that there was not a word in the orders—although it appeared in the report—that Stuart was to remain to guard the mountain passes or to harass and impede the enemy.

Mosby recounted the confusion and damage Stuart accomplished while he swung between the Army of the Potomac and Washington and repeated his indictment of Hill and Heth as perpetrators of the battle that Lee ordered them not to start.

Of Lee's ignorance of the whereabouts of the enemy, Mosby said, "It is not credible that General Lee should have stayed two days in Maryland, on the Potomac, and in the shadow of South Mountain, with Hooker's army on the other side and in the gaps, with their signal stations on the peaks, without discovering their presence. Such bucolic simplicity is inconsistent with the character of the Confederate commander. Every private in his army knew where Hooker was."[70]

Mosby did seem to back off on his theory that Lee did not read his Gettysburg reports: "Colonel Taylor says he read it. I am sorry to hear it." He also assailed Marshall, who said that Lee panicked upon hearing of Hooker's crossing the Potomac. Concluding, Mosby wrote, "It would have been far better for General Lee's military reputation if he had written his own report of events of the campaign just as they occurred, instead of having an acute lawyer to write a brief for him. I am aware that in Virginia there is a sentiment that tolerates only one side of a question which concerns General Lee."

Talcott replied to Mosby's response on March 7, 1910.[71] For some reason he first confused the issue by quoting Stuart's orders to the brigades he left behind (Robertson's and Jones') and saying that this is what *Stuart* was instructed to do. Talcott said that Lee "had a right" to expect to be advised as soon as the enemy crossed the Potomac, and that "all of Stuart's brigades would then be in the positions assigned them by his orders." Talcott continued, "Instead of that, Stuart and three of his best brigades were lost for a whole week, and, for all General Lee knew, were captured or destroyed; and the two brigades which should have been on his 'right and rear' in Pennsylvania assured him *by their absence* [Talcott's italics] that the enemy was still in their front until July 1st."

The rest of Talcott's article picked at Mosby's wording of his argument and tried stretching Lee's orders to Stuart to fit his argument. In refuting Mosby's contention that Lee did not read his reports (an argument that Mosby himself retreated from in his January 1910 article), Talcott quoted a letter by Lee in April 1868, which, to Talcott, proved that Lee authenticated his official reports and blamed Stuart for the failure at Gettysburg:

> General Lee accounts for the failure at Gettysburg and refers him [the recipient of his letter] to the official accounts, which is an assurance of the correctness of his official reports, as follows:
> "As to the Battle of Gettysburg, I must again refer you to the official accounts. Its loss was occasioned by a combination of circumstances. It was commenced in the absence of correct intelligence. It

was continued in the effort to overcome the difficulties by which we were surrounded, and it would have been gained could one determined and united blow have been delivered by our whole line."

Nowhere in the letter, except Lee's naming the lack of correct information as one of a combination of circumstances, did he name the cavalry or Stuart. Talcott, however, used this tenuous connection as proof of Stuart's guilt in Lee's eyes.

In order to deflate Mosby's argument that Heth and Hill brought on the battle, Talcott ended up doing what he was trying to avoid: blaming Lee. He wrote that on the night of June 30, "General Lee was not ready for a general engagement, for in the absence of his cavalry, he was not informed as to the disposition of Meade's army, and his own troops were not up; but there is no evidence that at that or any subsequent time he disapproved of General Hill's proposed advance on Gettysburg." Later, Talcott stated that Lee must have been on the field between 1:30 and 2:30 P.M. on July 1.

If, indeed, Lee were on the field at that time, and if he were not satisfied with his position, then he must take the blame for continuing the battle. By that time his reconnaissance in force was complete; Lee knew where the Federal army was—right before him. Lee made the decision—not Stuart—to stay and fight.

If Lee were not at Gettysburg at that time, then, as Mosby contends, Hill and Heth were to blame. Talcott tried to defend Hill and Heth and absolve Lee from the responsibility of Gettysburg. There was only one way: by blaming everything on Stuart.

If only Talcott, Marshall, and the rest could have, by saying it, changed Lee's orders of June 22–23 to Stuart, the arguments would have ended years before, with Stuart convicted. But the orders stood as written and Stuart and his three brigades were where Lee told them to go under the strictures on the movements of the enemy. Two brigades were left behind with definite orders.

CHAPTER ELEVEN

Marshall's Epitaph

"I can scarcely think of him without weeping."
—ROBERT E. LEE ON THE DEATH OF STUART

harles Marshall began making notes for an intended biography of Lee
shortly after the guns quieted. Since Lee's staff throughout the war had
always been small, Marshall, in his early thirties when he served Lee,
had a unique perspective, similar to that of Charles Venable, A. L. Long, and
Walter Taylor. He decided to await publication of the *Official Records* to finish
his work; by the time they came out, he was caught up in private law practice
and could not finish the biography.[1] His materials were placed in the hands of a
British officer, Major General Sir Frederick Maurice, who edited them and published them in 1927.

By then, of course, all the major participants in the Gettysburg/Stuart controversy were dead, yet Marshall's memoirs, as edited by Maurice, illuminated
Marshall's critical role in the affair and encouraged some latter-day historians
to resurrect it.

Marshall's comments were tainted by two factors. First was his desire to
correct what he perceived as a character flaw in Lee: that Lee refused to blame
anyone except himself for the shortcomings of the army. Maurice's introduction said that Marshall "was often disappointed and pained when an arduously
acquired piece of information, showing clearly that the responsibility for some
failure rested with a subordinate commander who had acted injudiciously or
failed to act judiciously, was struck out by Lee."[2] After the war, Marshall "burned
to use the special knowledge that he had acquired in the course of his duties, to
enhance the reputation of his chief," Maurice added. The second factor that tainted
the memoirs was Maurice's injection of his own prejudices, including some against
Longstreet and Stuart.

173

Marshall first related the purposes of the 1863 summer campaign, then narrated the invasion. Ewell's movement into Pennsylvania, he wrote, was "merely for the purpose of compelling the recall of Hooker from the Rappahannock."

By June 19th, Marshall said, Lee had resolved to cross the Potomac "with the object of compelling General Hooker to do the same so as to cover Washington." This coincides with Lee's June 25 letter to Davis in which he said, "I think I can throw General Hooker's army across the Potomac." But it also meant that Lee could not have been surprised, as Marshall and others wrote, when it actually happened.

Marshall then related having written the June 22 letter to Ewell and quoted it in its entirety. After the letter was sent, he said:

> General Lee explained to me that he had had a conversation with General Stuart when he left him near Paris [Virginia, near Ashby's Gap], and that his own view was to leave some cavalry in Snicker's and Ashby's Gaps to watch the army of General Hooker, and to take the main body of the cavalry with General Stuart to accompany the army into Pennsylvania. It is much to be regretted that this course was not pursued.

That course was not pursued because those were not Stuart's orders. This statement of the alleged conversation made no sense. That Stuart conversed with Lee in Paris was true; Mosby corroborates it. The rest of Marshall's recollection was suspect. Why would Lee explain this to Marshall, that he wanted to "take the main body of the cavalry with General Stuart to accompany the army into Pennsylvania," then turn around and issue orders (dated June 22) to Stuart telling him to leave two brigades and go with the other three into Maryland and take a position on Ewell's right?

Marshall wrote of this conversation:

> General Lee added that Stuart suggested that he could move down with his cavalry near Hooker, and annoy him if he attempted to cross the river, and when he found that he was crossing he could rejoin the army in good time.
>
> General Lee said that General Longstreet thought well of the suggestion and had assented, but he added that he had told General Stuart that, as soon as he found that General Hooker was crossing the Potomac, he must immediately cross himself and take his place on our right flank as we moved north. General Lee then told me that he was anxious that there should be no misunderstanding on General

Stuart's part, and that there should be no delay in his joining us as soon as General Hooker had crossed. He said that in reflection on the subject, while it had occurred to him that it might be possible for General Stuart, when the time came for him to cross the river, to cross east of the Blue Ridge and above General Hooker, thus avoiding the delay of returning through Snicker's or Ashby's Gap and crossing above Harpers Ferry, yet he added that circumstances might prevent Stuart from crossing east of the Blue Ridge.

Marshall then reprinted the orders he wrote June 22. They were the antithesis of what he said Lee wanted; they told Stuart to go to Ewell. They also said nothing about making no delay in joining them after Hooker had crossed; nothing about where to cross the Potomac; and nothing about the importance of rejoining the army quickly. If what Marshall said Lee expressed to him indeed was what Lee wanted, then Stuart did not disobey Lee's wishes because Marshall put none of Lee's spoken orders into writing.

Later, Marshall wrote that Lee's June 22 letter (containing Stuart's orders) showed that "when it was written he expected that General Stuart would pass, with all his cavalry except two brigades, to the west of the Blue Ridge, and cross the Potomac on that side of the mountains." Contrary to what Marshall said Lee expected, Stuart's orders of June 22 said nothing about Stuart crossing west of the Blue Ridge.

Marshall fell into the same pit that he had dug in his speech in 1896. Attacking Longstreet's letter of 7 P.M. June 22 endorsing Stuart's move, he said that Longstreet ignored the "positive instruction contained in General Lee's letter to General Stuart, that should the latter cross the Potomac he was to place himself as speedily as possible, after the enemy began to move northwards, upon General Ewell's right." It was not in the orders, but Marshall and others later talked and wrote again about the speed factor so often that it must have been discussed and perhaps even appeared in some orders to Stuart sometime. Again, perhaps the source for it and the other information mentioned in virtually all the reports but lacking in the published orders was in the "lengthy" sealed orders McClellan opened in Rector's Cross Roads.

Marshall referred to Stuart's report on the campaign, which mentioned that Lee wrote him authorizing the move through Hopewell or some other gap in the Bull Run Mountains, of passing between the Federal army and Washington, and crossing the Potomac. More important, Stuart referred to the information given him in that letter, "that one column would move via Gettysburg, the other by Carlisle," and that Lee directed Stuart after crossing the river *"to proceed with all dispatch to join the right (Early) in Pennsylvania."* (Author's italics.)

Marshall then stated in his memoirs, as he did in his 1896 speech, that:

> There is no letter as is mentioned by General Stuart contained in the book in which are found copies of all the other letters of General Lee to him, which letters I have cited, and it is inconsistent with those letters. General Stuart's report evidently refers to the letter of General Lee of June 23rd. That letter contains the instructions to be given to "the officer in command of the two brigades to be left in front of the enemy"; it also contains the information as to Ewell's movements referred to in the report. General Stuart constructed that letter to mean what he, in his report, states. That construction, however, is not justified by the letter itself.[3]

This was quite an accusation. He said Stuart invented a letter from Lee sometime between the end of July, when things quieted down after the campaign, and August 20, when he submitted his report. Of course, Marshall necessarily accused McClellan of going along with the story, since McClellan also mentioned it in speeches and his book. Yet McClellan included even more information than Stuart about the dispatch. All this pointed to an unpublished addendum to Stuart's copy of the June 23 published orders or even a different letter entirely, rather than a "construction" of orders by both Stuart and McClellan.

Marshall quoted a long passage from Stuart's report and concluded that it showed that Stuart crossed the river east of Hooker's army "so as to render it extremely difficult, if not impossible, for him to comply with the repeated injunctions he had received from General Lee to place himself on Ewell's right as soon as he entered Maryland." Having never gone to cavalry school, Marshall can be forgiven for not being able to calculate how long it would take cavalry to ride from Seneca (or even White's Ferry, where Marshall thought Stuart could have crossed) and the Pennsylvania line. But even Marshall had to leave to Stuart the definition of what was "impossible." Marshall repeated the account he had told to the McIntosh's dinner party in Baltimore.

> During the winter of 1863–4 while we lay on the Rapidan I was engaged in preparing the report on the Gettysburg campaign. I had received all the reports of the infantry and artillery commanders, and I was only waiting for General Stuart's, to complete General Lee's official report. Some delay took place, and General Stuart was applied to more than once. He said he was busy preparing it and promised me several times to send it in. General Lee was urging me to prepare his report before active operations should be resumed,

and I think that when I told him the cause of the delay, he either wrote or spoke to General Stuart on the subject himself. I know that I was unable to complete and forward General Lee's report until sometime in January or February, 1864. [The report is dated January, 1864.] At last General Stuart brought his report and asked me to read it carefully, and to tell him what I thought of his conduct.[4]

Stuart's report was dated August 20, 1863. Nearly half of all the reports were dated after his. Marshall continued:

In speaking of his having crossed the Potomac east of General Hooker on June 27th, instead of between Hooker and Harper's Ferry, General Stuart stated that he had at one time contemplated a dash on Washington, but did not undertake it [true] because his orders were to join the infantry as soon as possible. [Notice that the subject of speed of movement, though not mentioned in Stuart's published orders, comes up again.] He further stated that his orders had been to place his command on the right of our line of ranks, but argued that had he done so, he would have attracted the enemy's cavalry, which was more numerous than his, to that quarter.

Marshall must have been confused about what was said. He had Stuart misquoting his own orders to "place his command on the right of our line of ranks." Marshall went on to reveal:

He [Stuart] said they [the enemy cavalry] could have broken through the mountains at some pass, as he was not strong enough to hold all, and thus endangered our trains which were moving north on the west side of the Catoctin. General Stuart asked me if I did not consider his excuse for not putting himself on our right satisfactory, alleging that his movement had drawn the enemy's cavalry away from the Catoctin to watch him, and thus secured our trains.

I told him that I thought it would have been far better for him to have obeyed his orders; that General Lee had not ordered him to protect our trains, but had disposed his infantry to do that.

Marshall went on to dress down Stuart, pointing out the "disastrous consequence of our being without cavalry to get information for us and the fact that, owing to our not hearing from him, General Lee had been led to believe that General Hooker had not crossed the Potomac for several days after that event had occurred." He also repeated the theme so degrading to Lee, that since he had not heard from Stuart, he assumed that Hooker had not crossed, when Lee's own orders had told Stuart to ride around the Union army necessarily incommunicado, if the enemy were moving northward.

Marshall stated that they never got the dispatch Stuart said he sent informing Lee of Hooker's crossing, but that it would not have mattered anyway because they still "had no cavalry to get information for us." Again, this ignored Robertson's and Imboden's role. Marshall continued, "General Stuart admitted that he had made the movement at his own discretion, and that he had General Lee's letter written by me. He said that he was confident that he could get around Hooker and join us in Pennsylvania before the two armies could meet. I mention these facts to show that General Stuart felt it necessary to defend his course, which he would not have done had he been justified by his orders."

If Stuart ever conversed with Marshall, he certainly would not have stated that his orders were something that they were not. Stuart knew his orders because he followed them. Marshall was presenting what he *wanted* Stuart's orders to have been. The only way Marshall could indict Stuart was to have him misunderstand his orders the way Marshall did.

Marshall then returned to the narrative of the campaign, but continued to lash out at Stuart. He mentioned that Lee was apprehensive because he was concerned that Hooker would turn and attack Richmond, "and the apprehension was due entirely to his hearing nothing from Stuart." By not hearing from Stuart, Lee should have been assured that Hooker was not turning toward Richmond because Stuart was between Hooker and Richmond. Lee's only apprehension as to where Stuart was should have come when he was in communication with Ewell or Early, or days later when they arrived on the battlefield, because Lee had ordered Stuart to be with them.

Marshall then revealed the true purpose of his narrative:

> It has been my object to correct the impression that has prevailed that the movement of the cavalry was made by General Lee's orders, and that at a critical moment of the campaign he crossed the Potomac river and moved into Pennsylvania, sending the entire cavalry force of his army upon a useless raid. That this is not true I think the evidence I have produced abundantly establishes.

Marshall skewed the evidence so that if someone read only his account, they would believe that Lee's orders told Stuart to adhere to the right of his marching column and that only by disobeying Lee's "positive" orders could Stuart have done what he did.

During the segment on the Battle of Gettysburg, Marshall struck out again at Stuart, though his premise for this argument was an old and false one: that the Confederates were heading deliberately toward Gettysburg and if the movements of Meade's army had been known, they could have gotten there before the Federals did. Marshall blamed Stuart for the Confederates not winning the fictional race to Gettysburg. Then, strangely enough, Marshall praised Stuart for his role on the retreat.

Among Marshall's papers, Maurice found a memorandum dated April 15, 1868, by Colonel William Allan of a conversation Allan had had with Lee. Three questions were asked of Lee, the final one being why was Gettysburg fought and lost. In answer, the memorandum stated:

> [Lee] did not intend to give battle in Pennsylvania if he could avoid it. The South was too weak to carry on a war of invasion, and his offensive movements against the North were never intended except as parts of a defensive system. He did not know the Federal Army was at Gettysburg, *could not believe it* [italics in text], as Stuart had been specially ordered to cover his (Lee's) movements, and keep him informed of the enemy's position, and he (Stuart) had sent no word. He found himself engaged with the Federal Army, therefore, unexpectedly, and had to fight.

The letter continued that once engaged, "victory would have been won if he could have gotten one decided, simultaneous attack on the whole line. This he tried his uttermost for three days and failed."

Ewell, Rodes, Early, Edward Johnson, Longstreet, and Hill were named in the memorandum by Lee as having launched uncoordinated attacks. The memo then reviewed Lee's intentions for the summer campaign and followed other narratives of Lee's objectives. It mentioned that he accepted the fact that he would probably have to give battle before he returned in the fall, but "he had no idea of a permanent occupation of Pennsylvania."[5]

The memo said Lee was troubled as to gathering forage, so he "expected therefore to move about, maneuver, and alarm the enemy, threaten their cities, hit any blows he might be able to deliver without risking a general battle, and then, towards fall, return and recover his base." The next sentence was as amazing a leap as it was revealing: "Stuart's failure to carry out his intentions forced the battle of Gettysburg, and the imperfect, halting way in which his corps commanders, especially Ewell, fought the battle gave victory, which as he says trembled for three days in the balance, finally to the foe."

From narrating Lee's intentions, which were very similar to how the campaign was actually conducted, Allan jumped immediately to throwing the blame on Stuart—for forcing the battle upon Lee—and on Ewell for being cautious. Maurice editorialized:

> This memorandum is evidence that if Lee was careful to avoid in his dispatches, often to Marshall's grief, any appearance of defending his own reputation by casting blame upon subordinates, he was yet in general agreement with the criticisms and strictures which Marshall makes. It is also evidence that the prime cause of the Confederate failure in the campaign was Stuart's absence, and of their failure in the battle the lack of clear written orders, specifying how and when the attacks should be delivered.

Probably the best thing that can be said about Marshall's memoirs is that they were published after every major participant was dead. That was also the worst thing about them, since none could point out the irregularities, in particular that conversation with Stuart. Yet in attempting to take all blame from Lee, he turned the commander into a simpleton who could not remember his orders to Stuart from two days before and who did not have the sense to look in his own letter books for a copy of them.

Historians from Marshall beginning in July 1863 to historians today repeating the litany that "Stuart was late for the battle" have purposefully or inadvertently protected Lee. Gettysburg was Lee's fault. He tried to accept the blame. Allowing him to shoulder what he was willing to accept makes him all the greater.

CHAPTER TWELVE

Postmortem

"He never sent me a piece of false information."
—GENERAL ROBERT E. LEE ON STUART AFTER THE WAR

A number of modern historians, amateur and professional, have dealt with Stuart. Any thorough biography of Lee or book on the war or Battle of Gettysburg must include some reference to him. Most arguments blaming Stuart for the defeat originate from the same basic sources: Lee's staff including A. L. Long, but especially Charles Marshall, Henry Heth, and James Longstreet.

Three major biographies of Stuart have been published since the last of the original players died. A number of other works on the Gettysburg campaign have especially sought to make some sense of the controversy. Much of the twentieth-century criticism of Stuart has come as asides, often not documented or thoroughly analyzed, but more often merely accepted. The stories of Stuart disobeying Lee's orders had been repeated so often that they are considered the truth.

In his classic *Lee's Lieutenants,* published in 1944, Douglas Southall Freeman spent an entire chapter on Stuart in the campaign and titled it "The Price of 125 Wagons."[1] He began by recounting the number of newspapers that criticized Stuart for being surprised at Brandy Station. The *Richmond Whig* came out in defense of Stuart, predicting that soon he would make the Yankees regret it. Freeman thought that Stuart, after taking a beating from most of the other newspapers, resolved to do just that.

Stuart's desire for vindication at the cost of risking his command on another ride around the enemy has since been debunked by Wilbur S. Nye in *Here Come the Rebels!* Also, if Stuart were riding around the Union army only for fame, why did he pass up a raid on Washington on June 28?

Freeman interpreted Lee's June 23 published orders differently as well, which only indicated how confusing they were. He took "if General Hooker's army remains inactive, you can leave two brigades to watch him, and withdraw with the three others" to mean that Stuart should withdraw not *from* Lee's main body, but *to* the main body, emphasizing that "Stuart was free to determine whether he could 'pass around' the Federal army 'without hindrance'"[2] The logic and syntax in this made no sense, for Lee continued, "but if he should not appear to be moving northward, I think you had better withdraw this side of the mountains tomorrow night." According to Freeman, Lee seemingly repeated himself, ordering Stuart to stay with the army whether the enemy remained inactive or did "not appear to be moving northward."

Even Lee probably recognized how muddy these orders were, hence the letter McClellan recalls opening for Stuart at Rector's Cross Roads. Freeman failed to recognize the importance of this, in particular that Stuart should look for Early in York. Instead of suggesting that this communication was the reason for Stuart's move eastward, Freeman clung to the idea that Stuart was still to maintain contact with Lee, though Lee ordered him to contact Ewell or Early.

Freeman said Stuart spent too much time before crossing the Potomac and that once he did, "he did not know where Lee was."[3] Why Freeman should interject this is a mystery; Stuart was not looking for Lee but for Ewell or Early farther north. After he missed Early at York, assuming plans had changed, then he looked for Lee; it took one courier less than ten hours on July 1 to find him.[4] Freeman apparently was taking up Marshall's theme that Stuart was supposed to maintain contact with the main army. Freeman then contradicted the statement by repeating Lee's orders to "take position on Ewell's right."

Freeman recounted the capture of the wagon train and gave an inventory of its contents, yet wrote, "Singularly little of this ever reached the quartermasters." This appeared with no citation. Where did the food go? Though Stuart wrote nothing about his men feeding off the wagons, it is likely that he forbade it. Why cart 125 empty wagons around? Why did his men and horses stay up all night the very next day at Westminster, Maryland, after capturing the wagons, eating and feeding their horses from stores found there?[5]

Why, just two days after capturing the wagon train, was Stuart going to requisition food in Carlisle? If his 4,000 to 4,500 men consumed everything in the wagons, which could have fed nearly 10,000 Confederates, why did he not burn the empty wagons?

Freeman said that Stuart wrote about abstaining from attacking Washington "for hostile consumption," meaning for his critics at the newspapers. Perhaps, but a raid into the Northern capital would have gotten them scribbling sooner and on a much more positive note.

Freeman mentioned several times how long Stuart spent burning the railroad bridge at Sykesville, Maryland, and tearing up track and telegraph wire, but failed to acknowledge that Stuart had been ordered to do the enemy "all the damage you can." He also noted Heth's statement that Lee was continually asking for Stuart and his cavalry, as well as Lee's first post-battle report that it was a lack of cavalry that slowed the Confederate advance. (Remember, this was edited in the January 1864 report to read that the hot weather caused the leisurely pace.) Summing the two up, Freeman wrote:

> For his own part, Stuart would have been hurt and ashamed had he known how anxiously Lee was inquiring for news of him and how faltering was the movements of the Army in the absence of cavalry. Ignorant of his chief's distress, Stuart was not concerned that day, apparently, because of his wagon train.[6]

Freeman then gave a brief but excellent account of the fight at Hanover and an insightful introspective into Stuart's decision-making according to the intelligence at hand.

On the first day's battle at Gettysburg, Freeman mentioned Lee's reluctance to enter a large-scale fight until his divisions were up. This continued throughout the day until he finally ordered Ewell, who seemed merely to be carrying out Lee's wishes to avoid combat even after a major battle had been instigated, to take Cemetery and Culp's hills "if practicable." Stuart or any of Lee's concerns about him are not mentioned in connection with the opening of the battle.

In discussing how much intelligence the Confederates had on the Yankees' location up to that point in the battle, Freeman stated, "It was known that Stuart had been in a fight the previous day at Hanover."[7] This had no citation. Perhaps he was referring to the arrival of Major Venable, whom Stuart had sent to find Lee when he discovered Early had gone from York. But it confirmed that Stuart's location was generally known by the late afternoon of July 1. Later, Freeman said that Early thought the reports of cavalry behind the Confederate lines were merely "waifs from Stuart's fight at Hanover."[8]

Freeman did not mention Stuart in the decision-making for the second day's battle or the 250 troopers sent to Lee and Longstreet by Hampton, but he said Lee used his own two scouts to determine where the enemy was. Finally, after recounting the entire second day's battle, he began to discuss Stuart's whereabouts and arrival, saying it was afternoon on the 2nd when Stuart rode up to his "anxious" chief. Freeman acknowledged that there is no known record of the exchange between the two, but attributed Lee's statement about Stuart being "here at last" to tradition and cites John W. Thomason.

Freeman wrote that the "need of the presence of the cavalry was shown immediately by a clash at Hunterstown." This can be interpreted two ways: that Stuart had been needed all along and made it back just in time, or that thanks to

Stuart's active nature, he was again at the right place at the right time. Freeman did not elaborate, but did try to get into Stuart's mind when he said, "Stuart may have been disappointed that no applause greeted his return from his longest raid." Maybe, but Stuart immediately left Lee to ride out the railroad toward York to get shot at while discovering the enemy. It was back to business as usual.

In reviewing the defeat, Freeman wrote, "The approach of the Confederates to the battlefield was incautious. From the time the Army entered Pennsylvania, it was blinded by the absence of Stuart. Nothing was comparable to this in preparing the way for a tragedy." In this can be seen A. L. Long's argument that Gettysburg was a destination as well as Heth's parable about the well-trained giant being blinded and defeated.

In the next sentence, Freeman wrote, "On the 1st of July, having no information beyond that collected the previous day by Pettigrew, the van of the Third Corps advanced without cavalry. Contact by the front Division was with a strong Federal Corps. Another Union Corps was immediately at hand. Before the Confederates were aware of it, their leading Divisions were engaged beyond easy conclusion." But Pettigrew's information should have been enough to counsel extreme caution; if that had not been enough for Hill and Heth, the lack of cavalry should have made them more cautious. If that were still not enough, Lee's directive not to bring on a general engagement should have been obeyed.

Freeman concluded that the first day's battle was brought on by Stuart, who he said should have been on the scene scouting. "Obvious blame, also, would be charged against Powell Hill, if he had not been sick on the 1st,"[9] he added.

Of the battle on July 2, Freeman wrote, "Reconnaissance was inadequate. . . . Information concerning the enemy's left was scant and inaccurate."[10] He absolved Longstreet; by the time he had gotten his troops into position, the situation as Lee's scouts had observed it at dawn had changed. Union troops occupied the southern end of Cemetery Ridge. Freeman wrote, "There remains the consideration, not so easily determined, whether a thorough reconnaissance could have been made, and whether, in the absence of it, battle should have been joined. A small part only of the responsibility for this rests on Longstreet. The chief blame is that of Stuart, absent when most needed for reconnaissance."[11]

Why were Hampton's 250 troopers not used? Or those of E. V. White or Jenkins, both of whom arrived the day before? Would Stuart's 4,000 men have done any more good on the south end of the battlefield than did the 250 cavalrymen, Hood's Texas scouts, or Lee's engineers? If Lee and Longstreet felt that they did not know enough about the enemy, they should have done more. They were experienced officers. It is reasonable to conclude that they felt confident in their knowledge about the enemy and terrain and proceeded with the attack.

In the post-battle chapter, Freeman followed Marshall's memoirs, including the story that Stuart was late in writing his report and how Stuart allegedly admitted that he did not obey orders. Marshall's assertion at the Baltimore dinner party that Stuart should have been court-martialed also was included.

Freeman wrapped up his discussion of Stuart in the campaign by quoting Lee's official report on how the Army of Northern Virginia had been "embarrassed" by the absence of cavalry: "This was the measure of official criticism visited on Stuart. The full measure of historical criticism did not come in time to hurt his pride, though it impaired his fame." Freeman quoted himself from his earlier biography *R. E. Lee:*

> Stuart was innocent of most of the charges made against him, but he disregarded his principle mission of moving to the right flank of Ewell. . . . Orders were violated by Stuart when he encountered material "hindrance" and did not turn back. Lee had cherished the hope that "Jeb" could attack Hooker's trains and hamper the Federal operations, but the commanding General did not authorize or expect any such long raid as Stuart made. "Jeb's" worst shortcoming, ignored at the time, was his absence on the morning of July 2 when adoption of a sound battle-plan depended on careful reconnaissance of the Federal left.[12]

Although he had pretty much ignored them before, Freeman finally brought in Imboden and Robertson, concluding, "Imboden had angered Lee greatly by remaining at Hancock," which was exactly Longstreet's point as to the cavalry Lee missed on July 1. Freeman wrote, "Beverly Robertson had been slow in moving from the positions he had been left to defend in the Blue Ridge of Virginia. Not until July 3 did he join Lee."[13] Precisely Mosby's point, that Stuart left Robertson to do the tasks Lee wished done on the invasion.

One of the most highly esteemed modern historians of the Gettysburg campaign was Edwin Coddington. His *Gettysburg Campaign: A Study in Command* (1963, 1964, 1968) remains perhaps the most documented and well-respected work on the subject. Coddington also made an astute analysis of some controversies of the campaign. During a time when many historians bought into the arguments of Marshall, Long, and Heth, Coddington gave one of the more objective looks at Stuart's role in the campaign.

Coddington wrote that the effect of Brandy Station on Stuart's actions in the Gettysburg campaign was impossible to tell, in spite of the newspapers. He was fair to say that Jenkins and Imboden were taking care of the van of the invasion and that Lee was aware of their actions.

Coddington wrote that Lee had great faith in Stuart's judgment and gave him orders that seemed like suggestions. Stuart, as well, "was sanguine in temperament and experienced in semi-independent command, and he did not mind personal responsibility. On the contrary, he sought it."[14] Coddington wrote that, "without question," Lee wanted Stuart to take three of his five brigades, get ahead of the main army, and connect with Ewell.[15] More important, he wrote that whether Lee issued orders or suggestions, "the conditions upon which they are based should be made clear. Lee's orders to Stuart did not meet this standard."[16]

Coddington's interpretation of Stuart's June 22–23 orders differed from Freeman's. Lee's "first letter written on June 22 gave Stuart permission to join Ewell 'if you find that he [the enemy] is moving northward.' In a second letter sent at 5 P.M., June 23, the conditions Lee laid down were just the reverse." Concerning the confusing clause as to where Stuart should "withdraw" if Hooker's army remained inactive, Coddington thought Lee meant "presumably somewhere across the Potomac." What Lee meant by the second condition—"should he [Hooker] not appear to be moving northward"—Coddington thought was unclear. He did mention Lee's concern that Hooker might strike southward; perhaps that was the purpose for Lee's second contingency. But Stuart had to reach Ewell's troops.[17]

Coddington explained the change in Lee's orders by relating the effect Mosby's information given to Stuart on June 23 had on him. Tradition had Stuart discuss the move of cutting through the Yankee army with Lee and Longstreet and had them deciding that he should ride by way of Glasscock's Gap to the south, adding miles to the route but ensuring a safer passage. From this discussion, Coddington had Lee give Stuart a free hand in choosing the route, crossing the Potomac east or west of the Blue Ridge.

Coddington suspected that the dispatch H. B. McClellan opened for Stuart at Rector's Cross Roads late on June 23 was different from that of 5 P.M. that day. He placed the information in a note after his fifth chapter. Evidently, in a work as monumental as Coddington's, he apparently did not have time to analyze in depth the differences between the 5 P.M. letter and the one McClellan recalled. But his fine historian's mind sensed something and it was McClellan's "lengthy" missing dispatch.

He then discussed whether "Lee's approval of the Seneca Ford route was wise." He interpreted Lee's purposes for Stuart's mission: If Lee wanted Stuart to raid into the enemy's rear and do as much damage as possible, then reach Ewell, that was one thing; if he wished Stuart foremost to get into Pennsylvania and, on the way, incidentally harass the Yankees and gather supplies, that was another. The difference was the time Stuart was to spend in the enemy's rear. Coddington felt Lee's approval of Stuart's role should have been judged upon these criteria.

(McClellan's missing dispatch spoke of a time element, as did Stuart's report and Lee's report of January 1864, so perhaps Lee had second thoughts and later included a condition of time and speed in his orders. At least that was indicated in the dispatch McClellan remembered.)

Coddington related the problems with leaving Robertson and Jones but told of Stuart's explicit instructions. He followed Stuart's ride from 1 A.M. June 25 until early on June 28. To Coddington, that was the turning point for the invasion. He wrote, among other things, that Lee, late on June 28, was startled to learn from a spy that Hooker had crossed the Potomac. This is footnoted, however, to reports by Longstreet, Stuart, and Lee, none of which said anything about Lee being surprised or startled by the news.

Coddington then said that Lee had been "in the dark for almost a week about any major moves of the enemy."[18] Mosby, were he alive, would certainly disagree with him. To his credit as a historian, however, Coddington lumped the story of Harrison the spy finding the Union army for Lee together with the tale of the "shoeless brigade" starting the battle as "a mixture of truth and fiction," and pointed out that even the official versions in Lee's reports "both suffered from ambiguity and left certain questions unanswered." He also made an excellent point when he wrote that even though Lee had admitted giving Stuart discretion in his operations, oddly, Lee still held Stuart responsible for not reporting the enemy's movements. Only if Lee had been clear in his orders to definitely withdraw to the main army and cross at Shepherdstown could he "reasonably have made this inference" that Stuart would inform him of Hooker's movement.[19]

"Lee's surprise upon hearing of Hooker's crossing is therefore puzzling," was Coddington's conclusion. He also realized that as of June 23 Lee knew Hooker had thrown pontoon bridges across the Potomac, and that from Hooker's pattern of moves, he should have expected it. Coddington thought that the answer lay in Lee's comments about the absence of cavalry to provide him with accurate information, and then informed his readers how misleading these statements were: Lee had plenty of cavalry at his beckoning, "more than half of the troopers in Stuart's division."[20] He placed the blame for Lee's needing cavalry on Robertson, whose explicit orders left by Stuart told him to keep Lee and Longstreet informed of the enemy's movements. Coddington was just as perplexed as were Mosby and McClellan as to why Robertson did not follow Stuart's orders or why Lee allowed it to happen. Coddington also underestimated the effects of Stuart's ride (both in gathering supplies and upon the enemy) but absolved him of two of his critics' accusations:

> While Stuart's vainglorious ride around the Union army was a gross misuse of horseflesh and manpower, it neither stripped Lee of

cavalry nor deprived him of all opportunities to learn Hooker's whereabouts. There are no indications that Lee ordered the troopers still
available to him to look for the enemy at the obvious places.[21]

Coddington also included the controversy over the date of Harrison's arrival
at Lee's headquarters, but sided with those who thought Venable misdated the
dispatch, really meaning to date it "June 29." His opinion was that on June 29
Lee needed "effective cavalry support to screen his advance and to pinpoint the
location of enemy forces."[22] He mentioned Lee's use of "scouts" to obtain information as well as Pettigrew's report on June 30.

When Coddington said Lee believed the Union army was still in Maryland,
the endnotes lead right to Henry Heth's *Southern Historical Society Papers* article,
"The Causes of Lee's Defeat at Gettysburg," and A. L. Long's article of the same
name in the same publication.

Coddington wrote that on June 30, from the observations of others, if Lee were
concerned about cavalry or anything else, he kept it to himself. But since Imboden
and Robertson had not arrived, he had to leave behind infantry to do the work
cavalry could have done. "What troubled Lee more than anything else was the
absence of Stuart and his veteran brigades, for the time had come when they
could be most useful, if not indispensable," Coddington wrote. Still, Lee knew
he had given Stuart a mission; he was on it and Lee should have expected Stuart
to be looking for Ewell or Early in York. Coddington repeated Heth's story that
Lee asked over and over of Stuart's whereabouts.

Coddington mentioned Stuart capturing the wagon train outside of Rockville but attributed it to Stuart's "proclivity for the spectacular" rather than his
specific orders from Lee to gather provisions. "In this escapade if he did not
disobey Lee's orders, he at least went contrary to his commander's intentions. . . .
Stuart was furnished with a convenient excuse for delay." For the most part,
Coddington was sympathetic to—or at least objective about—Stuart's role, but
if he wanted to criticize something in Stuart's decision-making, this was the
wrong thing. Stuart was following both specific orders and the general purpose
of the campaign, and more than once considered burning the wagon train. He
did not jeopardize his mission for an excuse to delay; gathering supplies *was*
part of his mission.

Coddington called Hanover "a standoff affair" and followed Stuart's report,
in which he said he detoured around Hanover to save the wagons instead of heading toward York, where he was supposed to meet Early. He moved to accomplish
both. (Once again, McClellan's missing dispatch looms.) In an odd but literary
phrase, Coddington wrote, "Ewell and Early had kept their appointment at Gettysburg as decreed by the fates, but proud Stuart had missed it. The rest of his ride

was an anticlimax."[23] Here, as he did later in his book, Coddington echoed the sentiment of the post-war South over Gettysburg: The Yankees could not have beaten Lee in a fair fight, so fate did him in.

He bemoaned the fact that Stuart did not realize that he had crossed Early's path and did not follow it west; instead, he headed for Shippensburg via Carlisle. It was a little out of the way but the route would secure him provisions in the area's largest town.

Coddington did not see the advantage of Stuart's immobilizing Federal troops in Carlisle and frankly said that Stuart's role probably would not have been questioned if the Confederates had won at Gettysburg. But there are many things that might have changed had the Confederates won.

He saved his severest criticism for Stuart's own report, which he thought was mostly an apology. Stuart wrote too much, Coddington said. (Other historians have said the same, but his cavalry was more active, travelled farther, and fought more battles from June 15 to July 14 than any Confederate division of infantry or artillery. There was a lot to tell about.) In two revealing sentences, Coddington wrote that Stuart refused to admit that he was responsible for any delay and that "he implied that military necessity dictated his conduct and as a result he had no alternatives."[24] Surely Stuart's own personality showed through the ride as well as in the report on it; he refused to admit defeat or impediments a dozen times during the ride and many of his actions were dictated by Lee's orders.

Coddington repudiated Stuart's claims as to the damage he did or concern he caused the Yankees. Coddington quoted Brigadier General Henry J. Hunt, Union chief of artillery at Gettysburg, who called Stuart's ride "a good lesson on cavalry raids around armies, a thing easily done but of no particular use." Oddly, the cavalry in Hunt's own army, under flamboyant, hard-riding Major General Philip H. Sheridan, was a major force in the final undoing of the Confederate army in the spring of 1865. There are always at least two ways of listening to even the most respected of Civil War soldiers.

Coddington wrote that Stuart complained that the army was not where he thought it would be; to Coddington, that implied that Stuart thought its movement was conditional to his own. Stuart's complaint could also be taken to mean that he thought the invasion was to be a coordinated effort with himself and Ewell—or Early—cooperating once they reached Pennsylvania. Without proper communication, Ewell and Early marched to Gettysburg and Stuart, not hearing of it, continued to look for their juncture somewhere on the Susquehanna or at York.

Coddington correctly quoted Early as saying that he never received orders to send out scouts to communicate with Stuart. (The last orders concerning Stuart connecting with the advanced infantry went to Ewell on June 22.) Coddington then wrote that "beyond Stuart's report and the recollections of Major Henry B.

McClellan there is no evidence to indicate that Lee or Ewell told Early to watch for Stuart."[25]

Though tough in his review of Stuart's report, Coddington briefly commented on how Stuart's personal enemies made him a scapegoat. "As a result his role in the campaign became an object of scorn and derision, as well as the most generally accepted explanation for what went wrong for the rebels. To say that Stuart's late arrival was a major cause of Lee's defeat is a little too pat an answer."

In an endnote, Coddington called Charles Marshall, "the author of the letters of June 22 and 23 to Stuart, which were anything but models of clear, crisp, and definite English," Stuart's "bitterest critic." Too bad the comment was relegated to a note; Marshall's poorly written orders were the genesis of Stuart's actions during the campaign as well as the crux of the criticism later laid upon him.

In a fair summary, Coddington wrote:

> One thing is sure. On the eve of July 1 Lee had his forces in splendid shape to carry out his strategy of defeating the Army of the Potomac "in detail," that is, one part at a time. If, as Stuart's accusers insisted, the absence of cavalry permitted Lee to be surprised into an unfortunate encounter of major proportions at Gettysburg, they overlooked two important elements in the situation. Meade was just as surprised, and the initial advantage lay with Lee.[26]

Coddington later wrote that Lee was apparently satisfied with the intelligence gathered for him by Longstreet's engineer and the others he took along on the July 2 early-morning scout. Coddington reminded his readers that Lee, because of his Mexican War experiences, thought a small party of men best for such tactical reconnaissance work since they drew little attention. This answers Douglas Southall Freeman's charge that Stuart and his 4,000 cavalrymen were needed on the morning of July 2 to accomplish reconnaissance work for Lee.

A more recent biography of Stuart was *Bold Dragoon* by Emory Thomas, published in 1986. He came to some interesting conclusions about Stuart as his path led across the Potomac in June 1863. Stuart had had problems with Beverly Robertson before; he may have courted Flora Cooke Stuart at one time. Regardless, Robertson had been close to her father and waited until August 1861 to resign his commission and go with the Confederacy. Thomas discovered that Stuart once called Robertson "by far the most troublesome man I have to deal with."[27]

Thomas noted that Wade Hampton was also at odds with Stuart almost from the beginning, incensed that Virginia regiments got better duty or more glory that his Carolinians. Thomas said that Stuart learned to distance difficult subordinates from himself. By the time his ride around McClellan had brought him public adoration, Thomas assayed him as a man of action: "Stuart was not a contemplative man; he simply acted."[28]

Indeed, from the newspapers he had gained great fame for his ride around the Union army in 1862, but before that he had gained a reputation in the Confederate army of restlessness and untiring activity. The success, fame, and victories all came over a very short time. Thomas saw Stuart seeking promotion, as would any professional officer, and more fame. These desires, Thomas thought, stemmed from Stuart's adolescence and experiences at West Point and just after. The public infatuation with Stuart, in Thomas' view, began to fade after the Dumfries raid. After his great personal success leading Jackson's infantry at Chancellorsville, just as Stuart was thinking himself worthy of a lieutenant generalcy, came Brandy Station and the Gettysburg campaign.

Thomas used some letters to Flora and Stuart staff member Channing Price's brother Tom's diary (which fell into Federal hands and was partially published in the *New York Times*) to say that Stuart wore a mask as a defense mechanism to hide his flaws. From the diary excerpts that described him frolicking with his staff a number of times, Thomas concluded that Stuart was overacting. He wrote, "His romps and tickling and tales protested too much. This behavior was inappropriate for a hero. Stuart was becoming a boor."[29]

Thomas' analysis of the battles at Aldie, Upperville, and Middleburg concluded that Stuart helped screen the Confederate main force against a larger enemy while losing fewer men. However, Thomas called Stuart's reasons for not attacking on Sunday, June 21, uncharacteristic and found wanting the explanation to McClellan about allowing his brigade leaders more independent command in battle. "It would seem that Stuart's faith in himself may have indeed wavered. So he chose to rest upon his past laurels rather than seek new ones," Thomas wrote.[30]

His interpretation of Lee's orders to Stuart on June 22 was correct, and he included Mosby's role in Stuart's decisions. But he failed to mention anything about how confusing Lee's June 23 orders were. Instead, he used McClellan's version of Stuart's orders recalled in the "lengthy" dispatch. This choice of sources did not allow Thomas to compare the evidence, so he wrote, "Stuart had decided to do what he wanted to do."

Thomas praised Stuart for his actions during the retreat to Falling Waters. No sooner did he get Stuart across the Potomac than the wild gossip started, suggesting that Stuart be relieved of command.

Thomas well summarized Stuart's post-war defenders, especially McClellan and Mosby, but thought Mosby's only goal was Stuart's absolution. Mosby disliked scapegoating in order to raise Robert E. Lee to godhood at the expense of others. That he desired the truth to be told was just as strong a motive for Mosby and happened to coincide with defending Stuart.

Thomas noted that Fitz Lee, Rosser, and Hampton did not rush to Stuart's defense. He used Lee's article in the *Southern Historical Society Papers* for the source, but Lee later softened his attitude on Stuart in his book *General Lee*. Rosser praised Stuart and called him subject to error like all humans, but then went too far—perhaps inadvertently, perhaps for effect—by laying the entire blame for the failure of the campaign on Stuart. Hampton had had problems with Stuart all along.

Thomas thought that "perhaps the most damning piece of evidence in the case is Stuart's report," but fairly concluded, "Indeed some scholars have become so indignantly absorbed in Stuart's unfortunate explanations that they have judged him more for what he wrote rather than what he did."

Thomas pointed to the abnormal length of time Stuart's report took, but as the dates of other reports show, his was not any later than most. He thought the document too lengthy, but it was only several thousand words longer than Early's divisional report. Besides—as Thomas noted—Stuart's report of the Chickahominy Raid was verbose and flowery. Stuart's reports of major actions usually were lengthy.

In his summary of it all, Thomas remarked that Stuart's "report/apologia was indeed unfortunate" and contained fantasy. In a way, Thomas pointed out, Stuart's own success on this raid was his downfall: capturing the wagon train slowed him down even more, though Lee did give him the discretion to take the route in search of the enemy's lines of supply and communication. Stuart, Thomas said, underestimated the need for speed.

His criticism grew scathing: Stuart held on to the wagons because he was greedy, he underestimated the need for alacrity, and "gravely miscalculated the effect of his tardiness upon the campaign." Thomas compared Stuart's actions in the Gettysburg campaign, which he called timid and careless, with his other raids, which were a "rare blend of prudent audacity." He wrote that during this campaign, Stuart, who had redefined reconnaissance, lost two huge armies within his field of operations. Thomas threw out the idea that Stuart was merely trying to cleanse his record of Brandy Station; instead, he sought "to confirm his vision of himself."[31]

Thomas concluded with what he saw as Stuart's psychological problem: he had never learned to face failure, so feared it more than even death. His words to his men after his mortal wounding at Yellow Tavern, as he was being carried from the field, certainly reflected this analysis: "Go back! Go back and do your duty as I have done mine and our country will be safe. Go back! Go back! I had rather die than be whipped!"

But the personality "problem" Thomas saw was the same thing that was recognized and praised by others, including Lee, as it brought Stuart his successes.

Perhaps the most remarkable thing about such studies is that historians have the advantage of hindsight as well as plenty of time in which to analyze and decide, to weigh and ponder, to propose and condemn. Stuart had none of that. He made life-and-death decisions from the saddle, with the same aching back, empty stomach, and blurry, sleepy mind as the rest of his troopers, and he had to do it quickly.

It was easy for Coddington or Early to say that Stuart should have turned west upon crossing Early's track near Dover, but who knows what was going through Stuart's mind, what clutter or burden was occupying him at that moment? It is simple for Freeman to condemn him for not following orders, though even at his desk in his study, Freeman misunderstood Marshall's complicated, unclear directives. Stuart has been belittled for making immediate decisions, but had he not been the type to make them, and had he not made the correct ones so very often, he would never have attained his position before the Gettysburg campaign.

Decisions can be made only once, with the knowledge, experience, and limited foresight that is available at the time, then acted upon with iron resolve. Regardless of what men will say *someday*, there are orders to follow and duty *today*. Sometimes that is all a man can do. Sometimes that is all he needs to do. Certainly, it is all anyone can ask him to do.

Appendix

Cavalry Organization for the Gettysburg Campaign

UNION CAVALRY CORPS
MAJ. GEN. ALFRED PLEASONTON

First Division
Brig. Gen. John Buford

First Brigade *Col. William Gamble*
8th Illinois *Maj. John L. Beveridge*
12th Illinois (4 companies) *Col. George H. Chapman*
3rd Indiana (6 companies) *Col. George H. Chapman*
8th New York *Lt. Col. William L. Markell*

Second Brigade *Col. Thomas C. Devin*
6th New York *Maj. William E. Beardsley*
9th New York *Col. William Sackett*
17th Pennsylvania *Col. J. H. Kellogg*
3rd West Virginia (2 companies) *Capt. Seymour B. Conger*

Reserve Brigade *Brig. Gen. Wesley Merritt*
6th Pennsylvania *Maj. James H. Haseltine*
1st United States *Capt. Richard S. C. Lord*
2nd United States *Capt. T. F. Rodenbough*
5th United States *Capt. Julius W. Mason*
6th United States *Maj. Samuel H. Starr (wounded, July 3)*
　　　　　　　　Lt. Louis H. Carpenter
　　　　　　　　Lt. Nicholas Nolan
　　　　　　　　Capt. Ira W. Claflin (wounded, July 7)

Second Division
Brig. Gen. David McM. Gregg
1st Ohio, Company A (Headquarters Guard) *Capt. Noah Jones*

First Brigade *Col. John B. McIntosh*
1st Maryland (11 companies) *Lt. Col. James M. Deems*
Purnell (Maryland) Legion, Company A *Capt. Robert E. Duvall*
1st Massachusetts (detached to 6th Corps) *Lt. Col. G. S. Curtis*
1st New Jersey *Maj. M. H. Beaumont*
1st Pennsylvania *Col. John P. Taylor*
3rd Pennsylvania *Lt. Col. E. S. Jones*
3rd Pennsylvania Artillery, Section Battery H *Capt. W. D. Rank*

Second Brigade *Col. Pennock Huey*
2nd New York *Lt. Col. Otto Harhaus*
4th New York *Lt. Col. Augustus Pruyn*
6th Ohio (10 companies) *Maj. William Stedman*
8th Pennsylvania *Capt. William A. Corrie*

Third Brigade *Col. J. Irvin Gregg*
1st Maine (10 companies) *Lt. Col. Charles H. Smith*
10th New York *Maj. M. Henry Avery*
4th Pennsylvania *Lt. Col. William E. Doster*
16th Pennsylvania *Lt. Col. John K. Robison*

Third Division
Brig. Gen. Judson Kilpatrick
1st Ohio, Company C (Headquarters Guard) *Capt. S. N. Stanford*

First Brigade *Brig. Gen. Elon J. Farnsworth* (killed, July 3)
Col. Nathaniel P. Richmond
5th New York *Maj. John Hammond*
18th Pennsylvania *Lt. Col. William P. Brinton*
1st Vermont *Lt. Col. Addison W. Preston*
1st West Virginia (10 companies) *Col. Nathaniel P. Richmond*
                                    Maj. Charles E. Capehart

Second Brigade *Brig. Gen. George A. Custer*
1st Michigan *Col. Charles H. Town*
5th Michigan *Col. Russell A. Alger*
6th Michigan *Col. George Gray*
7th Michigan (10 companies) *Col. William D. Mann*

Horse Artillery

First Brigade *Capt. James M. Robertson*
9th Michigan Battery *Capt. Jabez J. Daniels*

6th New York Battery   *Capt. Joseph W. Martin*
2nd United States, Batteries B & L   *Lt. Edward Heaton*
2nd United States, Battery M   *Lt. A. C. M. Pennington, Jr.*
4th United States, Battery E   *Lt. Samuel S. Elder*

Second Brigade   *Capt. John C. Tidball*
1st United States, Batteries E & G   *Capt. Alanson M. Randol*
1st United States, Battery K   *Capt. William M. Graham*
2nd United States, Battery A   *Lt. John H. Calef*
3rd United States, Battery C (detached to Huey's Brigade)   *Lt. William D. Fuller*

Union Cavalry detached for headquarters guards and orderly work

General Headquarters   *Brig. Gen. Marsena R. Patrick*
2nd Pennsylvania Cavalry
6th Pennsylvania Cavalry, Companies E & I
United States Regular Cavalry (detachments from 1st, 2nd, 5th, and 6th)

Signal Corps   *Capt. Lemuel B. Norton*
Oneida (New York) Cavalry

First Army Corps General Headquarters
1st Maine Cavalry, Company L

Second Army Corps Headquarters
6th New York Cavalry, Companies D & K

Fifth Army Corps Headquarters
17th Pennsylvania Cavalry, Companies D & H

Sixth Army Corps Headquarters
1st New Jersey Cavalry, Company L
1st Pennsylvania Cavalry, Company H

Eleventh Army Corps Headquarters
1st Indiana Cavalry, Companies I & K
8th New York Cavalry (1 company)

CONFEDERATE CAVALRY DIVISION
Maj. Gen. J. E. B. Stuart

Hampton's Brigade   *Brig. Gen. Wade Hampton* (wounded, July 3)
Col. L. S. Baker
1st North Carolina   Col. L. S. Baker
1st South Carolina
2nd South Carolina
Cobb's (Georgia) Legion

Jefferson Davis Legion
Phillips (Georgia) Legion

Fitzhugh Lee's Brigade *Brig. Gen. Fitzhugh Lee*
1st Maryland Battalion (detached with Ewell's Corps)
                Maj. Harry Gilmor (captured)
                Maj. Ridgely Brown
1st Virginia *Col. James H. Drake*
2nd Virginia *Col. Thomas T. Munford*
3rd Virginia *Col. Thomas H. Owen*
4th Virginia *Col. Williams C. Wickham*
5th Virginia *Col. Thomas L. Rosser*

Robertson's Brigade Brig. Gen. Beverly H. Robertson
4th North Carolina *Col. D. D. Ferebee*
5th North Carolina

Jenkins' Brigade *Brig. Gen. A. G. Jenkins* (wounded July 2)
              Col. M. J. Ferguson
14th Virginia
16th Virginia
17th Virginia
34th Virginia Battalion *Lt. Col. Vincent A. Witcher*
36th Virginia Battalion
Jackson's (Virginia) Battery *Capt. Thomas E. Jackson*

Jones' Brigade *Brig. Gen. William E. Jones*
6th Virginia *Maj. C. E. Flournoy*
7th Virginia *Lt. Col. Thomas Marshall*
11th Virginia *Col. Lunsford L. Lomax*

W. H. F. Lee's Brigade *W. H. F. "Rooney" Lee* (wounded June 9)
              Col. J. R. Chambliss, Jr.
2nd North Carolina *Capt. William A. Graham*
9th Virginia *Col. R. L. T. Beale*
10th Virginia *Col. J. Lucius Davis*
13th Virginia

STUART HORSE ARTILLERY
Maj. R. F. Beckham
Breathed's (Virginia) Battery *Capt. James Breathed*
Chew's (Virginia) Battery *Capt. R. P. Chew*
Griffin's (Maryland) Battery *Capt. W. H. Griffin*
Hart's (South Carolina) Battery *Capt. J. F. Hart*
McGregor's (Virginia) Battery *Capt. W. M. McGregor*
Moorman's (Virginia) Battery *Capt. M. N. Moorman*

Imboden's Command *Brig. Gen. J. D. Imboden*

18th Virginia Cavalry *Col. George W. Imboden*
62nd Virginia Infantry (Mounted) *Col. George H. Smith*
Virginia Partisan Rangers *Capt. John H. McNeill*
Virginia Battery (McClanahan's) *Capt. J. H. McClanahan*

Confederate Cavalry detached for headquarters guards and orderly work

Second Army Corps
Randolph's Company Virginia Cavalry

Notes

INTRODUCTION

1. *War of the Rebellion: Official Records of the Union and Confederate Armies* (hereafter cited as *O. R.*), Ser. I, Vol. 27, Part iii, "Correspondence, etc."

2. The reports are found in Ibid., Ser. I, Vol. 27, Parts i and ii, "Reports."

CHAPTER ONE: SCHOOLING OF THE TROOPER

1. Much of Stuart's early life was taken from his biographers, H. B. McClellan, who served on Stuart's staff, and John Thomason, who knew and interviewed Stuart's family.

2. Adele H. Mitchell, ed., *The Letters of Major General James E. B. Stuart* (Stuart-Mosby Historical Society, 1990), 9–10. A vast source of personal information and precise documentation is available to the public thanks to this publication. Many dates can now be corrected and a much finer knowledge of Stuart gained through his personal correspondence. Hereafter cited as Stuart's Letters.

3. John W. Thomason, Jr., *J. E. B. Stuart* (New York: Charles Scribner's Sons, 1930), 19.

4. Stuart's Letters, 179.

5. Ibid., 13–16.

6. Ibid., 24–25.

7. Thomason, 19.

8. Stuart's Letters, 23.

9. *Southern Historical Society Papers* (hereafter cited as *SHSP*), Vol. 1, 100.

10. Ibid., 100.

11. Stuart's Letters, 3.

12. Ibid., 104.

13. Ibid., 8.

14. Ibid., 39.

15. Ibid., 70, 403.

16. Mary P. Coulling, *The Lee Girls* (Winston-Salem, N.C.: 1987), 41.

17. Stuart's Letters, 87.

18. Coulling, 94.

19. Stuart's Letters, 109.

20. Ibid., 108.

21. H. B. McClellan, *I Rode with Jeb Stuart* (Bloomington, IN: Indiana University Press, 1988 [reprint]), 9.

22. Stuart's Letters, 83; Burke Davis, *J. E. B. Stuart: The Last Cavalier* (New York: The Fairfax Press, 1988), 24–27.

23. Stuart's Letters, 32.

24. Davis, 24–27.

25. Stuart's Letters, 30.

26. Author's collection.

27. Stuart's Letters, 121.

28. Ibid., 120–21.

29. Ibid., 124.

30. Ibid., 126–47.

31. Thomason, 21–22.

32. Stuart's Letters, 143.

33. Ibid., 142–43.

34. Ibid., 153.

35. Ibid., 159–61.

36. Ibid., 166–75.

37. Davis, 38.

38. Stuart's Letters, 185.

39. Ibid.

40. Ibid., 186–87.

41. Ibid., 187.

42. Thomason, 55.

43. Stuart's Letters, 186.

44. *John Brown's Raid,* Government Printing Office, 49.

45. Ibid.

46. Stuart's Letters, 188–89.

47. Ibid., 178.

48. Ibid., 193–94.

49. Ibid., 193–94.

CHAPTER TWO: CIVIL WAR

1. Stuart's Letters, 193.

2. Ibid., 207.

3. W. W. Blackford, *War Years with Jeb Stuart* (New York, Charles Scribner's Sons, 1945), 16; McClellan, 320–21. Jones' hatred was personal. He appreciated Stuart's military sagacity. According to McClellan's book, when Jones heard of Stuart's death at Yellow Tavern, he paced his tent for a long while with downcast eyes. Finally, he said to his assistant adjutant general, Walter K. Martin, "By God, Martin! You know I had little love for Stuart, and he had just as little for me; but that is the greatest loss that army has sustained except the death of Jackson."

4. John Esten Cooke, "General Stuart in Camp and Field," *Annals of the War* (Philadelphia: Philadelphia Weekly Times, 1879), 666.

5. B. A. Botkin, ed., *A Civil War Treasury of Tales, Legends, and Folklore* (New York: Random House, 1960), 25.

6. Ibid.

7. Stuart's Letters, 210–11.

8. Blackford, 32.

9. Stuart's Letters, 212.

10. Blackford, 33.

11. McClellan, 39–40.
12. Ibid., 42.
13. Stuart's Letters, 218.
14. Stuart's Letters, 225.
15. Ibid., 228.
16. Ibid., 231. This statement is important historically. It meant that if Stuart were confident that he could get a personal note from his wife secretly to the wife of a Union general, he certainly must have had some connections in Washington. Could these connections have helped Stuart in his remarkable abilities of gathering information on the enemy?
17. Ibid., 237.
18. Ibid., 249.
19. Ibid., 250.
20. Ibid., 255.
21. McClellan, 60.
22. Ibid., 60.
23. Douglas S. Freeman, *Lee's Lieutenants* (New York: Charles Scribner's Sons, 1946), vol. I, 295.
24. Walter H. Taylor, *Four Years with General Lee* (1877. Reprint. New York: Bonanza Books, 1962), 41.
25. McClellan, 86.
26. Thomason, 225; McClellan, 90–91; Stuart's Letters, 260–61.
27. McClellan, 96–101.
28. Alan Gatt, *Brave Men's Tears* (Dayton, OH: Morningside, 1985).
29. Blackford, 125.
30. McClellan, 104–5.
31. Blackford, 127.
32. McClellan, 105–6.
33. Blackford, 141–42.
34. Stuart's Letters, 265.
35. McClellan, 115.
36. Ibid., 131–32.
37. *O. R.*, Ser. I, Vol. 19, Part ii, 55.
38. Blackford, 165.
39. McClellan, 146.
40. Davis, 216–34.
41. McClellan, 146–47.
42. Ibid., 163.
43. Ibid., 148.
44. Blackford, 180.
45. Thomason, 316–17.
46. Stuart's Letters, 267.
47. Ibid., 272.
48. Ibid., 279.
49. Davis, 251; Coulling, 113.
50. McClellan, 195.
51. Freeman, vol. II, 350.
52. Thomason, 347–52.
53. Stuart's Letters, 300.

54. Ibid., 301.
55. Ibid., 314.
56. McClellan, 232.
57. Thomason, 377.
58. McClellan, 236; from Cooke's *Life of Jackson,* 430.
59. Thomason, 384–85.
60. McClellan, 251.
61. Davis, 312.
62. McClellan, 255–56.
63. Blackford, 210.
64. McClellan, 261.
65. Thomason, 395.
66. Blackford, 211–12.
67. Ibid., 215.
68. Thomason, 409.
69. Freeman, vol. III, 19.
70. Stuart's Letters, 324.

CHAPTER THREE: RAIDING ON A GRAND SCALE

1. McClellan, 296.
2. *O. R.,* Ser. I, Vol. 27, Part ii, 688.
3. Ibid., 742–43.
4. McClellan, 297.
5. *O. R.,* Ser. I, Vol. 27, Part i, 952.
6. Ibid., Part ii, 739, 740, 742; McClellan, 297.
7. *O.R.,* Ser. I, Vol. 27, Part ii, 745.
8. Ibid., 746.
9. Ibid., 742.
10. McClellan, 300.
11. *O. R.,* Ser. I, Vol. 27, Part ii, 741.
12. McClellan, 301–2.
13. *O. R.,* Ser. I, Vol. 27, Part i, 963–64.
14. John S. Mosby, *War Reminiscences* (New York: Dodd, Mead, and Company, 1898), 164–67.
15. *O. R.,* Ser. I, Vol. 27, Part i, 975.
16. Ibid., Part ii, 690.
17. Ibid., Part i, 920–21.
18. Ibid., Part ii, 690.
19. Ibid., Part i, 1,035.
20. Ibid., Part ii, 690–91.
21. Ibid., Part i, 954.
22. Ibid., 921.
23. Nye, 204–5.
24. *O. R.,* Ser. I, Vol. 27, Part i, 954.
25. McClellan, 314.
26. Nye, 210–11.
27. Edwin B. Coddington, *The Gettysburg Campaign: A Study in Command* (New York: Charles Scribner's Sons, 1968), 162.
28. Ibid., 188.

29. Jacob Hoke, *The Great Invasion of 1863* (Gettysburg, PA: Stan Clark Military Books, 1992 [reprint]), 172–73.

30. Coddington, 105.

31. *O. R.,* Ser. I, Vol. 27, Part iii, 912–13.

CHAPTER FOUR: ORDERS

1. McClellan, 315.

2. Mosby, "Philadelphia Weekly Times" article, December 15, 1877, *B & L,* Vol. III, 251.

3. *O. R.,* Ser. I, Vol. 27, Part ii, 692. In his post-battle report, Stuart said, "I submitted to the commanding general" the plan of leaving at least a brigade and passing between the Union army and Washington. Lee's report (ibid., 316) says the same thing. Stuart's orders from Lee on June 22 (ibid., Part iii, 913) refer to a note of 7:45 A.M. to Longstreet and, for the first time in writing, suggest that Stuart move into Maryland with three brigades (leaving two behind) and take position on Ewell's right, if the enemy were moving northward. It is doubtful that Lee pulled this suggestion out of thin air; indeed, Stuart had suggested it to him earlier, as he wrote. Subsequent correspondence among Longstreet, Stuart, and Lee tighten up Stuart's orders to march around the Union army and Longstreet refers to Lee speaking of Stuart's leaving the army and passing to the rear of the enemy. See also *O. R.,* Part iii, 914, 915, and 923, and Mosby's December 1877 article in the *Philadelphia Weekly Times.*

4. Charles Marshall, *An Aide-de-Camp of Lee,* Sir Frederick Maurice, ed. (Boston: Little, Brown and Company, 1927), 201. Other parts of Marshall's recollection of what Lee told him about his meeting with Stuart are suspect; they contradict the orders issued subsequently by Lee to Stuart. When his memoirs were being written, Marshall had been for years building a case against Stuart. Perhaps some of his own prejudices had crept into his recollections by then.

5. *O. R.,* Ser. I, Vol. 27, Part iii, 913.

6. Ibid., 914.

7. Ibid., 914–15.

8. McClellan, 160. In the letter to his wife (Stuart's Letters, 267), Stuart estimated ninety miles in thirty-six hours.

9. *O. R.,* Ser. I, Vol. 27, Part iii, 915.

10. Ibid., 923.

11. Marshall, *Aide-De-Camp,* 207.

12. David G. McIntosh, *SHSP,* Vol. 37, 95.

13. *O. R.,* Ser. I, Vol. 27, Part ii, 297.

14. McClellan, 317–18.

15. Chiswell Dabney "Incedent" Letter, Virginia Historical Society.

16. Marshall mentioned it first in a speech he gave in January 1896 before the Confederate Veteran Association of Washington and subsequently published in Vol. 23, *SHSP,* 205. The recognition, or rather denial, of McClellan's recalled missing dispatch appears also in his posthumously published *Papers.*

17. Douglas Southall Freeman, *The South to Posterity* (New York: Charles Scribner's Sons, 1951), 87–88.

18. A perusal of the official correspondence during just a few days of the Gettysburg campaign (June 17–30) reveals well over a dozen references to "Your letter of June —, received" when no letter or note appears anywhere in the records. Add to that the unknown number of verbal communications that were sent, and there is truly a remarkably large amount of missing correspondence—both Union and Confederate.

19. *O. R.,* Ser. I, Vol. 27, Part iii, 927–28.

20. Thomason, 426; Davis, 324; McClellan, 319, all agree on size of Robertson's command.

21. See McClellan, 319n, for Early's contention in *SHSP*, Vol. 4, 245, that Jenkins had only 1,500 to 1,600 men. Thomason said 1,800.

22. Thomason, 426.

23. McClellan, 261.

24. Blackford, 214.

25. McClellan, 109.

26. Emory M. Thomas, *Bold Dragoon* (New York: Harper & Row, 1986; reprint, Vintage Books, 1988), 91–92.

27. McClellan, 319.

28. Cooke, 230.

29. Ibid., 231.

30. Ibid.

31. *O. R.*, Ser. I, Vol. 27, Part iii, 931.

32. Coddington, 165.

33. Mosby, *Stuart's Cavalry*, 109. Mosby wrote that with Jones on picket duty and considering his reputation, no one could doubt that he would report all he saw. The 12th Virginia was also detached from Jones and contained Baylor's company, recruited from near Charles Town. According to Mosby, Baylor "was an active partisan officer; with him were a number of men distinguished as scouts. Couriers were sent frequently from this regiment to General Lee." Mosby also said that Longstreet had his signal officer with him; if he had wanted to know where the enemy was, Longstreet could always have sent him to one of the mountaintops to find out.

34. Coddington, 166.

35. Ibid., 167.

36. Cooke, 233.

37. Marshall, 217; *O. R.*, Ser. I, Vol. 27, Part iii, 307, 316.

38. McClellan, 323–24.

CHAPTER FIVE: AROUND THE YANKEES AGAIN

1. Cooke, 237.

2. Jack Coggins, *Arms and Equipment of the Civil War* (New York: The Fairfax Press, 1962), 121.

3. Cooke, 239.

4. *Annals of the War*, 419 (pre-1879); *Manassas to Appomattox* (1896), 346–47.

5. Marshall, 219.

6. Arthur Fremantle, *Three Months in the Southern States* (London: William Blackwood and Sons, 1863), 255–56.

7. William G. Piston, *Lee's Tarnished Lieutenants* (Athens, GA: The University of Georgia Press, 1987), 131.

8. Marshall, 216. Why Marshall tried to imply that Stuart misled Lee can only be attributed to Marshall's dislike for him, which emerged in the years after the war. To say that Lee was purposely led to believe that the Union army had not crossed is ridiculous; it implies that Stuart virtually committed treason giving Lee false information, a charge belied by Stuart's devotion to his state, his country, and to Lee, and by Lee's own comment upon Stuart's death: "He never brought me a piece of false information." One can only hope, for Marshall's sake, that "misled" was merely a poor choice of word.

9. Edwin Coddington came to this same conclusion, in spite of Lee's reports, which said, "Nothing having been heard from him [Stuart] since our entrance into Maryland, it was inferred that

the enemy had not yet left Virginia." (*O. R.,* Ser. I, Vol. 27, Part ii, 316.) That was the wrong inference to have made.

10. *O. R.,* Ser. I, Vol. 27, Part iii, 925.

11. John S. Mosby, *Stuart's Cavalry in the Gettysburg Campaign* (New York: Moffat, Yard, and Company, 1908), 91, 99. See also Lee's and Davis' correspondence in *O. R.,* Ser. I, Vol. 27, Part i, 77; Ibid., Part iii, 904, 910–11, 925–26, 931–32. All of these letters address the safety of Richmond from Union troops north and south of the city and the formation of a Confederate force in Culpeper under General P. G. T. Beauregard to threaten Washington and alleviate that concern. Marshall wrote that "General Lee began to become uneasy as to the purpose of the Federal commander, and to fear that he contemplated a strong movement against Richmond. He remarked that such a proceeding on the part of the enemy would compel the immediate return of his own army to Virginia, if it could indeed reach Richmond in time to defend the city. I heard General Lee express this apprehension more than once while we lay at Chambersburg." *Aide-de-Camp,* 217–18.

12. *SHSP,* vol. 37, 210. McKim makes an interesting argument, using riding times of couriers and the time of the issuance of orders by Ewell, but concluded his argument by dropping names to support his thesis: "Either Colonel Venable in writing the letter from memory made a mistake in dating it the 28th, or General Lee and General Longstreet, and General Long and Colonel Marshall and Colonel Taylor were all mistaken in the belief that the change in the plans of the campaign was due to the arrival of a scout on the night of the 28th. Which is the more likely supposition?" Considering the confusion Longstreet's article and Fremantle's diary entry display, and the fact that Long and Taylor both used Lee's report (written by Marshall) for their information, they are hardly unimpeachable witnesses for McKim.

13. Jones' Report, *O. R.,* Ser. I, Vol. 27, Part ii, 751.

14. Coddington, 173.

15. *Encounter at Hanover* (Hanover, PA: Historical Publication Committee of the Hanover Chamber of Commerce, 1963), 44; Freeman, vol. iii, 69.

16. Blackford, 225; McClellan, 327.

17. *O. R.,* Ser. I, Vol. 27, Part i, reports of Colonel N. P. Richmond, 1st West Virginia, 1005; Major John Hammond, 5th New York, 1008; Major W. B. Darlington, 18th Pennsylvania, 1011.

18. Ibid., reports of Lieutenant Colonel A. W. Preston, 1st Vermont, 1013; Major C. E. Capehart, 1st West Virginia, 1018.

19. Ibid., 1008.

20. Ibid.

21. William A. Graham to McClellan, April 5, 1886, John B. Bachelder Papers, New Hampshire Historical Society in Gettysburg National Military Park library. Hereafter cited as Bachelder Papers.

22. Blackford, 226–27.

23. Coggins, 35.

24. *Encounter at Hanover,* 56.

25. *O. R.,* Ser. I, Vol. 27, Part ii, 696.

26. Cooke, 242.

CHAPTER SIX: TO GETTYSBURG

1. A. L. Long, *Memoirs of Robert E. Lee* (1886. Reprint. Secaucus, NJ: The Blue and Grey Press, 1983), 275.

2. James Longstreet, *From Manassas to Appomattox* (Philadelphia: J. B. Lippincott, 1896), 351.

3. Ibid., 351.

4. Ibid., 358–59.
5. Taylor, *Four Years with General Lee*, 92.
6. Ibid., 93.
7. Thomas G. Tousey, *Military History of Carlisle and Carlisle Barracks* (Richmond: The Dietz Press, 1939), 229.
8. D. W. Thompson, "Carlisle Is Bombarded," *Carlisle Sentinel* (Carlisle, Pennsylvania: July 1863).
9. Cooke, 245.
10. *O. R.,* Ser. I, Vol. 27, Part ii, 318.
11. Freeman, vol. iii, 111.
12. John L. Black, 1st South Carolina Cavalry, to Bachelder, March 22, 1886. Bachelder Papers, Gettysburg National Military Park.
13. Freeman, vol. iii, 119.
14. Heth, *SHSP,* vol. IV, 156–57, implied this and Long, 277, used it as his theme: that Lee for more than a month had wanted to fight near Gettysburg and Stuart's absence prevented him from gaining the proper ground.
15. Freeman, vol. iii, 139.
16. Interview with Robert J. Trout, October 1993.
17. Tucker, *High Tide,* 316–17. There are a number of errors in this account. It has Stuart arriving with Fitz Lee and H. B. McClellan at the Thompson House headquarters of Lee at 11 P.M. (Actually, Stuart arrived, probably alone, in the early afternoon; this came from McClellan himself [*Campaigns of Stuart's Cavalry,* 332] in 1885.)
18. Ibid.
19. Cooke, 246.
20. Robert J. Trout, author of *They Followed the Plume,* a comprehensive study of Stuart's staff officers, states that in all his years of research, he found no evidence from any to indicate they were present when Stuart met Lee.
21. Ibid., 246.
22. Paul Shevchuk, "The Battle of Hunterstown, Pennsylvania, July 2, 1863," *Gettysburg: Historical Articles of Lasting Interest* (Dayton, OH: Morningside, Inc., July 1989), 96.
23. Ibid., 99.
24. Ibid.
25. Ibid.

CHAPTER SEVEN: THE THIRD OF JULY

1. McClellan, 337. In 1906, in a letter to Jonathan W. Daniel, Witcher wrote, "It is wholly and absolutely untrue that Jenkins' brigade went into the Battle of Gettysburg with only ten rounds of ammunition. . . . My command had solitary and alone fought Griggs [Gregg's] dismounted men for hours before Stuart's command came." Daniel Papers, University of Virginia, Gettysburg National Military Park library.
2. McClellan, 337.
3. Witcher letter to Daniels, March 22, 1906. Daniel Papers, U. Va., GNMP library.
4. *O. R.,* Ser. I, Vol. 27, Part ii, 724.
5. J. H. Kidd, *Personal Recollections of a Cavalryman* (1908. Reprint. New York: Bantam Books, 1991) 79–80.
6. Bouldin to Bachelder, July 29, 1886, Bachelder Papers.
7. Bachelder map.
8. Confederate Colonel V. A. Witcher says he moved out to the Rummel barn between 8 and

10 A.M. George Briggs of the 7th Michigan, March 26, 1886, in the Bachelder Papers wrote that at 10 A.M. July 3, a force of Confederate cavalry and a battery appeared upon the army's right flank, that there was a short duel, and that the Confederate battery withdrew. Also, former artillery Captain Carle A. Woodruff wrote that the enemy battery near Rummel's (its position from his point of view) was silenced about 10 A.M. Former Lieutenant A. C. M. Pennington, whose guns were directly involved, could not recall twenty years after the battle in a letter to Woodruff even whether his battery was in sections or whether he had four or six guns.

9. Bachelder maps.

10. Witcher to Bachelder, April 7, 1886. Colonel John B. Bachelder was commissioned shortly after the Battle of Gettysburg to correspond with participants to ascertain their actions. He later produced detailed battle maps and the text for the government markers on the field. Much of his correspondence is in the "vertical files" of Gettysburg National Military Park and provides a fascinating, if sometimes contradictory, narrative of the battle. The correspondence on the cavalry action mostly dates from 1885–86 (with some as early as 1879), and so represents remembrances two decades after the fact. Most of the cavalrymen on both sides frankly concede that much of the fighting at Gettysburg was a blur, both at the time (because of exhaustion) and in the 1880s because of the time lapse. Yet, as primary sources go, for the cavalry battle, they are the best available. The Bachelder Papers regarding the cavalry battle east of Gettysburg are, to my knowledge, used extensively here in a book for the first time.

11. Witcher to McClellan, March 16, 1886, Bachelder Papers. "[We] held our position until towards 3 o'clock in the evening, when our ammunition being nearly exhausted as we had drawn none for some days."

12. Witcher to Bachelder, April 7, 1886, Bachelder Papers.

13. Woodruff to Bachelder, June 26, 1886, Bachelder Papers.

14. Robert K. Krick, *Ninth Virginia Cavalry* (The Virginia Regimental Histories Series) (Lynchburg, VA: H. E. Howard, Inc., 1982), 24; McClellan, 339.

15. This road, which crosses the cavalry battlefield, can now barely be seen. It lies abandoned— a trace road—from where Hampton's and Lee's brigades once joined toward the Low Dutch Road.

16. Kidd, 77.

17. Witcher to Bachelder, March 19, 1886, Bachelder Papers.

18. Robert J. Driver, Jr., *The Staunton Artillery—McClanahan's Battery* (Lynchburg, VA: H. E. Howard, Inc., 1988), 65.

19. William Brooke-Rawle, 1878 pamphlet "The Right Flank at Gettysburg" (Philadelphia: *The Philadelphia Weekly Times,* September 14, 1878), 21.

20. Dimitry letter, May 13, 1886, Bachelder Papers.

21. *B & L,* Vol. 3, 402.

22. Witcher to Bachelder, April 7, 1886, Bachelder Papers. Reading the accounts from the Bachelder Papers, one gets the impression that by July 3, the Confederate cavalry force was a shadow of the nearly 4,500 troopers who left Lee's army on June 25. The 2nd North Carolina, for example, was down to thirty-five men after Hanover, according to its commander, Colonel William Graham.

23. Witcher to Bachelder, March 19, 1886, Bachelder Papers.

24. Ibid.

25. Morgan to Bachelder, April 1886, Bachelder Papers.

26. Ibid.

27. Kidd, 83–84.

28. Trowbridge to Alger, February 19, 1886, Bachelder Papers.

29. Ibid.

30. *O. R.,* Ser. I, Vol. 27, Part ii, 698.

31. Statement of E. G. Fishburne, n.d., Bachelder Papers.

32. *O. R.*, Ser. I, Vol. 27, Part ii, 698.

33. *B & L*, Vol. 3, 404.

34. *O. R.*, Ser. I, Vol. 27, Part ii, 724–25.

35. Captain A. E. Mathews' account, n.d., Bachelder Papers.

36. Ibid.

37. *O. R.*, Ser. I, Vol. 27, Part ii, 725.

38. Ingram to McClellan, April 12, 1886, Bachelder Papers.

39. Lieutenant James I. Lee, Company F, 2nd Virginia Cavalry, to Bachelder; Edward Burgh to General T. T. Munford, July 5, 1885; *O. R.*, Ser. I, Vol. 27, Part ii, 345 (casualty returns) shows that the 2nd suffered one killed, three wounded, and one missing—about the same as other units not engaged in the final charge—as opposed to twenty-two casualties of the 1st Virginia.

40. Krick, 24; Daniel T. Balfour, *13th Virginia Cavalry* (Lynchburg, VA: H. E. Howard, Inc., 1986), 22.

41. Graham to McClellan, April 5, 1886.

42. *B & L*, Vol. 3, 404.

43. Ibid.

44. Speese, 9. He noted several other misstatements Miller made about people who were not even at Gettysburg. Speese bemoaned some published works, then being used at West Point, citing the apocryphal story of Miller's charge, and debunked two well-told stories of two pairs of enemies—two of whom Miller claimed were from the 3rd Pennsylvania—found clutched in one another's death grip. Speese pointed out that the records show not a man from the 3rd was killed on July 3. The little pamphlet is fascinating, but little known, for Miller's and Brooke-Rawle's works got into large publications. The pamphlet also illustrates that the controversies about Gettysburg began long ago and probably will continue.

45. Balfour, 22–24. Brooke-Rawle, *Annals* 482. Speese in his pamphlet mentioned that his men saw in the Confederate column "a color bearer . . . was a man of exceptional courage. Riding in the rear upon a gray horse, he waved the flag and defied the Yankees to take it. We tried hard to snipe him and secure the colors, but without success."

46. Morgan of the 1st Virginia gave another account of an officer who he thought was Hampton: "Suddenly, like an angel of deliverance, the noble and commanding form of Wade Hampton, waving the colors in his hand, came thundering up like a whirlwind. I hailed him as our deliverer. . . . Just as he came up to where I was standing, a shell struck his horse behind the saddle, and exploding almost cut it in two, and seriously wounding him. He was at once carried bleeding from the field." (To Bachelder, April 1886. Bachelder Papers.) Hampton himself said he was wounded by shrapnel in the body (which may have accounted for the blood seen on his thigh) and twice saber-slashed across the head. (Freeman, vol. 3, 195.)

47. Witcher to Bachelder, March 19, 1886. Referring to the area near the fence across which his troopers and the 7th Michigan fought, he wrote, "I went over this portion of the field with Gen. Stewart [sic] about sunset & he congratulated me on the stand I made."

48. At Fairfield, Pennsylvania, seven miles west of Gettysburg, as Stuart's final charge was receding, the 6th U.S. Cavalry was stopped from attacking the wagons and rear of the Confederate army by Grumble Jones' brigade.

CHAPTER EIGHT: COVERING THE WITHDRAWAL

1. Coddington, 543–44.

2. *B & L*, Vol. 3, 429.

3. *B & L*, Vol. 3, 424.

4. Bouldin to Bachelder, July 29, 1886, Bachelder Papers.

5. Fortesque Diary, Gettysburg National Military Park files, courtesy Gregory Coco.

6. Ted Alexander, co-author of *When War Passed This Way*, wrote that Imboden took the Pine Stump Road at Greenwood, then traveled to Greencastle and Williamsport via the Williamsport Road. (Correspondence with the author, November, 1993.)

7. W. P. Conrad and Ted Alexander, *When War Passed This Way* (Greencastle, PA: Greencastle Bicentennial Publication, 1982), 196.

8. *B & L*, Vol. 3, 425.

9. John W. Schildt, *Roads from Gettysburg* (Chewsville, MD: John W. Schildt, 1979), 37.

10. Stuart's exact route from Graceham through the Catoctin Mountains is debated to this day. The easiest way through the mountains just west of Thurmont is along Route 77, which goes directly to Smithburg. According to John Schildt in *Roads from Gettysburg,* Union cavalry was across that route, so the Confederates either took the Hampton Valley Road to Eyler's Valley, Deerfield, and Raven Rock, or could have gone north of Thurmont to Sabillasville to Deerfield and Raven Rock and along a mountain road. The problem is that the mountain road has all but disappeared.

11. *O. R.,* Ser. I, Vol. 27, Part ii, 701.

12. *O. R.,* Ser. I, Vol. 27, Part i, 928.

13. *B & L,* Vol. 3, 426–27.

14. Ibid.

15. Ibid.

16. *O. R.,* Ser. I, Vol. 27, Part i, 928.

17. Ibid.

18. Ibid., 996.

19. *O. R.,* Stuart's Report, 703. Conrad and Alexander (197) place this capture at Cunningham's Crossroads (now Cearfoss, Maryland). Colonel Lewis B. Pierce sent 200 cavalrymen of the 12th Pennsylvania and 1st New York who attacked the strung-out train. They place the capture at 100 wagons, three pieces of artillery, and 500 prisoners.

20. Coddington, 565.

21. *O. R.,* Ser. I, Vol. 27, Part ii, 703.

22. Daniel C. Toomey, *The Civil War in Maryland* (Baltimore: The Toomey Press, 1983), 86.

23. Alexander Correspondence, November 1993.

24. *O. R.,* Ser. I, Vol. 27, Part iii, 985. This is reminiscent of Longstreet's comment in his memoirs that Lee was "vexed . . . at the halt of the Imboden cavalry . . . in the opening of the campaign," that Lee still did not trust Imboden completely after his earlier actions.

25. Stuart's Letters, 326–27.

26. Schildt, 109.

27. Toomey, 88–89.

28. Ted Alexander, author and park historian at Antietam National Battlefield, recommends a visit to the Washington County Free Library and the Western Maryland Room there. Files of the battle at Funkstown document this action.

29. Clifford Dowdey and Louis Manarin, eds., *The Wartime Papers of Robert E. Lee* (New York: Bramhall House, 1961), 547.

30. McClellan, 364–66.

31. Stuart's Letters, 327.

32. Ibid., 328.

33. Coddington, 561.

34. *O. R. Atlas,* Pl XLII, 5; Coddington, 565–67.

35. Dowdey, *Wartime Papers,* 548.

36. Coddington, 567–68.

37. *O. R.*, Ser. I, Vol. 27, Part iii, 1001.

38. *O. R.*, Ser. I, Vol. 27, Part ii, 705.

39. Lieutenant Colonel S. G. Shepard of the 7th Tennessee Infantry wrote in his official report (*O. R.*, Ser. I, Vol. 27, Part ii, 648) that the Union force was a squadron of seventy-five to 100 men.

40. *O. R.*, Ser. I, Vol. 27, Part ii, 640–41.

41. Ibid., 644.

CHAPTER NINE: STUART UNDER ATTACK

1. Blackford, 234.

2. Cooke, 248–49.

3. Dowdey, *Wartime Papers*, 543.

4. Ibid., 548.

5. Longstreet, *Annals*, 421.

6. Lieutenant James P. Smith, Ewell's aide, recollected that Lee was "surprised and disturbed" that Stuart was still in Virginia on June 27. However, most of the major critics of this phase of Stuart's role wrote before Smith's 1906 publication date, thereby basing their arguments upon previously published recollections of Lee's comments.

7. This 10 A.M. time was one of the "typographical errors" in Longstreet's first article in the *Philadelphia Weekly*. Later, he published Anderson's letter in full, saying that Anderson met with Lee at noon.

8. Piston, 132.

9. Hill's report, *O. R.*, Ser. I, Vol. 27, Part ii, 607.

10. If Venable's published date of June 28 was correct, Ewell was told to concentrate his forces at Chambersburg even earlier, on the night of June 27.

11. Piston, 131. Henry M. Grady, a free-lance journalist from Atlanta, did the copying, editing, and the final drafts of Longstreet's originals. Perhaps, because of his wound, Longstreet's penmanship was so distorted that even Grady had problems with it. The real problem was that Longstreet never had a final look at the manuscript before it got into print and so a few mistakes were printed.

12. Longstreet, *Manassas to Appomattox*, 358.

13. Longstreet, 359.

14. *O. R.*, Ser. I, Vol. 27, Part iii, 923.

15. Ibid., 924.

16. Dowdey, 529–30.

17. Mosby, *Stuart's Cavalry*, 109.

18. *O. R.*, Ser. I, Vol. 27, Part iii, 948. E. E. Bouldin of the 14th Virginia Cavalry wrote to Bachelder July 29, 1886: "Jenkins Brig having had the advance of Lee's Army in Penn in 1863 . . . turned towards Gettysburg and some of his command was the first to Gettysburg 1 July 1863." Perhaps this is why Lee told Imboden not to rush.

19. Black to Bachelder, March 22, 1886, Bachelder Papers.

20. *O. R.*, Ser. I, Vol. 27, Part ii, 306.

21. For reference, here is the relevant section of Lee's June 22 orders: "If you find that he [the enemy] is moving northward, and that two brigades can guard the Blue Ridge and take care of your rear, you can move with the other three into Maryland, and take position on General Ewell's right, place yourself in communication with him, guard his flank, keep him informed of the enemy's movements, and collect all the supplies you can for the use of the army."

22. *O. R.*, Ser. I, Vol. 27, Part ii, 316.

23. Ibid., 307.

24. Ibid., 317.
25. Ibid., 316.
26. *O. R.,* Ser. I, Vol. 27, Part iii, 321.
27. Taylor, 77.
28. Marshall, xxiv.
29. *SHSP,* Vol. 4, 155.
30. Lee's orders, of course, were available with a little research. All the written records were in the process of being compiled by 1877. Though the first published volume was not issued until July 1881, many writers had delved into them before that; in fact, according to Freeman (*The South to Posterity,* 90), before the end of 1877, forty-seven volumes had already been typeset.
31. *SHSP,* Vol. 4, 156.
32. Longstreet, *Manassas to Appomattox,* 351.
33. Taylor, 92.
34. Long, 275.
35. Marshall, 218.
36. Tucker, *High Tide,* 100–101; N. C. Regiments, Vol. 5, 115–17.
37. Henry Heth, *The Memoirs of Henry Heth,* James L. Morrison, Jr., ed. (Westport, CT: Greenwood Press, 1974), 173.
38. *O. R.,* Ser. I, Vol. 27, Part ii, 607.
39. Ibid., 637.
40. Mosby, *Stuart's Cavalry,* 153.
41. Taylor, 92–93.
42. Mosby's work is excellent reading for anyone interested in the defense of Stuart in the campaign.
43. Piston, 134.
44. *SHSP,* Vol. 4, 269–70.
45. Coddington, 575–95.
46. Coddington, 197.
47. *O. R.,* Ser. I, Vol. 27, Part i. To Reynolds at 10:30 P.M. (923): "The road [from Cashtown to Oxford], however, is terribly infested with prowling cavalry parties." To Pleasonton at 10:40 P.M. (924): "There is a road from Cashtown running through Mummasburg and Hunterstown on to York Pike at Oxford, which is terribly infested with roving detachments of cavalry."
48. *SHSP,* Vol. 4, 145.
49. *SHSP,* Vol. 4, 122.

CHAPTER TEN: MOSBY PARRIES

1. McClellan, 314; Mosby's Letters, 51.
2. *Annals,* 433.
3. Longstreet, *Annals,* 434–35.
4. *SHSP,* Vol. 8, 446–50.
5. Ibid., 447.
6. *O. R.,* Ser. I, Vol. 27, Part ii, 467.
7. Ibid., 464–68.
8. *SHSP,* 448.
9. Ibid., 450.
10. McClellan, 317.
11. A search of the Confederate records in the Virginia Historical Society as late as October 1993 had not brought McClellan's "lengthy" sealed communication from Lee to light. Many Con-

federate records were destroyed in the evacuation of Richmond and the retreat afterward. Since it was a repeat and expansion of earlier orders, the "lengthy" letter may have been destroyed by Stuart himself as being too revealing of his mission should it have fallen into enemy hands. That it was sealed and that Stuart chastised McClellan for opening it gave a clue to its importance.

12. Mosby's Letters, 220.

13. McClellan, 336–37.

14. Freeman, *The South to Posterity,* p. 87.

15. Isaac Trimble remembered a similar occurrence except that it happened on June 26. According to historian Glenn Tucker, the story did not emerge in print until after 1893, when the *Confederate Veteran* began publication, and after, of course, Long's work was out. There was apparently a discussion between Lee and Trimble. Trimble recalled, "As he [Lee] brought the interview to a close, he put his hand to the map and touched Gettysburg. 'Hereabout we shall probably meet the enemy and fight a great battle, and if God give us victory, the war will be over and we shall achieve the recognition of our independence.'" (Tucker, 48.) Remove the dramatics inserted over the years and the Trimble story is a little more believable, mainly because of the date when it was allegedly told.

16. Long, 268.

17. Ibid., 275.

18. Ibid., 275–76.

19. Ibid., 277.

20. Ibid., 278.

21. Freeman, Vol. 3, 30. Quoting Jed Hotchkiss, "The land is full of everything and we have an abundance." Ibid., 37. "Besides all the food, mounts and quartermasters' supplies seized and issued in Pennsylvania to Ewell's own men, some 5,000 barrels of flour, in addition to 3,000 cattle, had been located for the Chief Commissary of the Army." Horses by the thousands were taken back to Virginia, as was much food. Confederates with Ewell even secured paper worth $150,000 at Mount Holly, Pennsylvania, and brought it back to the Confederacy (Major Frank Eakle, 14th Virginia Cavalry, to McClellan, April 7, 1886. Bachelder Papers). That does not include what Early gathered, what Jenkins seized, and the 125 wagons Stuart brought in.

22. Longstreet, "Lee's Invasion of Pennsylvania," *B & L,* Vol. 3, 251.

23. Mosby's letters, 219–20. Remarkably, this seems true. Though McClellan used Stuart's and Lee's reports, he did not use the subsequently published orders that were found in the Correspondence volume of which Mosby wrote. Mosby went on in this letter to Stuart's widow, "If I had then suspected that McClellan under some influence had suppressed such conclusive evidence in Stuart's favor I would not have written to him; I thought he had overlooked it."

24. *B & L,* Vol. 3, 251–52.

25. Ibid., 253.

26. Fitzhugh Lee, *General Lee* (Reprint. Greenwich, CT: Fawcett Publications, 1961), 254.

27. Ibid., 255.

28. Freeman, *South to Posterity,* 92.

29. Mosby's Letters, 85.

30. Ibid., 85–86.

31. *SHSP,* Vol. 23, 223.

31. Ibid., 225.

32. *O. R.,* Ser. I, Vol. 27, Part iii, 886.

33. Ibid., 904, 905, 925.

34. *SHSP,* Vol. 23, 227.

35. Mosby's Letters, 79.

36. Ibid., 85–86.

37. Ibid., 85.

38. In referring to his nearly completed work on Lee, Marshall, according to McIntosh's manuscript, "when pressed to know why he didn't allow its publication, and if it was because he was afraid it would hurt too many people, he frankly said it was . . . and he didn't know that he should ever publish it." (3–4, typescript, Virginia Historical Society.)

39. Longstreet, Manassas to Appomattox, 341.

40. Ibid., 343. "In the body of my note were orders . . . that he should assign General Hampton to command of the cavalry to be left with us, with orders to report at my headquarters." Longstreet's original note read, "Order General Hampton—whom I suppose you will leave here in command—to report to me." In any army, in any time period, "supposing" has never been considered orders.

41. Mosby, Reminiscences, 190–99.

42. Ibid., 193.

43. Ibid., 190.

44. Ibid., 187–88.

45. Sorrel, 136.

46. Ibid., 131.

47. Siepel, 175–76.

48. Mosby's Letters, 69.

49. Ibid., 152–53.

50. Ibid., 154.

51. Ibid., 158–59.

52. John S. Mosby, Stuart's Cavalry in the Gettysburg Campaign (New York: Moffat, Yard & Company, 1908), 68.

53. Ibid., 93.

54. Ibid., 94–95.

55. Ibid., 102–03.

56. Ibid., 106.

57. Ibid., 109–10.

58. Ibid., 112.

59. Ibid., 117.

60. McKim, SHSP, Vol. 37, 210–15.

61. Mosby, Stuart's Cavalry, 150.

62. Ibid., 171.

63. Ibid., 191.

64. Mosby (201) quotes a letter from Robertson to Heth of December 27, 1877, saying during the separation of his command from the army, there was constant communication between himself and Lee.

65. Mosby, Stuart's Cavalry, 198.

66. In his memoirs (180), Marshall himself said, "He struck from the original draft many statements which he thought might affect others injuriously."

67. Mosby, Stuart's Cavalry, 208.

68. SHSP, Vol. 37, 21–37.

69. SHSP, Vol. 38, 184–96.

70. Ibid., 192–93.

71. Ibid., 197.

CHAPTER ELEVEN: MARSHALL'S EPITAPH

1. Marshall, *Aide-de-Camp,* xxix.
2. Ibid., xvii–xviii.
3. Ibid., 210–11.
4. Ibid., 214–15.
5. Certainly Lee would have liked to have occupied Pennsylvania until the fall, because foraging in Maryland, a border state, would have been counterproductive politically. If Lee was to spend all summer in Pennsylvania and if he found the enemy at a disadvantage, he would have fought there. In fact, that is exactly what happened as Lee rode over the crest of Seminary Ridge at Gettysburg and saw the enemy in retreat before his army. Lee would not have continued the battle if he did not think he held the advantage.

CHAPTER TWELVE: POSTMORTEM

1. Freeman, Vol. 3, 51–72.
2. Ibid., 57.
3. Ibid., 64.
4. Stuart sent A. R. Venable on the morning of July 1, according to H. B. McClellan (330), and received word of the main army's location while preparing to bombard Carlisle that evening. Divide the daylight hours of July 1 in half and it probably took Venable less than ten hours to find the Confederate army and return.
5. Freeman, 68.
6. Ibid.
7. Ibid., 97.
8. Ibid., 98–99.
9. Freeman, 170–71.
10. Ibid., 173–74.
11. Ibid., 175.
12. Ibid., 208.
13. Ibid.
14. Coddington, 108.
15. Ibid., 107.
16. Ibid., 108.
17. Ibid.
18. Ibid., 181.
19. Ibid., 182.
20. Ibid., 184.
21. Ibid., 186.
22. Ibid., 196.
23. Ibid., 201.
24. Ibid., 202–03.
25. Ibid., 206.
26. Ibid., 207.
27. Thomas, 91.
28. Ibid., 141.
29. Ibid., 232–33.
30. Ibid., 239.
31. Ibid., 255.

Bibliography

Alexander, Ted. Interviews and correspondence with the author, October–December 1993.

Annals of the War Written by Leading Participants North and South Originally Published in the Philadelphia Weekly Times. Philadelphia: *Philadelphia Weekly Times,* 1879. Reprint. Dayton, OH: Morningside Bookshop Press, 1988.

Bachelder, John B. Papers. New Hampshire Historical Society, in possession of Gettysburg National Military Park.

Balfour, Daniel T. *13th Virginia Cavalry.* Lynchburg, VA: H. E. Howard, Inc., 1986.

Bandy, Ken, and Florence Freeland, compilers. *The Gettysburg Papers.* 2 vols. Dayton, OH: Morningside Bookshop Press, 1978.

Bates, Samuel P. *Martial Deeds of Pennsylvania.* Philadelphia: 1875.

Blackford, Susan Leigh, comp. *Letters from Lee's Army.* New York: Charles Scribner's Sons, 1947. Reprint. NY: A. S. Barnes & Company, Inc., 1962.

Blackford, W. W. *War Years with Jeb Stuart.* New York: Charles Scribner's Sons, 1945.

Botkin, B. A., ed. *A Civil War Treasury of Tales, Legends and Folklore.* 1960. Reprint. New York: Promontory Press, 1981.

Brooke-Rawle, William. *The Right Flank at Gettysburg.* Philadelphia: *Philadelphia Weekly Times,* September 14, 1878. Reprint. Pamphlet, November 1878.

Buel, C. C., and R. Johnson, eds. *Battles and Leaders of the Civil War.* 4 vols. New York, 1887–88.

Busey, John W., and David G. Martin. *Regimental Strengths and Losses at Gettysburg.* Hightstown, NJ: Longstreet House, 1986.

Coddington, Edwin B. *The Gettysburg Campaign: A Study in Command.* New York: Charles Scribner's Sons, 1968.

Coggins, Jack. *Arms and Equipment of the Civil War.* 1962. Reprint. New York: The Fairfax Press, 1983.

Connelly, Thomas L. *The Marble Man: Robert E. Lee and His Image in American*

Society. 1977. Reprint. Baton Rouge, LA: Louisiana State University Press, 1978.

Conrad, W. P., and Ted Alexander. *When War Passed This Way.* Greencastle, PA: Greencastle Bicentennial Publication, 1982.

Coulling, Mary P. *The Lee Girls.* Winston-Salem, NC: John F. Blair, Publisher, 1987.

Cowles, Calvin D., comp. *Atlas To Accompany the Official Records of the Union and Confederate Armies.* Washington: Government Printing Office, 1891–95.

Culpeper Historical Society. *Historic Culpeper.* Culpeper, VA: Culpeper Historical Society, 1974.

Dabney, Chiswell. Unpublished letter. Richmond, VA: Virginia Historical Society, n.d.

Daniel, Jonathan. Papers. University of Virginia, in possession of Gettysburg National Military Park.

Davis, Burke. *Jeb Stuart: The Last Cavalier.* New York: The Fairfax Press, 1988.

Dowdey, Clifford, and Louis H. Manarin, eds. *The Wartime Papers of R. E. Lee.* New York: Brambal House, 1961.

Driver, Robert J. Jr. *The Staunton Artillery—McClanahan's Battery.* Lynchburg, VA: H. E. Howard, Inc., 1988.

———. *1st Virginia Cavalry.* Lynchburg, VA: H. E. Howard, Inc., 1991.

Fortesque, Louis R. Unpublished diary. Gettysburg National Military Park files.

Freeman, Douglas Southall. *Lee's Lieutenants.* New York: Charles Scribner's Sons, 1946.

———. *The South to Posterity: An Introduction to the Writing of Confederate History.* New York: Charles Scribner's Sons, 1951.

Fremantle, Arthur. *Three Months in the Southern States.* London: William Blackwood and Sons, 1863.

Gaff, Alan D. *Brave Men's Tears: The Iron Brigade at Brawner Farm.* Dayton, OH: Morningside, 1985.

Gallant, T. Grady. *The Friendly Dead.* Garden City, NY: Doubleday, 1964.

Gettysburg National Military Park vertical files, Gettysburg, PA.

Hackley, Woodford B. *The Little Fork Rangers: A Sketch of Company "D" Fourth Virginia Cavalry.* Richmond, VA: The Dietz Printing Co., 1927.

Hahn, Thomas F. *Towpath Guide to the C & O Canal.* Shepherdstown, WV: The American Canal & Transportation Center, 1983.

Haines, Douglas Craig. "R. S. Ewell's Command June 29–July 1, 1863." *The Gettysburg Magazine: Historical Articles of Lasting Interest.* Dayton, OH: Morningside House, July 1993.

Hartwig, D. Scott. Interviews with the author, June–October 1993.

Hassler, Warren W. *Crises at the Crossroads: The First Day at Gettysburg.* 1970. Reprint. Gettysburg, PA: Stan Clark Military Books, 1991.

The Historical Publication Committee of the Hanover Chamber of Commerce. *Encounter at Hanover: Prelude to Gettysburg.* Hanover, PA: The Historical Publication Committee of the Hanover Chamber of Commerce, 1963.

Hitner Letter, July 6, 1863. Unpublished. U.S. Army Military History Institute, Carlisle Barracks, PA.

Hoke, Jacob. *The Great Invasion of 1863 or General Lee in Pennsylvania.* Reprint. Gettysburg, PA: Stan Clark Military Books, 1992.

Kidd, J. H. *A Cavalryman with Custer.* The Sentinel Press, 1908. (Originally published as *Personal Recollections of a Cavalryman.*) Reprint. New York: Bantam Books, 1991.

Krick, Robert K. *Ninth Virginia Cavalry* (The Virginia Regimental Histories Series). Lynchburg, VA: H. E. Howard, Inc., 1982.

Krolick, Marshall D. "Forgotten Fields: The Cavalry Battle East of Gettysburg on July 3, 1863." *Gettysburg: Historical Articles of Lasting Interest.* Dayton, OH: Morningside House, January 1991.

Lee, Fitzhugh. *General Lee.* 1894. Reprint. Greenwich, CT: Fawcett Publications, Inc., 1961.

Lee, Robert E. Headquarters papers, 1855–78. Virginia Historical Society.

Livermore, Thomas L. *Numbers and Losses in the Civil War.* Boston: Houghton, Mifflin & Co., 1900.

Long, A. L. *Memoirs of Robert E. Lee.* 1886. Reprint. Secaucus, NJ: The Blue and Grey Press, 1983.

Long, E. B., and Barbara Long. *The Civil War Day by Day: An Almanac.* Garden City, NY: Doubleday & Co., Inc., 1971.

Longstreet, James. *From Manassas to Appomattox: Memoirs of the Civil War in America.* Philadelphia: J. B. Lippincott, 1896. Reprint. New York: Mallard Press, 1991.

McCarthy, Carlton. *Detailed Minutiae of Soldier Life in the Army of Northern Virginia.* Richmond, VA: Carlton McCarthy and Company, 1882. Reprint. Alexandria, VA: Time-Life Books, Inc., 1981.

McClellan, H. B. *I Rode with Jeb Stuart: The Life and Campaigns of Major General J. E. B. Stuart.* Reprint. (Originally published as *The Campaigns of Stuart's Cavalry,* 1885.) Burke Davis, editor. Bloomington, IN: Indiana University Press, 1958.

McClure, A. K., ed. *The Annals of the War written by Leading Participants North and South.* 1879. Reprint. Dayton, OH: Morningside, 1988.

McIntosh, David Gregg. "Review of the Gettysburg Campaign." *Southern Historical Society Papers.* Volume 37. Richmond, VA: Southern Historical Society, 1909.

McKim, Randolph Harrison. "General J. E. B. Stuart in the Gettysburg Campaign." *Southern Historical Society Papers.* Volume 37. Richmond, VA: Southern Historical Society, 1909.

Marshall, Charles. Unpublished papers. Richmond, VA: Virginia Historical Society.

Maurice, Frederick, ed. *An Aide-de-Camp of Lee.* Boston: Little, Brown and Company, 1927.

Mitchell, Adele H. Interviews with the author, 1986.

———. ed. *The Letters of Major General J. E. B. Stuart.* The Stuart-Mosby Historical Society, 1990.

Morrison, James L. Jr., ed. *The Memoirs of Henry Heth.* Westport, CT: Greenwood Press, 1974.

Mosby, John S. *The Letters of John S. Mosby.* The Stuart-Mosby Historical Society, 1986.

———. *Mosby's War Reminiscences, Stuart's Cavalry Campaigns.* New York: Dodd, Mead and Company, 1898.

———. *Stuart's Cavalry in the Gettysburg Campaign.* New York: Moffat, Yard & Company, 1908. Reprint. Falls Church, VA: Confederate Printers, 1984.

Murfin, James V. *The Gleam of Bayonets: The Battle of Antietam and Robert E. Lee's Maryland Campaign, September 1862.* Cranbury, NJ: Thomas Yoseloff, 1965.

Nanzig, Thomas P. *3rd Virginia Cavalry.* Lynchburg, VA: H. E. Howard, Inc., 1989.

Nesbitt, Mark. *If the South Won Gettysburg.* Gettysburg: Reliance Publishing Co., 1980. Reprint. Gettysburg, PA: Thomas Publications, 1993.

———. *Rebel Rivers: A Guide to the Civil War Sites on the Potomac, Rappahannock, York, and James.* Harrisburg, PA: Stackpole Books, 1993.

———. *35 Days to Gettysburg: The Campaign Diaries of Two American Enemies.* Harrisburg, PA: Stackpole Books, 1992.

Nye, Wilbur S. *Here Come the Rebels!* Baton Rouge, LA: Louisiana State University Press, 1965.

Office of Publications Staff, National Park Service. *John Brown's Raid.* Washington: U.S. Department of the Interior, 1973.

Paris, Comte de (Louis Philippe Albert d'Orleans). *The Battle of Gettysburg: From the History of the Civil War in America.* Philadelphia: Porter & Coates, 1886. Reprint. Baltimore: Butternut and Blue, 1987.

Piston, William Garrett. *Lee's Tarnished Lieutenant: James Longstreet and His Place in Southern History.* Athens, GA: The University of Georgia Press, 1987.

Robertson, James I., Jr. *General A. P. Hill: The Story of a Confederate Warrior.* New York: Random House, Inc., 1987. Reprint. New York: Vintage Books, 1992.

Sauers, Richard Allen. "John B. Bachelder: Government Historian of the Battle of Gettysburg." *Gettysburg: Historical Articles of Lasting Interest.* Dayton, OH: Morningside House, Inc., July 1990.

Schildt, John W. *Roads from Gettysburg.* Chewsville, MD: John W. Schildt, 1979.

Shevchuk, Paul M. "The Battle of Hunterstown, Pennsylvania, July 2, 1863." *Gettysburg: Historical Articles of Lasting Interest.* Dayton, OH: Morningside House, July 1989.

———. "Cut to Pieces: The Cavalry Fight at Fairfield, Pennsylvania, July 3rd, 1863." *Gettysburg: Historical Articles of Lasting Interest.* Dayton, OH: Morningside House, January 1991.

———. "The Lost Hours of 'JEB' Stuart." *Gettysburg: Historical Articles of Lasting Interest.* Dayton, OH: Morningside House, January 1991.

———. "The Wounding of Albert Jenkins, July 2, 1863." *Gettysburg: Historical Articles of Lasting Interest.* Dayton, OH: Morningside House, Inc., July 1990.

Siepel, Kevin H. *Rebel: The Life and Times of John Singleton Mosby.* New York: St. Martin's Press, 1983.

Sorrel, G. Moxley. *Recollections of a Confederate Staff Officer.* The Neale Publishing Company, 1905. Reprint. New York: Bantam Books, 1992.

Speese, Andrew J. S*tory of Companies H, A and C Third Pennsylvania Cavalry at Gettysburg, July 3, 1863.* Germantown, PA: Privately published, 1906.

Taylor, Walter H. *Four Years with General Lee.* 1877. Reprint. James I. Robertson, Jr., ed. New York: Bonanza Books, 1962.

———. Unpublished papers, 1861–1916. Richmond, VA: Virginia Historical Society.

Thomas, Emory M. *Bold Dragoon: The Life of J. E. B. Stuart.* New York: Harper & Row, 1986. Reprint. New York: Vintage Books, 1988.

Thomason, John W. Jr. *Jeb Stuart.* New York: Charles Scribner's Sons, 1930.

Thompson, D.W. "Carlisle is Bombarded." *Carlisle Sentinel.* Carlisle, PA: July 1863.

Tilberg, Frederick. *Vignettes of the Battlefield.* Unpublished paper, Gettysburg National Military Park files.

Todd, Frederick P. *American Military Equipage: 1851–1872.* New York: Charles Scribner's Sons, 1978.

Toomey, Daniel Carroll. *The Civil War in Maryland.* Toomey Press, Baltimore: 1983.

Tousey, Thomas G. *Military History of Carlisle and Carlisle Barracks.* Richmond, VA: The Dietz Press, 1939.

Trout, Robert J. *They Followed the Plume: The Story of J. E. B. Stuart and His Staff.* Mechanicsburg, PA: Stackpole Books, 1993.

Trout, Robert J. Interviews with the author, July–November 1993.

Tucker, Glenn. *High Tide at Gettysburg: The Campaign in Pennsylvania.* Indianapolis, IN: The Bobbs-Merrill Co., Inc., 1958.

———. *Lee and Longstreet at Gettysburg.* Indianapolis, IN: The Bobbs-Merril Co., Inc., 1968.

U.S. War Department. *War of the Rebellion: A Compilation of the Official Records of the War of the Rebellion.* Series I, Volume 27, Parts i, ii, iii. Washington: Government Printing Office, 1889.

Von Borcke, Heros. *Memoirs of the Confederate War for Independence.* Blackwood's Magazine, 1866. Reprint. New York: Peter Smith, 1938.

Wiley, Bell I. *The Life of Billy Yank: The Common Soldier of the Union.* Indianapolis, IN: The Bobbs-Merrill Co., Inc., 1952.

———. *The Life of Johnny Reb: The Common Soldier of the Confederacy.* Indianapolis, IN: The Bobbs-Merrill Co., Inc., 1962 (Charter Edition).

Index